taste of home

5-Ingredient
Cookbook

taste of home

BOOKS

REIMAN MEDIA GROUP, LLC • GREENDALE, WISCONSIN

taste of home

A TASTE OF HOME/READER'S DIGEST BOOK

Editor-in-Chief: Catherine Cassidy
Vice President, Executive Editor/Books: Heidi Reuter Lloyd
Creative Director: Howard Greenberg
North American Chief Marketing Officer: Lisa Karpinski
Food Director: Diane Werner, RD
Senior Editor/Retail Books: Faithann Stoner
Editor: Jean Duerst
Associate Editor: Beth Kong
Associate Creative Director: Edwin Robles Jr.
Art Director: Lori Arndt
Layout Designer: Catherine Fletcher
Recipe Asset System Manager: Coleen Martin
Recipe Testing & Editing: Taste of Home Test Kitchen
Food Photography: Taste of Home Photo Studio
Administrative Assistant: Barb Czysz

The Reader's Digest Association, Inc.
President and Chief Executive Officer: Robert E. Guth
Executive Vice President, RDA, & President, North America: Dan Lagani
President/Publisher, Trade Publishing: Harold Clarke
Associate Publisher: Rosanne McManus
Vice President, Sales & Marketing: Stacey Ashton

For other Taste of Home books and products, visit us at tasteofhome.com.

For more Reader's Digest products and information, visit
rd.com (in the United States)
or rd.ca (in Canada).
ISBN 978-1-61765-247-9
Library of Congress Control Number: 2007925731

Pictured on front cover: Bacon-Wrapped Chicken, p. 56.

Printed in China.
1   3   5   7   9   10   8   6   4   2

taste of home
5-Ingredient Cookbook

|TABLE OF CONTENTS|

Snacks & Beverages

Fruity Sherbet Punch (p. 17), Ham Roll-Ups (p. 6), Turkey Meatballs (p. 8) and Sausage Biscuit Bites (p. 9)

| BEVERAGES |

Blackberry Banana Smoothies, p. 10

Creamy Thyme Spread, p. 12

Ham Roll-Ups

(Pictured on page 4)

Green onions and ripe olives give lively flavor to these bite-size appetizers. They're quick to assemble and can be made the day before they're needed. They're very popular with my friends and family.

—*Kathleen Green, Republic, Missouri*

 Uses less fat, sugar or salt. Includes Nutritional Analysis and Diabetic Exchanges.

  1 **package (8 ounces) cream cheese, softened**
  1 **can (2-1/4 ounces) chopped ripe olives, drained**
1/3 **cup thinly sliced green onions**
  8 **to 10 thin slices fully cooked ham**

In a mixing bowl, beat cream cheese until smooth; stir in the olives and onions. Spread over ham slices. Roll up, jelly-roll style, starting with a short side. Chill for at least 1 hour. Just before serving, cut into 1-in. pieces. **Yield:** 40 appetizers.

Nutritional Analysis: One serving of 2 roll-ups (prepared with fat-free cream cheese and reduced-fat ham) equals 27 calories, 259 mg sodium, 7 mg cholesterol, 1 g carbohydrate, 4 g protein, 1 g fat. **Diabetic Exchange:** 1/2 meat.

Raspberry Iced Tea

A co-worker of mine from England gave me a tip on making the best iced tea: The sugar should be added first to make a syrup before adding the tea bags. I often serve Raspberry Iced Tea with lemon slices and prepare it with fresh raspberries from my backyard bushes.

—*Christine Wilson*
Sellersville, Pennsylvania

8-1/4 **cups water, *divided***
 2/3 **cup sugar**
   5 **individual tea bags**
   3 **to 4 cups unsweetened raspberries**

In a large saucepan, bring 4 cups water to a boil. Stir in sugar until dissolved. Remove from the heat; add tea bags. Steep for 5-8 minutes. Discard tea bags. Add 4 cups water.

In another saucepan, bring raspberries and remaining water to a boil. Reduce heat; simmer, uncovered, for 3 minutes. Strain and discard pulp. Add raspberry juice to the tea mixture. Serve over ice. **Yield:** about 2 quarts.

Smoky Bacon Wraps

These cute little sausage and bacon bites are finger-licking good. They have a sweet and salty taste that's fun for an appetizer. I've even served them for breakfast and brunch, and everyone gobbles them up!
—*Cara Flora, Kokomo, Indiana*

1 pound sliced bacon
1 package (16 ounces) miniature smoked sausage links
1 cup packed brown sugar

Cut each bacon strip in half widthwise. Wrap one piece of bacon around each sausage. Place in a foil-lined 15-in. x 10-in. x 1-in. baking pan. Sprinkle with brown sugar.

Bake, uncovered, at 400° for 30-40 minutes or until bacon is crisp and sausage is heated through. **Yield:** about 3-1/2 dozen.

Salsa Strips

I rely on refrigerated crescent rolls to make these crisp Southwestern appetizers. Choose mild, medium or hot salsa to suit your taste. I often use the hot variety for my own family and a milder salsa when I serve them to guests.
—*Joann Woloszyn*
Fredonia, New York

1 tube (8 ounces) refrigerated crescent rolls
2 tablespoons Dijon mustard
3/4 cup salsa
1 cup (4 ounces) shredded mozzarella cheese
Minced fresh cilantro

Unroll crescent roll dough and separate into four rectangles. Place on greased baking sheets. Spread mustard and salsa on each rectangle.

Bake at 350° for 10 minutes. Sprinkle with cheese; bake 8-10 minutes longer or until golden brown. Cool for 10 minutes. Cut each into four strips; sprinkle with cilantro. **Yield:** 16 appetizers.

Glazed Chicken Wings

I received the recipe for these yummy chicken wings from a cousin on Vancouver Island during a visit there a number of years ago. They're an appealing appetizer but also a favorite for Sunday lunch with rice and a salad. We love the glaze that coats each wing.
—Joan Airey
Rivers, Manitoba

12 whole chicken wings (about 2-1/2 pounds)
1/2 cup barbecue sauce
1/2 cup honey
1/2 cup soy sauce

Cut chicken wings into three sections; discard wing tip section. Place in a greased 13-in. x 9-in. x 2-in. baking dish. Combine barbecue sauce, honey and soy sauce; pour over wings. Bake, uncovered, at 350° for 50-60 minutes or until chicken juices run clear. **Yield:** 4 servings.

Editor's Note: 2-1/2 pounds of uncooked chicken wing sections may be substituted for the whole chicken wings. Omit the first step of the recipe.

Turkey Meatballs

(Pictured on page 4)

I hate to cook, so I'm always looking for fast and easy recipes like this one. A sweet sauce coats these firm meatballs that are made with ground turkey for a nice change of pace.
—Hazel Bates
Clinton, Oklahoma

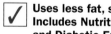 **Uses less fat, sugar or salt. Includes Nutritional Analysis and Diabetic Exchanges.**

1 pound ground turkey
1/4 cup oat bran cereal
1 bottle (14 ounces) ketchup
1 cup grape jelly
3 to 4 tablespoons lemon juice

In a bowl, combine turkey and cereal; mix well. Shape into 1-in. balls. In a Dutch oven, combine ketchup, jelly and lemon juice; bring to a boil. Add meatballs. Reduce heat; simmer, uncovered, for 30-35 minutes or until meat is no longer pink, stirring several times. **Yield:** 4-1/2 dozen.

Nutritional Analysis: One serving of 5 meatballs (prepared with ground turkey breast, no-salt-added ketchup and reduced-sugar grape jelly) equals 137 calories, 36 mg sodium, 20 mg cholesterol, 24 g carbohydrate, 11 g protein, 1 g fat. **Diabetic Exchanges:** 1 very lean meat, 1 starch, 1/2 fruit.

Sausage Biscuit Bites

(Pictured on page 4)

I sometimes bake these delightful little morsels the night before, refrigerate them, then put them in the slow cooker in the morning so my husband can share them with his co-workers. They're always gone in a hurry. —*Audrey Marler, Kokomo, Indiana*

1 tube (7-1/2 ounces) refrigerated buttermilk biscuits
1 tablespoon butter, melted
4-1/2 teaspoons grated Parmesan cheese
1 teaspoon dried oregano
1 package (8 ounces) brown-and-serve sausage links

On a lightly floured surface, roll out each biscuit into a 4-in. circle; brush with butter. Combine Parmesan cheese and oregano; sprinkle over butter. Place a sausage link in the center of each; roll up.

Cut each widthwise into four pieces; insert a toothpick into each. Place on an ungreased baking sheet. Bake at 375° for 8-10 minutes or until golden brown. **Yield:** 40 appetizers.

Fluffy Hot Chocolate

Melted marshmallows provide the frothy texture that you'll savor in this sweet and speedy warm beverage. They're also what makes this hot chocolate different from (and better than) the instant kind you make from a store-bought mix. Chocolaty and comforting, it's our daughter's favorite. —*Jo Ann Schimcek Weimar, Texas*

8 teaspoons sugar
4 teaspoons baking cocoa
4 cups milk
1-1/2 cups miniature marshmallows
1 teaspoon vanilla extract

In a saucepan, combine the first four ingredients. Cook and stir over medium heat until the marshmallows are melted, about 8 minutes. Remove from the heat; stir in vanilla. Ladle into mugs. **Yield:** 4 servings.

Blackberry Banana Smoothies

(Pictured on page 5)

I originally began blending up this simple beverage when our young girls shied away from berries. Now they're thrilled whenever I serve it. The thick fruity drink is a refreshing treat no matter what kind of berries you use.

—*Heidi Butts, Streetsboro, Ohio*

☑ **Uses less fat, sugar or salt. Includes Nutritional Analysis and Diabetic Exchanges.**

> **2 cups orange juice**
> **1/3 cup vanilla yogurt**
> **2 medium ripe bananas, cut into thirds and frozen**
> **1/2 cup fresh *or* frozen blackberries**

In a blender, combine all ingredients. Cover and process until blended. Serve immediately. **Yield:** 4 servings.

Nutritional Analysis: One 3/4-cup serving (prepared with reduced-fat yogurt) equals 136 calories, 1 g fat (trace saturated fat), 1 mg cholesterol, 14 mg sodium, 32 g carbohydrate, 2 g fiber, 2 g protein. **Diabetic Exchanges:** 1 starch, 1 fruit.

Reuben Roll-Ups

This recipe turns the popular Reuben sandwich into an interesting and hearty snack. We love these roll-ups at our house. Company quickly reaches for them as well. —*Patty Kile Greentown, Pennsylvania*

> **1 tube (10 ounces) refrigerated pizza dough**
> **1 cup sauerkraut, well drained**
> **1 tablespoon Thousand Island salad dressing**
> **4 slices corned beef, halved**
> **4 slices Swiss cheese, halved**

Roll dough into a 12-in. x 9-in. rectangle. Cut into eight 3-in. x 4-1/2-in. rectangles. Combine sauerkraut and salad dressing. Place a slice of beef on each rectangle. Top with about 2 tablespoons of the sauerkraut mixture and a slice of cheese. Roll up.

Place with seam side down on a greased baking sheet. Bake at 425° for 12-14 minutes or until golden. **Yield:** 8 roll-ups.

Cucumber Pita Wedges

I first tasted these delicious snacks at a basket party in a friend's home. (I work as a sales consultant for a hand-crafted basket company.) Of the finger foods she served, this platter was the first to become empty.
—Grace Yaskovic
Branchville, New Jersey

1 package (8 ounces) cream cheese, softened
2 tablespoons Italian salad dressing mix
4 whole pita breads
1 to 2 medium cucumbers, peeled and cut into 1/8-inch slices
Lemon-pepper seasoning

In a mixing bowl, beat cream cheese and salad dressing mix until combined. Split pita breads in half, forming two circles. Spread cream cheese mixture over pita circles; cut each into six wedges. Top with cucumbers. Sprinkle with lemon-pepper. **Yield:** 4 dozen.

Easy Cheese Nachos

There's no need to brown ground beef when fixing this satisfying snack. I simply top crunchy tortilla chips with warm canned chili and melted cheese, then sprinkle it all with chopped tomato and onion for fresh flavor and color.
—Laura Jirasek
White Lake, Michigan

1 package (14-1/2 ounces) tortilla chips
2 cans (15 ounces *each*) chili without beans
1 pound process cheese (Velveeta), cubed
4 green onions, sliced
1 medium tomato, chopped

Divide the tortilla chips between six plates and set aside. In a saucepan, warm chili until heated through. Meanwhile, in another saucepan, heat the cheese over medium-low heat until melted, stirring frequently. Spoon chili over chips; drizzle with cheese. Sprinkle with onions and tomato. **Yield:** 6 servings.

Hot Diggety Dogs

My family has always enjoyed this quick and easy snack. When our children were young, they used to help me fix these. Now they prepare them with their own families. And their kids enjoy them as much if not more!
—Linda Blankenmyer
Conestoga, Pennsylvania

20 saltine crackers
5 slices process American cheese, quartered
Ketchup, mustard *and/or* pickle relish
2 hot dogs

Place crackers on a lightly greased baking sheet. Top with cheese and ketchup, mustard and/or relish. Cut each hot dog into 10 slices; place one slice on each cracker. Bake at 350° for 10-12 minutes or until the cheese is melted. **Yield:** 20 snacks.

Editor's Note: If serving small children, cut hot dog slices in half; double the amount of crackers and cheese.

Creamy Thyme Spread

(Pictured on page 5)

This make-ahead cracker spread showcases thyme and garlic. A neighbor who has an herb garden gave me the recipe. It's simple to stir up and makes a special appetizer for company. It's also great to serve at a party.
—*Mary Steiner, West Bend, Wisconsin*

1 package (8 ounces) cream cheese, softened
1 tablespoon minced fresh thyme *or* 1 teaspoon dried thyme
1 tablespoon minced fresh parsley *or* 1 teaspoon dried parsley flakes
1 garlic clove, minced
Assorted crackers

In a bowl, combine the cream cheese, thyme, parsley and garlic; mix well. Cover and refrigerate until serving. Serve with crackers. **Yield:** about 1 cup.

|IT'S ABOUT THYME| Thyme has a bold earthy taste and a strong aroma. There are many varieties of fresh thyme, including the popular lemon-flavored plant. Use fresh or dried thyme to season fish, potato dishes, soups, stuffing, stews, rice pilaf, wild rice dishes, poultry and meat marinades.

Chocolate Quivers

These smooth, cool snacks are more fun than chocolate pudding! They're a nice make-ahead treat that I keep on hand for kids of all ages.

—Shirley Kidd, New London, Minnesota

2 envelopes unflavored gelatin
2 cups milk, *divided*
1/2 cup instant chocolate drink mix
1/4 cup sugar

In a bowl, dissolve gelatin in 1 cup milk. In a small saucepan over medium-high heat, combine drink mix, sugar and remaining milk; bring to a boil, stirring until chocolate and sugar are dissolved. Add to gelatin mixture and mix well.

Pour into an 8-in. square pan. Cool at room temperature for 30 minutes. Cover and refrigerate until firm, about 5 hours (do not freeze). Cut with a knife or cookie cutter. **Yield:** about 1 dozen.

Apricot Wraps

I accumulated a large recipe collection from around the world while my husband served in the Air Force for 25 years. This mouth-watering appetizer is one of our favorites, and we enjoy sharing it with friends.

—Jane Ashworth, Beavercreek, Ohio

1 package (14 ounces) dried apricots
1/2 cup whole almonds
1 pound sliced bacon
1/4 cup plum *or* apple jelly
2 tablespoons soy sauce

Fold each apricot around an almond. Cut bacon strips into thirds; wrap a strip around each apricot and secure with a toothpick. Place on two ungreased 15-in. x 10-in. x 1-in. baking pans. Bake, uncovered, at 375° for 25 minutes or until bacon is crisp, turning once.

In a small saucepan, combine jelly and soy sauce; cook and stir over low heat for 5 minutes or until warmed and smooth. Remove apricots to paper towels; drain. Serve with sauce for dipping. **Yield:** about 4-1/2 dozen.

Granola Chip Shakes

Packed with irresistible ingredients and served with a spoon, this shake is a super summertime treat. Treat your family and friends to this blended beverage soon!

—Elaine Anderson
Aliquippa, Pennsylvania

3/4 to 1 cup milk
4 tablespoons butterscotch ice cream topping, *divided*
2 cups vanilla ice cream, softened
1/2 cup granola cereal
2 tablespoons miniature semisweet chocolate chips

In a blender, combine milk, 2 tablespoons butterscotch topping and ice cream; cover and process until smooth. Pour into chilled glasses.

Drizzle with remaining topping; sprinkle with half of the granola and chocolate chips. Use a knife to swirl topping into shake. Top with remaining granola and chips. **Yield:** 2-1/2 cups.

Orange Marmalade Turnovers

A church friend prepares these delicate pastries for gatherings, but they're usually gone before she gets the platter to the serving table.

—Anna Jean Allen
West Liberty, Kentucky

1/2 cup butter, softened
1 jar (5 ounces) sharp American cheese spread
1 cup all-purpose flour
1/3 cup orange marmalade

In a bowl, combine butter and cheese. Add flour; stir until mixture forms a ball. Cover and refrigerate for 1 hour.

On a lightly floured surface, roll dough to 1/8-in. thickness; cut into 2-3/4-in. circles. Place 1/2 teaspoon marmalade on each circle. Fold pastry over and seal edges with a fork. Cut slits in top of pastry.

Place 2 in. apart on ungreased baking sheets. Bake at 350° for 5-9 minutes or until lightly browned. Remove to wire racks to cool. **Yield:** 2-1/2 dozen.

Picnic Fruit Punch

This pink cooler is deliciously thirst-quenching on a warm day. Seeing its color, folks guess it might be pink lemonade. They're pleasantly surprised to discover the bubbly blend includes cranberry, pineapple, orange and lemon juices.
—*Marion Lowery*
Medford, Oregon

  2 quarts cranberry juice
  3 cups pineapple juice
  3 cups orange juice
1/4 cup lemon juice
  1 liter ginger ale, chilled
  1 medium navel orange,
    sliced, optional

Combine the juices in a large container. Refrigerate. Just before serving, stir in ginger ale and orange slices if desired. **Yield:** 5 quarts.

Icebox Sandwiches

My mother liked making these cool, creamy treats when I was growing up in the States because they're so quick to fix. Now my three kids enjoy them.
—*Sandy Armijo, Naples, Italy*

  1 package (3.4 ounces)
    instant vanilla pudding
    mix
  2 cups cold milk
  2 cups whipped topping
  1 cup (6 ounces) miniature
    semisweet chocolate
    chips
 48 graham cracker squares

Mix pudding and milk according to package directions and refrigerate until set. Fold in whipped topping and chocolate chips.

Place 24 graham crackers on a baking sheet; top each with about 3 tablespoons filling. Place another graham cracker on top. Freeze for 1 hour or until firm. Wrap individually in plastic wrap; freeze. Serve sandwiches frozen. **Yield:** 2 dozen.

Pineapple Orange Drink

Living in the Sunshine State gives me a sunny outlook on life, as this drink deliciously proves! The delightful beverage featuring our famous orange juice is not too sweet but is so easy to make...just throw it in a blender and it's done.
—*LaChelle Olivet, Pace, Florida*

6 cups orange juice
2 cans (8 ounces *each*) crushed unsweetened pineapple, undrained
16 ice cubes

Place half of the orange juice, pineapple and ice cubes in a blender; cover and process until smooth. Repeat with remaining ingredients. Pour into chilled glasses. Serve immediately. **Yield:** 8 servings.

Grilled Jalapenos

When barbecuing with my friends, I also use the grill to serve up hot appetizers. These crowd-pleasing stuffed peppers have a bit of bite. They were concocted by my son.
—*Catherine Hollie
Cleveland, Texas*

24 fresh jalapeno peppers
12 ounces bulk pork sausage
12 bacon strips, halved

Wash peppers and remove stems. Cut a slit along one side of each pepper. Remove seeds; rinse and dry peppers. In a skillet over medium heat, cook sausage until no longer pink; drain. Stuff peppers with sausage and wrap with bacon; secure with a toothpick.

On an uncovered grill over medium heat, grill peppers for about 15 minutes or until tender and bacon is crisp, turning frequently. **Yield:** 2 dozen.

Editor's Note: When cutting or seeding hot peppers, use rubber or plastic gloves to protect your hands. Avoid touching your face.

One of the most common hot peppers, jalapenos are usually moderately to very hot and are sold at their green stage. At the red stage of full maturity, the jalapeno is super hot.

Fruity Sherbet Punch

(Pictured on page 4)

Everybody loves glasses of this sweet fruit punch. When entertaining, I start with a quart of sherbet, then add more later so it all doesn't melt right away. —*Betty Eberly, Palmyra, Pennsylvania*

4 cups apple juice, chilled
4 cups pineapple juice, chilled
4 cups orange juice, chilled
2 liters ginger ale, chilled
1 to 2 quarts orange *or* pineapple sherbet

Combine juices in a punch bowl. Stir in ginger ale. Top with sherbet. Serve immediately. **Yield:** 15-20 servings (about 5 quarts).

Veggie Dip

I always serve a colorful array of vegetables with this delicious dip. This popular appetizer is a welcome snack just about anytime. —*Sue Schuller*
Brainerd, Minnesota

1 cup mayonnaise
1 cup (8 ounces) sour cream
1 envelope vegetable soup mix
1 package (10 ounces) frozen chopped spinach, thawed and squeezed dry
1 can (8 ounces) water chestnuts, drained and chopped

In a bowl, combine mayonnaise, sour cream and soup mix. Stir in spinach and water chestnuts. Cover and refrigerate for at least 2 hours. **Yield:** 3 cups.

Harvest Apple Drink

My family loves this spiced apple drink, especially during the cooler fall months. I like that I can hand out mugfuls of it in a hurry.

—*Linda Young, Longmont, Colorado*

>   1 can (46 ounces) apple
>   juice
> 1/3 cup packed brown sugar
>   2 cinnamon sticks
>   6 whole cloves

In a medium saucepan, bring all ingredients to a boil. Reduce heat; simmer for 15 minutes. Strain. Serve warm. **Yield:** 4-6 servings.

Bacon-Broccoli Cheese Ball

Needing a quick appetizer one night when dinner was running late, I combined a few leftovers into this easy cheese ball. For variety, you can shape it into a log or substitute favorite herbs for the pepper. However er you make it, it's delicious served with a variety of crackers.

—*Tamara Rickard*
Bartlett, Tennessee

>   1 package (8 ounces)
>   cream cheese, softened
>   1 cup (4 ounces) finely
>   shredded cheddar
>   cheese
> 1/2 teaspoon pepper
>   1 cup finely chopped
>   broccoli florets
>   6 bacon strips, cooked and
>   crumbled

In a mixing bowl, beat cream cheese, cheddar cheese and pepper until blended. Stir in broccoli. Shape into a ball and roll in bacon. Cover and refrigerate. Remove from the refrigerator 15 minutes before serving. **Yield:** 2-1/2 cups.

|SHAPING A CHEESE BALL| To keep your hands and the countertop clean, spoon the cheese mixture onto a piece of plastic wrap. Working from the underside of the wrap, pat the mixture into a ball. Complete the recipe as directed.

Caramel Peanut Butter Dip

When crisp autumn apples are available, I make this quick delicious dip. My family loves the combination of caramel and peanut butter, and the consistency is perfect for dipping. —*Sandra McKenzie Braham, Minnesota*

30 caramels
1 to 2 tablespoons water
1/4 cup plus 2 tablespoons creamy peanut butter
1/4 cup finely crushed peanuts, optional
Sliced apples

In a microwave-safe bowl, microwave the caramels and water on high for 1 minute; stir. Microwave 1 minute more or until smooth. Add peanut butter and mix well; microwave for 30 seconds or until smooth. Stir in peanuts if desired. Serve warm with apples. **Yield:** 1 cup.

Editor's Note: This recipe was tested in a 700-watt microwave.

Pizza Roll-Ups

Since receiving this recipe through 4-H, it's been a regular after-school snack. These bite-size pizza treats, made with refrigerated crescent rolls, are especially good served with spaghetti sauce for dipping. —*Donna Klettke, Wheatland, Missouri*

1/2 pound ground beef
1 can (8 ounces) tomato sauce
1/2 cup shredded mozzarella cheese
1/2 teaspoon dried oregano
2 tubes (8 ounces *each*) refrigerated crescent rolls

In a skillet, cook beef over medium heat until no longer pink; drain. Remove from the heat. Add tomato sauce, mozzarella cheese and oregano; mix well.

Separate crescent dough into eight rectangles, pinching seams together. Place about 3 tablespoons of meat mixture along one long side of each rectangle. Roll up, jelly-roll style, starting with a long side. Cut each roll into three pieces. Place, seam side down, 2 in. apart on greased baking sheets. Bake at 375° for 15 minutes or until golden brown. **Yield:** 2 dozen.

Mushroom Bacon Bites

This is the perfect appetizer for most any occasion. The tasty bites are easy to assemble and brush with prepared barbecue sauce. When we have a big cookout, they're always a hit...but they make a nice little "extra" for a family dinner, too.
—Gina Roesner, Ashland, Missouri

24 medium fresh
    mushrooms
12 bacon strips, halved
1 cup barbecue sauce

Wrap each mushroom with a piece of bacon; secure with a toothpick. Thread onto metal or soaked bamboo skewers; brush with barbecue sauce.

Grill, uncovered, over indirect medium heat for 10-15 minutes or until the bacon is crisp and the mushrooms are tender, turning and basting occasionally with remaining barbecue sauce. **Yield:** 2 dozen.

|MUSHROOM HINT| Clean mushrooms just before using. Never immerse them in water, as they're very absorbent and become mushy. Simply rinse mushrooms under cold running water and blot dry with paper towels.

Cranberry Quencher

This tart, fruity punch has such a pretty color. I got the recipe while visiting Hawaii, so it's no surprise pineapple juice is a main ingredient. I like to serve it for the holidays.
—Dorothy Smith
El Dorado, Arkansas

1 bottle (1 gallon)
    cranberry-apple juice,
    chilled
1 can (46 ounces)
    pineapple juice, chilled
3/4 cup (6 ounces) lemonade
    or orange juice
    concentrate
Pineapple rings *or* tidbits, fresh
    cranberries *and/or* mint,
    optional

Combine cranberry-apple and pineapple juices in a large container or punch bowl. Stir in lemonade concentrate. Garnish glasses with pineapple, cranberries and/or mint if desired. **Yield:** 6 quarts.

Pineapple Ham Spread

This is a recipe I served my kids when time was short…and so was leftover ham. Spread the sweet ham mixture on rye bread or crunchy crackers for an effortless appetizer.
—*Delia Kennedy*
Deer Park, Washington

4 ounces cream cheese, softened
1 can (8 ounces) crushed pineapple, drained
1/2 cup ground fully cooked ham
Crackers *or* snack rye bread

In a bowl, combine the cream cheese, pineapple and ham. Serve with crackers or bread. **Yield:** 1-1/3 cups.

Editor's Note: See your local butcher to purchase ground ham.

Raspberry Lemonade

This crisp, tart beverage is a real thirst-quencher on a hot day. Pretty enough to serve at a bridal shower and refreshing enough to pour at a picnic, it's a fun change from iced tea or regular lemonade.
—*Dorothy Jennings, Waterloo, Iowa*

2 cans (12 ounces *each*) frozen lemonade concentrate, thawed
2 packages (10 ounces *each*) frozen sweetened raspberries, partially thawed
2 to 4 tablespoons sugar
2 liters club soda, chilled
Ice cubes

In a blender, combine lemonade concentrate, raspberries and sugar. Cover and process until blended. Strain to remove seeds. In a 4-1/2-qt. container, combine raspberry mixture, club soda and ice cubes; mix well. Serve immediately. **Yield:** 3-1/2 quarts.

Ham Pickle Pinwheels

My mom introduced me to these appetizers a number of years ago, and I've been serving them for parties ever since. They're easy to make and are always well received by guests. —*Gloria Jarrett*
Loveland, Ohio

1 package (8 ounces) cream cheese, cubed
1/4 pound sliced Genoa salami
1 tablespoon prepared horseradish
7 slices deli ham
14 to 21 okra pickles *or* dill pickle spears

Place cream cheese, salami and horseradish in a blender or food processor; cover and process until smooth. Spread over ham slices.

Remove stems and ends of okra pickles. Place two or three okra pickles or one dill pickle down the center of each ham slice. Roll up tightly and wrap in plastic wrap. Refrigerate for at least 2 hours. Cut into 1-in. slices. **Yield:** about 3-1/2 dozen.

|MAKE-AHEAD ADVICE| Ham Pickle Pinwheels can be prepared a day or two before you serve them. Simply store the uncut appetizer in the refrigerator tightly wrapped in plastic wrap.

Frothy Apricot Drink

Four simple ingredients make this drink as refreshing as it is pretty. It's especially great to sip this treat on a hot day.
—*Diane Hixon*
Niceville, Florida

1 can (15-1/4 ounces) apricot halves, undrained
1/2 cup milk
1/4 cup orange juice concentrate
1 pint lemon sherbet

In a blender, place apricot halves with juice, milk and orange juice concentrate. Cover and process until smooth. Add sherbet; cover and process just until combined. Pour into glasses; serve immediately. **Yield:** 4 cups.

Chocolate Cream Fruit Dip

This recipe was truly an accident. While hosting a graduation party, I realized I'd forgotten the fruit dip. So I raided my cabinets and slapped this combination together. It was a surprising success and has since become one of our family's favorites.
—Debbie Bond, Richwood, West Virginia

1 package (8 ounces)
    cream cheese, softened
1/4 cup chocolate syrup
1 jar (7 ounces)
    marshmallow creme
Apple wedges, fresh strawberries
    and/or banana chunks

In a small mixing bowl, beat cream cheese and chocolate syrup. Fold in marshmallow creme. Cover and refrigerate until serving. Serve with fruit. **Yield:** about 2 cups.

Lunch Box Pizzas

It's a challenge finding lunch fare that both our children enjoy. These mini pizzas are fun to make. They pack nicely in plastic sandwich bags and travel well, so there's no mess. They also make a tasty after-school snack. —Rhonda Cliett, Belton, Texas

1 tube (7-1/2 ounces)
    refrigerated buttermilk
    biscuits (10 biscuits)
1/4 cup tomato sauce
1 teaspoon Italian
    seasoning
10 slices pepperoni
3/4 cup shredded Monterey
    Jack cheese

Flatten each biscuit into a 3-in. circle and press into a greased muffin cup. Combine the tomato sauce and Italian seasoning; spoon 1 teaspoonful into each cup. Top each with a slice of pepperoni and about 1 tablespoon of cheese.

Bake at 425° for 10-15 minutes or until golden brown. Serve immediately or store in the refrigerator. **Yield:** 10 servings.

Creamy Swiss Spinach Dip

A few items and a microwave oven are all you need to throw together this warm cheesy dip. It's always gone at the party's end. My favorite way to serve the dip is in a bread bowl with bread cubes, but it's also good with tortilla chips or French bread slices. —*Heather Millican*
Fort Myers, Florida

1 package (8 ounces) cream cheese, softened
1 teaspoon garlic powder
1 package (9 ounces) frozen creamed spinach, thawed
2 cups diced Swiss cheese
2 unsliced round loaves (1 pound *each*) Italian *or* French bread

In a small microwave-safe mixing bowl, beat cream cheese and garlic powder until smooth. Stir in spinach and Swiss cheese. Cover and microwave on high for 5-8 minutes or until cheese is melted, stirring occasionally.

Meanwhile, cut a 4-in. circle in the center of one loaf of bread. Remove bread, leaving 1 in. at bottom of loaf. Cut removed bread and the second loaf into 1-1/2-in. cubes. Spoon hot spinach dip into bread shell. Serve with bread cubes. **Yield:** 3-1/2 cups.

Editor's Note: This recipe was tested in an 850-watt microwave.

After-School Treats

These delicious no-bake bars satisfy my craving for chocolate and are much easier to whip up than brownies or cookies from scratch. Requiring just five ingredients, they're especially handy for a bake sale or after-school treat.
—*Andrea Neilson, East Dundee, Illinois*

2 cups (12 ounces) semisweet chocolate chips
1/4 cup butter-flavored shortening
5 cups crisp rice cereal
1 package (10 ounces) Milk Duds
1 tablespoon water

In a large microwave-safe bowl, combine chocolate chips and shortening. Cover and microwave on high until chocolate is melted, about 2 minutes; stir until well blended. Stir in cereal until well coated.

In another microwave-safe bowl, combine Milk Duds and water. Cover and microwave on high for 1 minute or until mixture is pourable; mix well. Stir into cereal mixture. Spread into a buttered 13-in. x 9-in. x 2-in. pan. Cover and refrigerate for 30 minutes or until firm. Cut into bars. **Yield:** 2 dozen.

Editor's Note: This recipe was tested in an 850-watt microwave.

Skewered Shrimp

I combine four ingredients to create a ginger mixture that's used as both a marinade and a sauce for these barbecued shrimp. Serve them with toothpicks as an appetizer or stir the shrimp into pasta for an entree.

—*Joan Morris, Lillian, Alabama*

3 tablespoons soy sauce
2 tablespoons lemon juice
1 tablespoon chili sauce
1 tablespoon minced fresh gingerroot
1 pound uncooked medium shrimp, peeled and deveined

In a bowl, combine the soy sauce, lemon juice, chili sauce and ginger; mix well. Pour half into a large resealable plastic bag; add the shrimp. Seal bag and turn to coat; refrigerate for 2 hours. Cover and refrigerate remaining marinade.

Drain and discard marinade from shrimp. Thread onto metal or soaked wooden skewers. Grill, uncovered, over medium heat for 6-8 minutes or until shrimp turn pink, turning once. Serve with reserved marinade. **Yield:** 4 servings.

|PEELING AND DEVEINING SHRIMP| Remove the shell by opening the shell at the underside or leg area and peeling it back. A gentle pull may be necessary to release the shell from the tail area. To remove the black vein, make a slit with a paring knife along the back from the head area to the tail. Rinse shrimp under cold water to remove the exposed vein.

Peach Smoothies

Nothing could be sweeter than starting the day off with this refreshing beverage. But I enjoy the smoothies so much, I make them throughout the day.

—*Dana Tittle, Forrest City, Arkansas*

2 cups milk
2 cups frozen unsweetened sliced peaches
1/4 cup orange juice concentrate
2 tablespoons sugar
5 ice cubes

In a blender, combine all ingredients; cover and process until smooth. Pour into glasses; serve immediately. **Yield:** 4 servings.

Ranch Chicken Bites

These zesty bites are a fun and easy way to serve chicken. Only two simple ingredients make the savory ranch coating.
—*Ann Brunkhorst, Masonville, Iowa*

1 **pound boneless skinless chicken breasts**
1/2 **cup ranch salad dressing**
2-1/2 **cups finely crushed sour cream and onion potato chips**

Cut chicken into bite-size pieces; place in a bowl. Add salad dressing and stir to coat. Let stand for 10 minutes. Add potato chips and toss well. Place on a greased baking sheet. Bake, uncovered, at 350° for 18-20 minutes or until juices run clear. **Yield:** 4 servings.

Fried Cinnamon Strips

I first made these crispy strips for a special family night at our church. Most of them were snapped up before dinner!
—*Nancy Johnson*
Laverne, Oklahoma

1 **cup sugar**
1 **teaspoon ground cinnamon**
1/4 **teaspoon ground nutmeg**
10 **flour tortillas (8 inches)**
Vegetable oil

In a large resealable plastic bag, combine sugar, cinnamon and nutmeg; set aside. Cut tortillas into 3-in. x 2-in. strips. Heat 1 in. of oil in a skillet or electric fry pan to 375°; fry 4-5 strips at a time for 30 seconds on each side or until golden brown. Drain on paper towels.

While still warm, place strips in bag with sugar mixture; shake gently to coat. Serve immediately or store in an airtight container. **Yield:** 5 dozen.

|DEEP-FRYING FACT| It's best to fry food in small batches. Large amounts of food lower the oil's temperature, which means that it's more likely to soak into the food.

Sugar-Coated Pecans

It's impossible to stop snacking on these sweet crispy nuts, so I make several batches over the holidays to keep a supply on hand. They also make a mouth-watering homemade Christmas gift. People tend to eat them by the handful.   —*Carol Crowley*
West Haven, Connecticut

1 tablespoon egg white
2 cups pecan halves
1/4 cup sugar
2 teaspoons ground cinnamon

In a bowl, beat egg white until foamy. Add pecans and toss until well coated. Combine sugar and cinnamon; sprinkle over pecans and toss to coat.

Spread in a single layer on an ungreased baking sheet. Bake at 300° for 25-30 minutes or until browned, stirring occasionally. Cool on waxed paper. **Yield:** 3 cups.

Nutty Cracker Delights

I always receive compliments when I serve these crispy snacks. Both sweet and salty, they're fun as appetizers or for munching. They freeze well, too, so you can make them ahead if you're planning a party.
—*Carla Lee, Devils Lake, North Dakota*

42 Club crackers (2-1/2 inches x 1 inch)
1/2 cup butter
1/2 cup sugar
1 teaspoon vanilla extract
1 cup slivered almonds

Place crackers in a single layer in a foil-lined 15-in. x 10-in. x 1-in. baking pan. In a saucepan over medium heat, melt butter. Add sugar; bring to a boil, stirring constantly. Boil for 2 minutes. Remove from the heat; add vanilla. Pour evenly over crackers; sprinkle with nuts.

Bake at 350° for 10-12 minutes or until lightly browned. Immediately remove from the pan, cutting between crackers if necessary, and cool on wire racks. Store in an airtight container. **Yield:** 3-1/2 dozen.

Mozzarella Puffs

These savory cheesy biscuits go over great at my house. Since they're so quick to make, I can whip up a batch anytime. They're full of pizza flavor but are more fun to serve!
—Joan Mousley Dziuba
Waupaca, Wisconsin

1 tube (7-1/2 ounces) refrigerated buttermilk biscuits
1 teaspoon dried oregano
1 block (2 to 3 ounces) mozzarella cheese
2 tablespoons pizza sauce

Make an indentation in the center of each biscuit; sprinkle with oregano. Cut the mozzarella into 10 cubes, 3/4 in. each; place a cube in the center of each biscuit. Pinch dough tightly around cheese to seal.

Place seam side down on an ungreased baking sheet. Spread pizza sauce over tops. Bake at 375° for 10-12 minutes or until golden brown. **Yield:** 10 servings.

Simple Guacamole

This homemade guacamole is pretty basic, but it always gets compliments. A jar of salsa makes it a breeze to stir up and serve with crunchy tortilla chips for an effortless appetizer.   —Heidi Main
Anchorage, Alaska

2 medium ripe avocados
1 tablespoon lemon juice
1/4 cup chunky salsa
1/8 to 1/4 teaspoon salt

Peel and chop avocados; place in a small bowl. Sprinkle with lemon juice. Add salsa and salt; mash coarsely with a fork. Refrigerate until serving. **Yield:** 1-1/2 cups.

|AVOCADO ADVICE| To peel an avocado half, use the point of a sharp paring knife to make a lengthwise cut down the middle of the skin. At the stem end, grasp one piece of the skin between your thumb and the knife edge; pull the skin down and off the avocado. Repeat with the other strip of skin. For guacamole or other dips, choose slightly over-ripe avocados—they'll mash more easily. Always add lemon juice to guacamole. The acid not only helps keep the avocado from browning, it also brightens the flavor.

Purple Cows

Kids will need only three ingredients to whip up this bright beverage. The sweet blend gets its purple color and refreshing flavor from grape juice concentrate.

—Renee Schwebach
Dumont, Minnesota

1-1/2 cups milk
  3/4 cup grape juice
      concentrate
    2 cups vanilla ice cream

In a blender, combine milk and grape juice concentrate. Add ice cream; cover and blend until smooth. Serve immediately. **Yield:** 4 servings.

|WHAT'S IN A NAME?| A Purple Cow consists, basically, of purple grape juice and milk and/or milk products. There are more variations than breeds of real cows! Kids love it, partly because it turns their tongue purple and gives them a violet mustache.

Tiger Tea

"Tee time" was deliciously refreshing when we poured this thirst-quenching iced tea at a golf party we had a few years ago. I enjoyed coming up with the recipe titles for our theme foods. Even non-golfers know this bright beverage is named for famous young pro Tiger Woods.

—Sue Ann O'Buck
Sinking Spring, Pennsylvania

    3 quarts water, *divided*
    6 individual tea bags
  3/4 cup lemonade
      concentrate
  3/4 cup orange juice
      concentrate
    1 cup sugar

In a large kettle, bring 1 quart water to a boil. Remove from the heat; add tea bags. Steep for 5 minutes. Discard the tea bags.

Stir in the lemonade and orange juice concentrates, sugar and remaining water. Serve over ice. **Yield:** about 3 quarts.

Chocolate Malts

I can whip up this decadent ice cream drink in just minutes. It's a favorite with kids after a day in the pool or for dessert after a barbecue.
—*Marion Lowery, Medford, Oregon*

3/4 cup milk
1/2 cup caramel ice cream topping
2 cups chocolate ice cream, softened
3 tablespoons malted milk powder
2 tablespoons chopped pecans, optional
Grated chocolate, optional

In a blender, combine the first five ingredients; cover and process until blended. Pour into chilled glasses. Sprinkle with grated chocolate if desired. **Yield:** 2-1/2 cups.

|SCOOPING ICE CREAM| Dip your ice cream scoop in hot water before removing ice cream from the carton, and the ice cream will easily slip off the scoop.

Pizza Corn Dog Snacks

I dress up frozen corn dogs to create these tasty bite-size treats. Just slice 'em and spread 'em with pizza sauce and other toppings for a fun snack for kids or an easy appetizer for adults.
—*Linda Knopp*
Camas, Washington

1 package (16 ounces) frozen corn dogs, thawed
1/2 cup pizza sauce
3 tablespoons chopped ripe olives
1 jar (4-1/2 ounces) sliced mushrooms, drained
1/4 cup shredded mozzarella cheese

Remove stick from each corn dog; cut into 1-in. slices. Place on an ungreased baking sheet. Spread with pizza sauce. Top with olives, mushrooms and cheese.

Bake at 350° for 15-20 minutes or until the cheese is melted and corn dogs are heated through. **Yield:** 30 snacks.

Buttermilk Shakes

These rich shakes taste like liquid cheesecake! With just a few ingredients, they're a snap to prepare at a moment's notice any time of the day.
—*Gloria Jarrett, Loveland, Ohio*

1 pint vanilla ice cream, softened
1 cup buttermilk
1 teaspoon grated lemon peel
1/2 teaspoon vanilla extract
1 drop lemon extract

Place all ingredients in a blender container. Cover and process on high until smooth. Pour into glasses. Refrigerate any leftovers. **Yield:** 2 servings.

Honey-Glazed Snack Mix

Short and sweet sums up the recipe for this munchable snack mix. It's a cinch to package it in individual snack bags, too.
—*Jan Olson*
New Hope, Minnesota

8 cups Crispix cereal
3 cups miniature pretzels
2 cups pecan halves
2/3 cup butter
1/2 cup honey

In a large bowl, combine the cereal, pretzels and pecans; set aside. In a small saucepan, melt butter; stir in honey until well blended. Pour over cereal mixture and stir to coat. Spread into two greased 15-in. x 10-in. x 1-in. baking pans.

Bake at 350° for 12-15 minutes or until mixture is lightly glazed, stirring occasionally. Cool in pan for 3 minutes; remove from pan and spread on waxed paper to cool completely. Store in an airtight container. **Yield:** about 12 cups.

Low-Fat Eggnog

Everyone can enjoy a traditional taste of the season with this smooth, creamy eggnog. Although it's made with low-fat ingredients, the easy-to-fix recipe retains the thick and creamy consistency of the classic Christmas beverage. Our kids love it.

—*Paula Zsiray, Logan, Utah*

✓ **Uses less fat, sugar or salt. Includes Nutritional Analysis and Diabetic Exchanges.**

**11 cups cold fat-free milk
2 teaspoons vanilla extract
2 packages (1.5 ounces each) instant sugar-free vanilla pudding mix
Artificial sweetener equivalent to 1/3 cup sugar
1/2 teaspoon ground nutmeg**

In a large bowl, combine the milk and vanilla. In another bowl, combine dry pudding mix, sweetener and nutmeg. Whisk into milk mixture until smooth. Refrigerate until serving. **Yield:** 12 servings.

Nutritional Analysis: One 1-cup serving equals 105 calories, 408 mg sodium, 4 mg cholesterol, 17 g carbohydrate, 8 g protein, trace fat. **Diabetic Exchanges:** 1 skim milk, 1/2 starch.

|EGGNOG IQ| A takeoff on similar European egg-and-milk drinks, eggnog was a popular wintertime beverage in Colonial America. It was made in large quantities and was nearly always served for social occasions, especially on Christmas.

Cherry Berry Smoothies

We have three young children, so we always have fruit juices on hand to experiment with when making smoothies. I turn cherry juice, fruit and yogurt into this colorful family favorite.

—*Shonna Thibodeau, Fort Huachuca, Arizona*

**1 cup cherry juice
1 carton (8 ounces) vanilla yogurt
1 cup frozen unsweetened raspberries
1/2 cup seedless red grapes
3 to 4 teaspoons sugar**

In a blender, combine all ingredients. Cover and process until well blended. Pour into glasses; serve immediately. **Yield:** 3 servings.

Reuben Party Spread

This speedy sandwich spread makes an appearance at almost all of our family gatherings. It tastes like a traditional Reuben sandwich, but it's easier to assemble.
—*Connie Thompson*
Racine, Wisconsin

1 pound fully cooked ham, chopped
4 cups (1 pound) shredded Swiss cheese
1 can (8 ounces) sauerkraut, drained
1/2 cup Thousand Island salad dressing
Cocktail rye bread

In a microwave-safe bowl, combine the ham, cheese, sauerkraut and salad dressing. Cover and microwave on high for 1 to 1-1/2 minutes or until cheese is melted, stirring once. Serve on rye bread. **Yield:** 6 cups.

Editor's Note: This recipe was tested in an 850-watt microwave.

Sweet Pretzel Nuggets

This crowd-pleasing snack has been a tremendous hit both at home and at work. The fun crunchy bites have a sweet cinnamon-toast taste and just a hint of saltiness that make them very munchable.
—*Billie Sue Ebinger, Holton, Indiana*

1 package (15 to 18 ounces) sourdough pretzel nuggets
2/3 cup vegetable oil
1/3 cup sugar
1 to 2 teaspoons ground cinnamon

Place pretzels in a microwave-safe bowl. In a small bowl, combine the oil, sugar and cinnamon; pour over the pretzels and toss to coat. Microwave, uncovered, on high for 2 minutes; stir. Microwave 3-4 minutes longer, stirring after each minute or until oil is absorbed. Cool to room temperature. **Yield:** 12-16 servings.

Editor's Note: This recipe was tested in an 850-watt microwave.

Salsa Sausage Quiche

A prepared pastry crust hurries along the assembly of this hearty appetizer. Served with sour cream and additional salsa, it's a party favorite in our retirement community. If you're feeding a crowd, bring two—they disappear fast!
—*Dorothy Sorensen, Naples, Florida*

3/4 pound bulk pork sausage
1 unbaked pastry shell (9 inches)
2 cups (8 ounces) shredded cheddar cheese, *divided*
3 eggs
1 cup salsa

In a skillet, cook the sausage over medium heat until no longer pink; drain. Transfer to the pastry shell. Sprinkle with half of the cheese. In a small bowl, lightly beat the eggs; stir in salsa. Pour over cheese.

Bake at 375° for 30-35 minutes or until a knife inserted near the center comes out clean. Sprinkle with the remaining cheese. Bake 5 minutes longer or until the cheese is melted. **Yield:** 6-8 servings.

|STORING SAUSAGE| Refrigerator storage for sausages depends on the type: uncooked fresh sausages (like pork sausage) are very perishable and should be refrigerated, well wrapped, for no more than 2 days; uncooked smoked (mettwurst) for up to 1 week; cooked smoked (knockwurst) in unopened package for 2 weeks; dry sausage (pepperoni) for up to 3 weeks.

Strawberry Banana Shakes

This very thick, not-too-sweet shake packs a big strawberry and banana taste. It's easy to mix together in the blender. I especially like it topped with whipped cream. —*Grant Dixon Roseburg, Oregon*

1/4 cup milk
1 cup strawberry ice cream
1 medium firm banana, sliced
Whipped cream and two fresh strawberries, optional

Place milk, ice cream and banana in a blender; cover and process until smooth. Pour into glasses. Garnish with whipped cream and a strawberry if desired. **Yield:** 2 servings.

Cheese Wedges

These easy cheesy treats are a hit at evening gatherings. They're a zesty change of pace from mozzarella sticks, plus they're great for dipping in pizza sauce.
—*Jennifer Eilts, Omaha, Nebraska*

1 package (7 ounces) extra sharp cheddar cheese
1/3 cup seasoned dry bread crumbs
1/2 teaspoon crushed red pepper flakes, optional
1 egg
1 can (8 ounces) pizza sauce, warmed

Cut cheese into 1/2-in. slices; cut each slice in half diagonally. In a shallow bowl, combine bread crumbs and red pepper flakes if desired. In another bowl, beat egg. Dip cheese triangles into egg, then in crumb mixture.

Place on a greased baking sheet. Broil 4 in. from the heat for 2-3 minutes or until browned and cheese begins to melt. Serve cheese wedges warm with pizza sauce for dipping. **Yield:** 6 servings.

Hot Mustard Pretzel Dip

It's a snap to stir together this zippy dip. With its hint of honey, the mixture is great with pretzels...or try it anywhere you'd use a hot-and-spicy sauce.
—*Kim Barrick, Lincoln, Illinois*

1/4 cup ground mustard
1/4 cup vinegar
1/4 cup sugar
1 egg yolk
2 tablespoons honey

In a small saucepan, combine mustard and vinegar; let stand for 30 minutes. Whisk in the sugar and egg yolk until smooth.

Cook over medium heat, whisking constantly, until mixture just begins to simmer and is thickened, about 7 minutes. Remove from the heat; whisk in honey. Store in the refrigerator. **Yield:** 1/2 cup.

Trail Mix

With nuts, raisins, M&M's and coconut, this is a super snack. In small gingham bags, it made wonderful party favors for each guest at the cowboy-theme wedding shower I hosted a number of years ago. This mix is a tasty treat anytime, so I always keep batches on hand in my cupboard. —Sandra Thorn
Sonora, California

2 pounds dry roasted peanuts
2 pounds cashews
1 pound raisins
1 pound M&M's
1/2 pound flaked coconut

Combine all ingredients in a large bowl. Store in an airtight container. **Yield:** 6 quarts.

|DEFINING RAISINS| Dark raisins are sun-dried for several weeks, thereby gaining their dark color and shriveled appearance. Golden raisins have been treated with sulphur dioxide (to prevent darkening) and dried with artificial heat, which leaves them plumper and moister than dark raisins. Raisins can be stored in a tightly sealed plastic bag at room temperature for several months.

Mock Champagne Punch

Every Christmas, I place holly from our own trees around my punch bowl filled with Mock Champagne Punch. Even the children can enjoy this nonalcoholic beverage. Of all the punch recipes I've tried, I keep coming back to this one. It's so easy to keep the ingredients in the refrigerator and mix as much as needed. —Betty Claycomb, Alverton, Pennsylvania

1 quart white grape juice, chilled
1 quart ginger ale, chilled
Strawberries *or* raspberries

Combine grape juice and ginger ale; pour into a punch bowl or glasses. Garnish with strawberries or raspberries. **Yield:** 16 (1/2-cup) servings.

|PUNCH POINTER| Chill all punch ingredients before mixing so that you don't have to dilute the punch with ice to get it cold. Or garnish a cold punch with an ice ring made from punch ingredients instead of water.

Roasted Mixed Nuts

It's impossible to stop eating these savory nuts once you start. We love to munch on them as an evening snack.

—*Carolyn Zimmerman, Fairbury, Illinois*

1 pound mixed nuts
1/4 cup maple syrup
2 tablespoons brown sugar
1 envelope ranch salad
dressing mix

In a bowl, combine the nuts and maple syrup; mix well. Sprinkle with brown sugar and salad dressing mix; stir gently to coat.

Spread in a greased 15-in. x 10-in. x 1-in. baking pan. Bake at 300° for 20-25 minutes or until lightly browned. Cool. Store in an airtight container. **Yield:** 3 cups.

|STOVETOP SNACK| You can also make cocktail nuts in a skillet. Saute 2 cups nuts in 2 tablespoons oil or melted butter over medium-high heat, stirring often, until they begin to brown. Sprinkle with your choice of seasonings (salt, pepper, cayenne pepper, curry powder, etc.), tossing the nuts with a wooden spoon. Turn out onto paper towels to cool, then store in an airtight container.

Cool Waters Shakes

Ride a wave of approval when you serve this refreshing berry-flavored beverage. Kids will love its pastel blue color and sea-foamy consistency...and with just three simple ingredients, it's a breeze to whip up in the blender.

—*Taste of Home*
Test Kitchen

4 cups cold milk
2 packages (3 ounces
each) berry blue gelatin
1 quart vanilla ice cream

In a blender, combine 2 cups of milk, one package of gelatin and 2 cups of ice cream. Cover and process for 30 seconds or until smooth. Repeat. Pour into glasses and serve immediately. **Yield:** 6 servings.

Lemonade Slush

I used to make a similar beverage with orange juice concentrate, but I enjoy lemonade so much that I altered the recipe a bit. My family loved the results and now I fix this lemon version all the time. Not only is the drink fast and refreshing, but it's perfect at breakfast, after school or any time of the day.
—*Tracy Brousseau, Orem, Utah*

✓ **Uses less fat, sugar or salt. Includes Nutritional Analysis and Diabetic Exchanges.**

  2/3 cup lemonade
     concentrate, partially
     thawed
    1 cup milk
  2/3 cup water
    1 teaspoon vanilla extract
Yellow food coloring, optional
  12 ice cubes, crushed

In a blender, combine lemonade concentrate, milk, water, vanilla and food coloring if desired; cover and process until blended. While processing, slowly add crushed ice. Process until slushy. Serve immediately. **Yield:** 8 servings.

Nutritional Analysis: One 3/4-cup serving (prepared with fat-free milk) equals 56 calories, trace fat (trace saturated fat), 1 mg cholesterol, 17 mg sodium, 13 g carbohydrate, trace fiber, 1 g protein. **Diabetic Exchange:** 1 fruit.

Minted Iced Tea Cooler

This cool rose-colored tea quenches your thirst in the most delightful way. It's a pleasant blend of fruit and mint flavors. It's easy to make but more special than traditional iced tea.
—*Debbie Terenzini Wilkerson*
Lusby, Maryland

    3 peppermint-flavored tea
     bags
    7 cups boiling water
    1 cup cranberry juice
  3/4 cup pink lemonade
     concentrate

Steep tea bags in boiling water for 5-10 minutes. Discard tea bags. Pour tea into a pitcher or large bowl; stir in cranberry juice and lemonade concentrate. Cover and refrigerate overnight. Serve over ice. **Yield:** 8 servings.

Cheerio Treats

I use peanut butter, Cheerios and candies to put a tooth-tingling spin on marshmallow-cereal bars. Whether I take them to picnics or bake sales, I'm always asked for the recipe. —*Penny Reifenrath*
Wynot, Nebraska

3 tablespoons butter
1 package (10-1/2 ounces) miniature marshmallows
1/2 cup peanut butter
5 cups Cheerios
1 cup plain M&M's

Place the butter and marshmallows in a large microwave-safe bowl. Microwave, uncovered, on high for 2 minutes or until puffed. Stir in the peanut butter until blended. Add the cereal and M&M's; mix well. Spoon into a greased 13-in. x 9-in. x 2-in. pan; press down gently. Cool slightly before cutting. **Yield:** 15 servings.

Corny Snack Mix

It's hard to stop munching on this yummy snack mix! Melted vanilla chips make a delightful coating for the crisp corn chips, cereal and popcorn. This mix is quick and easy to toss together. I like to keep it on hand for when our five grandchildren visit.
—*Sandy Wehring, Fremont, Ohio*

3 quarts popped popcorn
1 package (15 ounces) Corn Pops
1 package (15 ounces) corn chips
2 packages (10 to 12 ounces *each*) vanilla *or* white chips

In several large bowls, combine the popcorn, Corn Pops and corn chips. In a saucepan over medium-low heat, melt chips; stir until smooth. Pour over popcorn mixture and toss to coat. Spread in two 15-in. x 10-in. x 1-in. pans. Cool. Store in airtight containers. **Yield:** 7-1/2 quarts.

Pineapple Cooler

I stir up this mild and refreshing beverage in a jiffy. Lemon juice cuts the sweetness you might expect from pineapple juice and lemon-lime soda.
—*Michelle Blumberg*
Littlerock, California

✓ **Uses less fat, sugar or salt. Includes Nutritional Analysis and Diabetic Exchanges.**

1 cup unsweetened pineapple juice, chilled
1 to 2 tablespoons lemon juice
1 can (12 ounces) lemon-lime soda, chilled

Combine all ingredients in a pitcher; stir well. Serve over ice. **Yield:** 2-2/3 cups.

Nutritional Analysis: One 1-cup serving (prepared with diet soda) equals 48 calories, 13 mg sodium, 0 cholesterol, 12 g carbohydrate, trace protein, trace fat. **Diabetic Exchange:** 1 fruit.

Mocha Morning Drink

When I'm sipping this delicious coffee in the morning, I almost feel like I've been to my favorite coffeehouse instead of to my own kitchen to whip it up.
—*Jill Rodriguez, Gonzales, Louisiana*

6 cups hot brewed coffee
3/4 cup half-and-half cream
6 tablespoons chocolate syrup
7 teaspoons sugar
6 cinnamon sticks (3 inches)
Whipped cream in a can, optional

In a saucepan, combine the coffee, cream, chocolate syrup and sugar. Cook and stir over medium heat until sugar is dissolved and mixture is heated through. Ladle into six large mugs. Stir with a cinnamon stick. Garnish with whipped cream if desired. **Yield:** 6 servings.

|COFFEE FACTS| For maximum flavor, grind only as many beans as needed to brew each pot of coffee. Generally, the finer the grind, the fuller the flavor. The flavor of coffee begins to deteriorate within 15 minutes after it's brewed.

Lo-Cal Apple Snack

This quick snack is often requested as an office treat. It's a simple and harvest-fresh way to serve autumn's best apples—kids also love it.
—*Nancy Horan, Sioux Falls, South Dakota*

 Uses less fat, sugar or salt. Includes Nutritional Analysis and Diabetic Exchanges.

- 4 medium Golden Delicious apples, peeled, cored and sliced into rounds
- 1/2 cup apple juice
- 1/4 teaspoon ground cinnamon
- 1 tablespoon grated lemon peel

In an ungreased 11-in. x 7-in. x 2-in. microwave-safe baking dish, arrange apples in two rows. Pour apple juice over apples. Sprinkle with cinnamon and lemon peel. Cover and microwave on high for 7 minutes or until apples are tender, turning after 3-1/2 minutes. **Yield:** 4 servings.

Nutritional Analysis: One serving equals 88 calories, 1 mg sodium, 0 cholesterol, 23 g carbohydrate, trace protein, trace fat. **Diabetic Exchange:** 1-1/2 fruit.

Editor's Note: This recipe was tested in a 700-watt microwave.

Taco Tidbits

This four-ingredient combination is a great change of pace from typical snack mixes. It's a good thing the crispy treat is so simple to throw together because your family will empty the bowl in no time.
—*Sharon Mensing, Greenfield, Iowa*

- 6 tablespoons butter
- 2 to 3 tablespoons taco seasoning
- 8 cups Corn Chex
- 1/4 cup grated Parmesan cheese

Place butter in an 11-in. x 7-in. x 2-in. microwave-safe dish. Cover and microwave on high for 60-70 seconds or until melted. Add taco seasoning. Stir in the cereal until evenly coated.

Microwave on high for 1 minute; stir. Heat 1 to 1-1/2 minutes longer; stir. Sprinkle with Parmesan cheese; microwave for 1 minute. Stir; heat 1 minute longer. Cool. **Yield:** 8 cups.

Editor's Note: This recipe was tested in an 850-watt microwave.

Banana Pops

Frozen pops, kids and summer just naturally seem to go together. Not only do kids like eating the sweet treats, they also can have fun making them. Making a batch of Banana Pops is easy. My little granddaughter likes scooping the yogurt and pouring in the orange juice. The hardest part for her is waiting for the pops to freeze so she can enjoy one down to the last refreshing lick!

—*Elaine Carver, Portland, Maine*

1 cup vanilla yogurt
1/2 cup orange juice
1 medium ripe banana, cut into chunks

In a blender, combine the yogurt, orange juice and banana; cover and process until smooth. Pour into Popsicle trays, or pour into small plastic disposable cups and insert Popsicle sticks. Freeze until firm, about 5 hours or overnight. **Yield:** 6 servings.

Sunny Citrus Cooler

The sunny color of this refreshing punch matched the bright yellow sunflower decorations for my theme dinner I hosted a few years ago. It's easy to stir up, too, which is good news because a few sips may quench your thirst, but your taste buds are sure to be asking for more.

—*Holly Joyce*
Jackson, Minnesota

1 can (46 ounces) pineapple juice
2 cans (12 ounces *each*) frozen orange juice concentrate, thawed
3/4 cup lemonade concentrate
6 cups ginger ale *or* white soda, chilled
Orange slices, optional

In a 1-gal. pitcher, combine pineapple juice, orange juice concentrate and lemonade concentrate. Add ginger ale and mix well. Serve over ice. Garnish with orange slices if desired. Refrigerate leftovers. **Yield:** 1 gallon.

Peanut Butter Popcorn Bars

If you're looking for a fun snack for kids, try these chewy popcorn treats that have a mild peanut butter taste. They're easy to stir up and can be pressed into a pan to form bars or shaped into balls.
—*Kathy Oswald, Wauzeka, Wisconsin*

10 cups popped popcorn
1/2 cup sugar
1/2 cup light corn syrup
1/2 cup creamy peanut
    butter
1/2 teaspoon vanilla extract

Place popcorn in a large bowl; set aside. In a saucepan over medium heat, bring sugar and corn syrup to a boil, stirring constantly. Boil for 1 minute. Remove from the heat.

Stir in peanut butter and vanilla; mix well. Pour over popcorn and mix until well coated. Press into a buttered 13-in. x 9-in. x 2-in. pan. Cool slightly before cutting. **Yield:** 2 dozen.

Cinnamon 'n' Spice Fruit Dip

Cinnamon, nutmeg and brown sugar dress up whipped topping in this extremely easy party pleaser. My gang especially likes the dip with apples and pears, but feel free to try it with pineapple slices, strawberries and other fresh fruit. —*Julie Bertha
Pittsburgh, Pennsylvania*

✓ Uses less fat, sugar or salt. Includes Nutritional Analysis and Diabetic Exchanges.

2 cups whipped topping
1/4 cup packed brown sugar
1/8 to 1/4 teaspoon ground
    cinnamon
Dash ground nutmeg
Assorted fresh fruit

In a small bowl, combine the whipped topping, brown sugar, cinnamon and nutmeg. Store in the refrigerator. Serve with fruit. **Yield:** about 2 cups.

Nutritional Analysis: 2 tablespoons dip (prepared with reduced-fat whipped topping; calculated without fruit) equals 66 calories, 2 g fat (2 g saturated fat), 0 cholesterol, 3 mg sodium, 11 g carbohydrate, trace fiber, 0 protein. **Diabetic Exchange:** 1/2 starch.

Main Dishes

Bacon Cheeseburger Pasta, p. 47

Apricot Round Steak, p. 48

Tuscan Pork Roast, p. 49

Almond-Topped Chicken, p. 52

Creole Salmon
Fillets, p. 46

Main Dishes   45

Creole Salmon Fillets

(Pictured on page 45)

My crusty salmon fillets bake up moist and golden brown. Our grown daughters and grandsons like their food on the spicy side, so I knew Creole seasoning would make this entree a family favorite.
—*Florine Bruns, Fredericksburg, Texas*

4 **teaspoons Creole seasoning**
2 **garlic cloves, minced**
2 **teaspoons pepper**
4 **salmon fillets (6 ounces each)**
1/4 **cup minced fresh parsley**

In a large resealable plastic bag, combine the first three ingredients. Add salmon; shake to coat. Place salmon on a broiler pan or baking sheet. Broil 6 in. from the heat for 10-14 minutes or until fish flakes easily with a fork. Sprinkle with parsley. **Yield:** 4 servings.

Citrus Sirloin Steak

The mild citrus flavor of the marinade offers a nice change of pace from the usual steak seasonings. It's easy to prepare the steak the night before, then throw it on the grill. —*Carol Towey Pasadena, California*

2 **medium unpeeled lemons, quartered**
1 **medium unpeeled orange, quartered**
1/2 **cup vegetable oil**
1 **garlic clove, minced**
1 **boneless sirloin steak (about 2-1/2 pounds and 1-3/4 inches thick)**

In a skillet, cook the lemon and orange wedges in oil over medium heat for 10-15 minutes, stirring often. Add garlic; cook and stir 1-2 minutes longer. Place steak in a shallow glass baking dish; pierce meat every inch with a fork. Pour citrus mixture over meat; turn to coat. Cover and refrigerate overnight, turning three or four times.

Drain and discard marinade. On a covered grill over medium-hot heat, cook steak for 9-10 minutes on each side or until meat reaches desired doneness (for medium-rare, a meat thermometer should read 145°; medium, 160°; well-done, 170°). **Yield:** 6-8 servings.

Apple Kielbasa Coins

The juice, jelly and syrup add sweetness to sliced sausage in this stovetop sensation. My grown children look forward to this breakfast dish on special occasions such as Christmas. Slices of toast are tasty served with it. —JoAnn Lee
Kerhonkson, New York

 Uses less fat, sugar or salt. Includes Nutritional Analysis and Diabetic Exchanges.

1-1/2 pounds fully cooked kielbasa *or* Polish sausage, cut into 1/4-inch slices
1/4 cup apple juice
1/4 cup apple jelly
2 tablespoons maple syrup

In a large skillet, bring sausage and apple juice to a boil. Cover and cook for 5 minutes. Uncover and cook 5 minutes longer. Drain. Add jelly and syrup; cook and stir until jelly is melted and sausage is coated. **Yield:** 6 servings.

Nutritional Analysis: One 4-ounce serving (prepared with smoked turkey sausage) equals 224 calories, 5 g fat (2 g saturated fat), 51 mg cholesterol, 980 mg sodium, 27 g carbohydrate, trace fiber, 14 g protein. **Diabetic Exchanges:** 2 lean meat, 2 fruit.

Bacon Cheeseburger Pasta

(Pictured on page 44)

Children of all ages are sure to enjoy Bacon Cheeseburger Pasta, an effortless entree I concocted to duplicate all the wonderful flavors of my favorite hamburger. —Melissa Stevens
Elk River, Minnesota

8 ounces uncooked tube *or* spiral pasta
1 pound ground beef
6 bacon strips, diced
1 can (10-3/4 ounces) condensed tomato soup, undiluted
1 cup (4 ounces) shredded cheddar cheese
Barbecue sauce and prepared mustard, optional

Cook pasta according to package directions. Meanwhile, in a skillet, cook beef over medium heat until no longer pink; drain and set aside. In the same skillet, cook bacon until crisp; remove with a slotted spoon to paper towels. Discard drippings.

Drain pasta; add to the skillet. Add soup, beef and bacon; heat through. Sprinkle with cheese; cover and cook until the cheese is melted. Serve with barbecue sauce and mustard if desired. **Yield:** 4-6 servings.

Grilled Wild Turkey Breast

With only two ingredients, this is definitely the easiest recipe I have for cooking the wild turkey that my husband, Richard, brings home during spring hunting season. The grilled meat takes on a wonderful sweet smoky flavor. This recipe is equally delicious made with Italian salad dressing in place of the honey mustard variety.
—Michelle Kaase
Tomball, Texas

1 bone-in wild turkey breast (about 1-1/2 pounds), split
1 cup honey mustard salad dressing

Place turkey in a large resealable plastic bag; add salad dressing. Seal bag and turn to coat; refrigerate overnight, turning occasionally.

Drain and discard marinade. Grill turkey, covered, over indirect medium heat for 45-55 minutes or until juices run clear and a meat thermometer reads 170°. **Yield:** 2 servings.

|GRILLING GUIDE| With the indirect grilling method, foods are not cooked directly over the heat. On a charcoal grill, the hot coals are moved or "banked" to opposite sides of the grill, and a shallow foil pan is placed between the coals to catch the drippings. The food is placed on the center of the grill rack above the pan.

Apricot Round Steak

(Pictured on page 44)

Looking for a fun alternative to traditional steak sauce? Serve tender slices of round steak with a sweet apricot sauce that has a hint of pepper. The broiled entree is a snap to prepare.
—Bernadine Dirmeyer, Harpster, Ohio

1-3/4 pounds boneless top round steak (3/4 inch thick)
3/4 cup apricot preserves
1 tablespoon lemon juice
1/2 teaspoon salt
1/8 teaspoon hot pepper sauce

Place steak on broiler pan rack; broil for 6-8 minutes on each side. Meanwhile, in a saucepan or microwave-safe bowl, combine remaining ingredients. Cook until preserves are melted. Set aside 1/2 cup; brush remaining sauce over steak.

Broil 2-3 minutes longer or until meat reaches desired doneness (for medium-rare, a meat thermometer should read 145°; medium, 160°; well-done, 170°). Slice meat on the diagonal; serve with reserved apricot sauce. **Yield:** 8 servings.

Tuscan Pork Roast

(Pictured on page 44)

Everyone's eager to eat after the wonderful aroma of this roast tempts us all afternoon. This is a great Sunday dinner with little fuss. Since I found this recipe a few years ago, it's become a favorite with our seven grown children and their families.
—*Elinor Stabile, Canmore, Alberta*

5 to 8 garlic cloves, peeled
1 tablespoon dried rosemary
1 tablespoon olive oil
1/2 teaspoon salt
1 boneless pork loin roast (3 to 4 pounds)

In a blender or food processor, combine garlic, rosemary, oil and salt; blend until mixture turns to paste. Rub over the roast; cover and let stand for 30 minutes.

Place roast fat side up on a greased baking rack in a shallow roasting pan. Bake, uncovered, at 350° for 1 to 1-1/4 hours or until a meat thermometer reads 160°. Let stand for 15 minutes before slicing. **Yield:** 10-12 servings.

Stuffed Pasta Shells

These savory shells never fail to make a big impression, even though the recipe is very easy. One or two of these shells makes a great individual serving at a potluck, so a single batch goes a long way.
—*Jena Coffey, St. Louis, Missouri*

4 cups (16 ounces) shredded mozzarella cheese
1 carton (15 ounces) ricotta cheese
1 package (10 ounces) frozen chopped spinach, thawed and drained
1 package (12 ounces) jumbo pasta shells, cooked and drained
1 jar (28 ounces) spaghetti sauce

Combine cheeses and spinach; stuff into shells. Arrange in a greased 13-in. x 9-in. x 2-in. baking dish. Pour spaghetti sauce over the shells. Cover and bake at 350° for 30 minutes or until heated through. **Yield:** 12-14 servings.

|PASTA POINTER| Instead of draining jumbo pasta shells in a colander, which can cause them to tear, carefully remove them from the boiling water with a tongs. Pour out any water inside the shells and drain on lightly greased waxed paper until you're ready to stuff them.

Supreme Roast Beef

This fix-and-forget roast is one of our family's favorite Sunday meals. It's simple to prepare and leaves plenty of leftovers to enjoy later in the week.
—*Jackie Holland, Gillette, Wyoming*

1 large onion, sliced into rings
2 tablespoons Worcestershire sauce
4 to 5 teaspoons coarsely ground pepper
1 boneless rump roast (4 to 5 pounds)
6 to 8 bay leaves

Place onion in a greased shallow roasting pan. Rub Worcestershire sauce and pepper over the roast. Place over the onion; top with bay leaves.

Cover and bake at 325° for 1-3/4 to 2-1/4 hours or until meat reaches desired doneness (for rare, a meat thermometer should read 140°; medium, 160°; well-done, 170°). Discard bay leaves. Let stand for 10-15 minutes before carving. Thicken pan juices if desired. **Yield:** 8 servings.

Cheesy Chicken

This tender chicken with its cheesy crumb coating is one of my husband's favorites. It's always a hit with company, too, because it comes out juicy and great-tasting every time.
—*Joan Ergle*
Woodstock, Georgia

5 tablespoons butter, melted, *divided*
1 cup crushed cheese-flavored snack crackers
1/4 teaspoon pepper
4 boneless skinless chicken breast halves
1/2 cup sour cream

Place 1 tablespoon of butter in an 11-in. x 7-in. x 2-in. microwave-safe dish; set aside. Combine cracker crumbs and pepper. Dip chicken in remaining butter, then spread with sour cream. Roll in the crumb mixture.

Place in prepared dish. Cover loosely and microwave on high for 6-7 minutes or until chicken juices run clear. Let stand for 5-10 minutes before serving. **Yield:** 4 servings.

Editor's Note: This recipe was tested in an 850-watt microwave.

Maple French Toast Bake

This scrumptious French toast casserole is a breeze to whip up the night before a busy morning. My family loves the richness it gets from cream cheese and maple syrup.

—*Cindy Steffen*
Cedarburg, Wisconsin

12 slices bread, cubed
1 package (8 ounces) cream cheese, cubed
8 eggs
1 cup milk
1/2 cup maple syrup
Additional maple syrup

Arrange half of the bread cubes in a greased shallow 2-qt. baking dish. Top with the cream cheese and remaining bread. In a bowl, whisk eggs, milk and syrup; pour over bread. Cover and refrigerate overnight. Remove from the refrigerator 30 minutes before baking.

Cover and bake at 350° for 30 minutes. Uncover; bake 20-25 minutes longer or until golden brown. Serve with additional syrup. **Yield:** 8 servings.

Turkey Stuffing Roll-Ups

When I worked at a local deli, a customer gave me this family-pleasing recipe. After a busy day, I tried it with quicker boxed stuffing mix in place of homemade dressing. It's wonderful with salad and green beans.
—*Darlene Ward, Hot Springs, Arkansas*

1 package (6 ounces) stuffing mix
1 can (10-3/4 ounces) condensed cream of chicken soup, undiluted
3/4 cup milk
1 pound sliced deli smoked turkey
1 can (2.8 ounces) french-fried onions, crushed

Prepare stuffing mix according to package directions. Meanwhile, in a bowl, combine soup and milk; set aside. Spoon about 1/4 cup stuffing onto each turkey slice. Roll up and place in a greased 13-in. x 9-in. x 2-in. baking dish. Pour soup mixture over roll-ups.

Bake, uncovered, at 350° for 20 minutes. Sprinkle with onions. Bake 5 minutes longer or until heated through. **Yield:** 6 servings.

Editor's Note: 3 cups of any prepared stuffing can be substituted for the stuffing mix.

Almond-Topped Chicken

(Pictured on page 45)

Lemon juice adds a pleasant tartness to the buttery sauce I serve over this chicken. My family loves this easy-to-make entree. I often toss in more almonds for extra crunch.
—*Karen Zink*
Grand Island, Nebraska

4 **boneless skinless chicken breast halves**
5 **tablespoons butter, *divided***
1/3 **cup slivered almonds**
3 **tablespoons lemon juice**

In a skillet, cook the chicken in 2 tablespoons of butter until juices run clear, about 20 minutes. Transfer to serving plate and keep warm. Add almonds and remaining butter to skillet; cook and stir just until almonds are lightly browned. Stir in lemon juice; heat through. Spoon over chicken. **Yield:** 4 servings.

Salmon with Dill Sauce

This moist, tender salmon is a savory treat draped with a creamy dill sauce. When my daughter served this tempting main dish for dinner, I was surprised to learn how easy the recipe is.
—*Janet Painter*
Three Springs, Pennsylvania

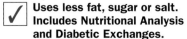 **Uses less fat, sugar or salt. Includes Nutritional Analysis and Diabetic Exchanges.**

1 **salmon fillet (1 pound)**
1-1/2 **teaspoons dill weed, *divided***
1/2 **cup reduced-fat plain yogurt**
1/2 **teaspoon sugar**
1/2 **teaspoon salt-free seasoning blend**

Place salmon in a 13-in. x 9-in. x 2-in. baking dish coated with nonstick cooking spray; sprinkle with 1/2 teaspoon dill. Cover and bake at 375° for 20-25 minutes or until fish flakes easily with a fork.

Meanwhile, in a small saucepan, combine the yogurt, sugar, seasoning blend and remaining dill. Cook and stir over low heat until warmed. Serve with the salmon. **Yield:** 4 servings.

Nutritional Analysis: One serving equals 227 calories, 12 g fat (3 g saturated fat), 77 mg cholesterol, 76 mg sodium, 3 g carbohydrate, 0 fiber, 24 g protein. **Diabetic Exchanges:** 2-1/2 lean meat, 2 fat.

Hawaiian Pork Roast

Preparing a pork roast with bananas, Liquid Smoke and soy sauce produces a wonderfully tender meat. If you garnish the roast with flowers, as shown in the photo, make sure they are edible and have not been chemically treated; wash and pat dry before using.

—Mary Gaylord, Balsam Lake, Wisconsin

1 boneless pork shoulder
  roast (3 to 4 pounds),
  trimmed
4 teaspoons Liquid Smoke,
  optional
4 teaspoons soy sauce
2 unpeeled ripe bananas
1/2 cup water

Place roast on a 22-in. x 18-in. piece of heavy-duty foil; sprinkle with Liquid Smoke if desired and soy sauce. Wash bananas and place at the base of each side of roast. Pull sides of foil up around meat; add water. Seal foil tightly; wrap again with another large piece of foil. Place in a shallow baking pan; refrigerate overnight, turning several times.

Place foil-wrapped meat in a roasting pan. Bake at 400° for 1 hour. Reduce heat to 325°; continue baking for 3-1/2 hours. Drain; discard bananas and liquid. Shred meat with a fork. **Yield:** 8-10 servings.

Garlic Potatoes And Ham

Not even my finicky little eaters can resist the veggies in this main dish when they're seasoned with soup mix. I sometimes replace the ham with cooked kielbasa or smoked sausage for a change of pace.

—Melody Williamson, Blaine, Washington

8 small red potatoes, cut
  into wedges
1 tablespoon vegetable oil
1 package (16 ounces)
  frozen broccoli cuts,
  partially thawed
1 cup cubed fully cooked
  ham
1 envelope herb with garlic
  soup mix

In a large skillet, cook potatoes in oil over medium-high heat for 10 minutes or until lightly browned. Stir in broccoli, ham and soup mix. Reduce heat; cover and cook for 25 minutes or until potatoes are tender. **Yield:** 4 servings.

Editor's Note: This recipe was tested with Lipton Recipe Secrets Savory Herb with Garlic soup mix.

Reuben Dogs

My husband and children enjoy Reuben sandwiches, and this quick casserole is as close as you can get without the mess.
—*Colleen Hawkins, Monrovia, Maryland*

1 can (27 ounces) sauerkraut, rinsed and drained
1 to 2 teaspoons caraway seeds
8 hot dogs, halved lengthwise
1 cup (4 ounces) shredded Swiss cheese
Thousand Island salad dressing

Place sauerkraut in a greased 2-qt. baking dish. Sprinkle with caraway seeds. Top with hot dogs. Bake, uncovered, at 350° for 15-20 minutes or until heated through. Sprinkle with cheese. Bake 3-5 minutes longer or until cheese is melted. Serve with salad dressing. **Yield:** 4-6 servings.

| SAUERKRAUT SUGGESTIONS | Apples are also delicious with sauerkraut. Simply cut them into chunks and cook with the kraut. Or add chopped apples and onions to cooked and cooled sauerkraut and serve cold as a salad.

Seasoned Flank Steak

I always keep a flank steak in the freezer for unexpected company. This recipe has often saved me when our son appears on the doorstep. The easy marinade provides delicious flavor. —*Betty Graham Sun City, California*

1/4 cup vegetable oil
2 tablespoons water
1 to 2 tablespoons lemon-pepper seasoning
1 to 2 teaspoons seasoned salt
1 beef flank steak (about 1-1/2 pounds)

In a large resealable plastic bag, combine the first four ingredients; add steak. Seal bag and turn to coat; refrigerate for 1-2 hours, turning occasionally.

Grill steak, uncovered, over medium-hot heat for 6-12 minutes or until meat reaches desired doneness (for medium-rare, a meat thermometer should read 145°; medium, 160°; well-done, 170°). **Yield:** 6 servings.

Honey-Lime Grilled Chicken

You don't need a lot of ingredients to stir up my easy marinade. It requires only three items and gives fabulous lime flavor to tender chicken breasts.
—*Dorothy Smith*
El Dorado, Arkansas

1/2 cup honey
1/3 cup soy sauce
1/4 cup lime juice
  4 boneless skinless
    chicken breast halves

In a resealable plastic bag or shallow glass container, combine the honey, soy sauce and lime juice; mix well. Add chicken and turn to coat. Seal or cover and refrigerate for 30-45 minutes.

Drain and discard marinade. Grill chicken, uncovered, over medium heat for 6-7 minutes on each side or until juices run clear. **Yield:** 4 servings.

Ham and Rice Bake

I can put a satisfying meal on the supper table in a jiffy. I just add a can of soup, rice and a few convenience items to leftover ham for a flavorful no-fuss casserole. —*Sharol Binger, Tulare, South Dakota*

1 can (10-3/4 ounces)
  condensed cream of
  chicken soup, undiluted
1 cup (4 ounces) shredded
  cheddar cheese, *divided*
1 package (16 ounces)
  frozen California-blend
  vegetables, thawed
1 cup cooked rice
1 cup cubed fully cooked
  ham

In a large saucepan, combine the soup and 1/2 cup cheese; cook and stir until cheese is melted. Stir in the vegetables, rice and ham.

Transfer to a greased 1-1/2-qt. baking dish. Sprinkle with remaining cheese. Bake, uncovered, at 350° for 25-30 minutes or until heated through. **Yield:** 4 servings.

|HAM HINTS| Choose firm, plump ham that is rosy pink and finely grained. When using ham as a flavoring in soups, casseroles, bean dishes or stir-fries, finely chop the meat. You'll get more intense, evenly distributed flavor than with a few large chunks.

Bacon-Wrapped Chicken

Tender chicken gets a special treatment when spread with a creamy filling and wrapped with tasty bacon strips. This easy entree is frequently requested by my bunch. I'm happy to make it for them as often as they like because I keep the ingredients on hand and can have it on the dinner table in less than an hour.
—*MarlaKaye Skinner*
Tucson, Arizona

6 **boneless skinless chicken breast halves**
1 **carton (8 ounces) whipped cream cheese with onion and chives**
1 **tablespoon butter, cubed**
Salt to taste
6 **bacon strips**

Flatten chicken to 1/2-in. thickness. Spread 3 tablespoons cream cheese over each. Dot with butter and sprinkle with salt; roll up. Wrap each with a bacon strip. Place, seam side down, in a greased 13-in. x 9-in. x 2-in. baking pan.

Bake, uncovered, at 400° for 35-40 minutes or until juices run clear. Broil 6 in. from the heat for 5 minutes or until bacon is crisp. **Yield:** 6 servings.

|FLATTENING CHICKEN| Place one chicken breast between two pieces of waxed paper. Starting in the center and working out to the edges, pound lightly with the flat side of a meat mallet until the chicken is even in thickness.

Peppy Macaroni

I like to keep an extra box of macaroni and cheese on the pantry shelf to make this fun pizza-flavored casserole for unexpected guests. Because it's a snap to prepare, older kids could assemble it to give Mom and Dad a break from dinner duties.   —*Helen Cluts, Sioux Falls, South Dakota*

1 **package (7-1/4 ounces) macaroni and cheese dinner**
2 **eggs, lightly beaten**
1 **jar (8 ounces) pizza sauce**
40 **slices pepperoni (about 2-1/2 ounces)**
2 **cups (8 ounces) shredded mozzarella cheese**

Prepare macaroni and cheese according to package directions. Fold in eggs. Spread into a greased 13-in. x 9-in. x 2-in. baking dish. Top with pizza sauce, pepperoni and mozzarella.

Bake, uncovered, at 350° for 30-35 minutes or until lightly browned and cheese is melted. Let stand for 5 minutes before serving. **Yield:** 4 servings.

Fish Nuggets

My family loves to camp and fish. We developed this different breading made with saltines and graham crackers to coat our "catch of the day". It fries to a tasty golden brown and has become a campground favorite.   —*Deana Brandenburg, Great Bend, Kansas*

2 **pounds haddock** *or* **cod fillets**
1 **cup finely crushed graham crackers (about 16 squares)**
3/4 **cup finely crushed saltines (about 25 crackers)**
1-1/2 **to 2 teaspoons seasoned salt**
Oil for deep-fat frying

Cut fish into 1-in. cubes; secure with a toothpick if necessary. Combine cracker crumbs and seasoned salt in a shallow bowl; roll fish in crumb mixture until coated.

In an electric skillet or deep-fat fryer, heat oil to 375°. Fry nuggets, a few at time, for 3 minutes or until browned. Drain on paper towels. **Yield:** 4-6 servings.

Shrimp Newberg

A friend gave me the recipe for this tasty time-saving dish that takes advantage of cooked shrimp. It's a quick company meal when served over rice with a tossed salad and dessert.   —*Donna Souders Hagerstown, Maryland*

1 **can (10-3/4 ounces) condensed cream of shrimp** *or* **mushroom soup, undiluted**
1/4 **cup water**
1 **teaspoon seafood seasoning**
1 **package (1 pound) frozen cooked medium salad shrimp, thawed**
Hot cooked rice

In a saucepan, combine soup, water and seafood seasoning. Bring to a boil. Reduce heat; stir in shrimp. Heat through. Serve over rice. **Yield:** 4 servings.

|RELY ON RICE| Instant rice has been fully or partially cooked, then dehydrated, that's why it only takes a few minutes to prepare. Make a double batch of rice so you can use the leftovers for another night's meal. It will keep in the refrigerator for up to 4 days.

Apricot Sausage Kabobs

Basted with a simple sweet-sour sauce, these tasty kabobs make a quick meal that's elegant enough for company.
—*Susie Lindquist, Ellijay, Georgia*

3/4 **cup apricot preserves**
3/4 **cup Dijon mustard**
1 **pound fully cooked kielbasa *or* Polish sausage, cut into 12 pieces**
12 **dried apricots**
12 **medium fresh mushrooms**
Hot cooked rice, optional

In a small bowl, combine preserves and mustard; mix well. Remove 1/2 cup for serving; set aside. Alternate sausage, apricots and mushrooms on four metal or soaked bamboo skewers.

Grill, covered, over indirect heat for 15-20 minutes or until meat juices run clear. Turn frequently and baste with remaining apricot sauce. Warm the reserved sauce; serve with kabobs and rice if desired. **Yield:** 4 servings.

Taco Chicken Rolls

I always keep the ingredients for this tender and flavorful chicken on hand. The cheese-stuffed rolls are nice with a green salad or plate of fresh vegetables and Spanish rice.
—*Kara De la vega*
Suisun City, California

1 **cup finely crushed cheese-flavored crackers**
1 **envelope taco seasoning**
6 **boneless skinless chicken breast halves (about 2 pounds)**
2 **ounces Monterey Jack cheese, cut into six 2-inch x 1/2-inch sticks**
1 **can (4 ounces) chopped green chilies**

In a shallow dish, combine the cracker crumbs and taco seasoning; set aside. Flatten chicken between two sheets of waxed paper to 1/4-in. thickness. Place a cheese stick and about 1 tablespoon of chilies on each piece of chicken. Tuck ends of chicken in and roll up; secure with a toothpick.

Coat chicken with crumb mixture. Place in a greased 13-in. x 9-in. x 2-in. baking dish. Bake, uncovered, at 350° for 35-40 minutes or until chicken juices run clear. Remove toothpicks. **Yield:** 6 servings.

Festive Fillets

(Also pictured on front cover)

When the weather's not right for outdoor cooking and you want an outstanding steak, this recipe is the answer. We like the zippy gravy so much that we don't wait for inclement evenings to fix this. It's a cinch to prepare on the stovetop.

—Donna Cline
Pensacola, Florida

✓ Uses less fat, sugar or salt. Includes Nutritional Analysis and Diabetic Exchanges.

1 envelope brown gravy mix
1 jar (4-1/2 ounces) sliced mushrooms, drained
2 teaspoons prepared horseradish
4 beef tenderloin fillets (5 ounces *each*)
1/8 teaspoon pepper

Prepare gravy according to package directions; add mushrooms and horseradish. Set aside and keep warm. In a non-stick skillet, cook fillets over medium-high heat until meat reaches desired doneness (for rare, a meat thermometer should read 140°; medium, 160°; well-done 170°), turning once. Season with pepper. Serve with the gravy. **Yield:** 4 servings.

Nutritional Analysis: One serving equals 268 calories, 714 mg sodium, 88 mg cholesterol, 7 g carbohydrate, 33 g protein, 11 g fat. **Diabetic Exchanges:** 4 lean meat, 1/2 starch.

Editor's Note: Fillets can be baked. First brown in a skillet for 1 minute on each side, then transfer to an 8-in. square baking pan. Bake, uncovered, at 350° for 10-20 minutes or until meat reaches desired doneness.

Crabby Alfredo

Supper couldn't be easier when you put this quick, creamy entree on the menu. My mother-in-law gave me this wonderful recipe. The whole family loves it and everyone asks for more.

—Tara Kampman, Manchester, Iowa

4 cups cooked egg noodles
1 package (16 ounces) imitation crabmeat, chopped
1 jar (16 ounces) Alfredo sauce
Seafood seasoning *or* minced chives

In a large saucepan, combine the noodles, crab and Alfredo sauce. Cook and stir until heated through. Sprinkle with seafood seasoning or chives. **Yield:** 4 servings.

Italian Sausage Skillet

Served over rice or pasta, this skillet is a hearty favorite. This garden-fresh dish gets extra color from a can of stewed tomatoes. The Italian sausage has so many wonderful flavors you don't need to add any other seasonings. —*Eve Gauger Vargas*
Prairie Village, Kansas

1-1/4 **pounds uncooked Italian sausage links**
   3 **small zucchini** *or* **yellow summer squash, cubed**
1/2 **cup chopped onion**
   1 **can (14-1/2 ounces) stewed tomatoes**
Hot cooked rice *or* **pasta**

In a skillet over medium heat, brown the sausage until no longer pink; drain. Cut sausage into 1/4-in. slices; return to the skillet to brown completely.

Add zucchini and onion; cook and stir for 2 minutes. Stir in the tomatoes. Reduce heat; cover and simmer for 10-15 minutes or until the zucchini is tender. Serve over rice or pasta. **Yield:** 4-6 servings.

Perch Fillets

Guests will never guess that lemon-lime soda and pancake mix are the secret ingredients behind these tasty perch fillets in a golden coating. If perch isn't available, try substituting haddock.
—*Connie Tibbetts, Wilton, Maine*

1-1/2 **cups lemon-lime soda**
   1 **pound perch fillets**
   2 **cups pancake mix**
1/4 **teaspoon pepper**
Oil for frying

Pour soda into a shallow bowl; add fish fillets and let stand for 15 minutes. In another shallow bowl, combine pancake mix and pepper. Remove fish from soda and coat with pancake mix.

In a large skillet, heat 1/4 in. of oil over medium-high heat. Fry fish for 2-3 minutes on each side or until fish flakes with a fork. Drain on paper towels. **Yield:** 4 servings.

|BREADING FISH| When buying fresh fish fillets, look for firm flesh that has a moist look; don't purchase fish that looks dried out. To bread fish, combine the dry ingredients in a pie plate or shallow bowl. In another pie plate or bowl, whisk egg, milk and/or other liquid ingredients. Dip fish into liquid mixture, then gently roll in dry ingredients. Fry as directed.

Noodle Pepperoni Pizza

My family would eat wedges of this great-tasting skillet dinner without any complaint several nights a week. I love it because it's inexpensive and can be made in a snap.

—Gayle Lizotte
Merrimack, New Hampshire

4 packages (3 ounces *each*) ramen noodles
1 tablespoon olive oil
1 cup spaghetti *or* pizza sauce
1 cup (4 ounces) shredded mozzarella cheese
1 package (3 ounces) sliced pepperoni, cut into strips

Discard seasoning packets from noodles or save for another use. Cook noodles according to package directions; drain. Heat oil in a 10-in. ovenproof skillet. Press noodles into skillet, evenly covering the bottom of pan. Cook until bottom of crust is lightly browned, about 5 minutes.

Pour spaghetti sauce over the crust. Sprinkle with cheese and pepperoni. Broil 4 to 6 in. from the heat for 3-4 minutes or until heated through and cheese is melted. **Yield:** 4-6 servings.

Marinated Baked Chicken

This tender, flavorful chicken is one of my mom's specialties. Soy sauce and bottled Italian dressing combine in a mouth-watering marinade that nicely complements the meat.

—Cindy Kufeldt
Orlando, Florida

1/2 cup Italian salad dressing
1/2 cup soy sauce
6 bone-in chicken breast halves
1/8 teaspoon onion salt
1/8 teaspoon garlic salt
Kale and spiced apple rings, optional

In a measuring cup, combine salad dressing and soy sauce. Pour 3/4 cup into a large resealable plastic bag; add chicken. Seal the bag and turn to coat; refrigerate for 4 hours or overnight, turning several times. Refrigerate remaining marinade for basting.

Drain chicken, discarding marinade. Place chicken, skin side up, on a rack in a roasting pan. Sprinkle with onion salt and garlic salt. Bake, uncovered, at 350° for 45-60 minutes or until juices run clear and a meat thermometer reads 170°, brushing occasionally with reserved marinade. Garnish platter with kale and apple rings if desired. **Yield:** 6 servings.

Crumb-Coated Cod

Fish fillets get fast flavor from Italian salad dressing mix and a breading made with seasoned stuffing mix. I serve this baked fish with a tossed salad or relishes. —*Julia Bruce, Tuscola, Illinois*

2 tablespoons vegetable oil
2 tablespoons water
1 envelope Italian salad dressing mix
2 cups crushed stuffing mix
4 cod fillets (about 6 ounces *each*)

In a shallow bowl, combine the oil, water and salad dressing mix. Place the stuffing mix in another bowl. Dip fillets in salad dressing mixture, then in stuffing.

Place on a greased baking sheet. Bake at 425° for 15-20 minutes or until the fish flakes easily with a fork. **Yield:** 4 servings.

Pizza Chicken Roll-Ups

I love the chicken roll-ups my mom made for special occasions, filled with spinach and cream cheese. My own kids wouldn't eat those, so I came up with this pizza-flavored variety the whole family enjoys. —*Tanja Penquite, Oregon, Ohio*

4 boneless skinless chicken breast halves
12 pepperoni slices
8 mozzarella cheese slices, *divided*
1 can (15 ounces) pizza sauce
Minced fresh parsley, optional

Flatten chicken to 1/4-in. thickness. Place three slices of pepperoni and one slice of cheese on each. Roll up tightly; secure with toothpicks. Place in a greased 11-in. x 7-in. x 2-in. baking dish. Spoon pizza sauce over roll-ups.

Cover and bake at 350° for 35-40 minutes. Uncover; top with the remaining cheese. Bake 5-10 minutes longer or until cheese is melted. Sprinkle with parsley if desired. **Yield:** 4 servings.

Thanksgiving In a Pan

This meal-in-one tastes like a big holiday dinner without the work. It's a great way to use up leftover turkey, but I often use thick slices of deli turkey instead with equally delicious results. —*Lynne Hahn*
Temecula, California

1 package (6 ounces) stuffing mix
2-1/2 cups cubed cooked turkey
2 cups frozen cut green beans, thawed
1 jar (12 ounces) turkey gravy
Pepper to taste

Prepare stuffing mix according to package directions. Transfer to a greased 11-in. x 7-in. x 2-in. baking dish. Top with turkey, beans, gravy and pepper. Cover and bake at 350° for 30-35 minutes or until heated through. **Yield:** 6 servings.

Editor's Note: Any poultry, herb seasoned or corn bread stuffing mix would work in this recipe.

Pork Chop Casserole

I rely on orange juice and canned soup to boost the flavor of this tender pork chop and rice bake. It's very good...and a little different from your usual fare. —*Wanda Plinsky, Wichita, Kansas*

4 bone-in pork loin chops (1/2 inch thick)
1 tablespoon vegetable oil
1-1/3 cups uncooked long grain rice
1 cup orange juice
1 can (10-1/2 ounces) condensed chicken with rice soup, undiluted

In a large skillet, brown pork chops in oil; drain. Place the rice in an ungreased shallow 3-qt. baking dish; pour orange juice over rice. Top with pork chops and soup.

Cover and bake at 350° for 40-45 minutes or until pork juices run clear and rice is tender. **Yield:** 4 servings.

|SIZING IT UP| Casserole dishes are measured by volume. If you're unsure of how large a dish is, fill it with water, then measure the liquid. Casserole dishes are most commonly found in the following sizes: 1, 1-1/2, 2 and 3 quarts.

Chili Casserole

I threw together this main dish when my husband unexpectedly invited his hunting buddies for dinner. It was on the table by the time they'd unpacked their gear and washed up. —*Karen Bruggman*
Edmonds, Washington

1 can (40 ounces) chili with beans
1 can (4 ounces) chopped green chilies
1 can (2-1/4 ounces) sliced ripe olives, drained
2 cups (8 ounces) shredded cheddar cheese
2 cups ranch-flavored tortilla chips, crushed

In a bowl, combine all ingredients. Transfer to a greased 2-1/2-qt. baking dish. Bake, uncovered, at 350° for 30-35 minutes or until bubbly. **Yield:** 6 servings.

|CRUSHING TORTILLA CHIPS| Place tortilla chips in a resealable plastic bag and seal. Then simply crush the chips with your hands. Crushing them with a rolling pin will produce pieces that are too fine.

Saucy Apricot Chicken

The tangy glaze on this tender chicken entree is just as wonderful with ham or turkey. Leftovers reheat nicely in the microwave. —*Dee Gray*
Kokomo, Indiana

6 boneless skinless chicken breast halves (about 1-1/2 pounds)
2 jars (12 ounces *each*) apricot preserves
1 envelope onion soup mix
Hot cooked rice

Place chicken in a slow cooker. Combine the preserves and soup mix; spoon over chicken. Cover and cook on low for 4-5 hours or until tender. Serve over rice. **Yield:** 6 servings.

Biscuit Tostadas

Refrigerated biscuits and just four other ingredients make it easy for little hands to assemble these cute kid-size tostadas. I enjoy the time our gang spends together in the kitchen making these Mexican mini main dishes. They're best eaten on a plate with a fork.
—Terrie Stampor
Sterling Heights, Michigan

1 pound ground beef
1 jar (16 ounces) salsa, *divided*
1 tube (17.3 ounces) large refrigerated biscuits
2 cups (8 ounces) shredded Colby-Monterey Jack cheese
2 cups shredded lettuce

In a skillet, cook beef over medium heat until no longer pink; drain. Add 1-1/2 cups salsa; heat through.

Split each biscuit in half; flatten into 4-in. rounds on ungreased baking sheets. Bake at 350° for 10-12 minutes or until golden brown. Top with meat mixture, cheese, lettuce and remaining salsa. **Yield:** 16 servings.

Tangy Ham Steak

This glazed ham steak is a yummy quick-and-easy main dish. It tastes especially good heated on the grill but works well in the oven broiler, too. Dad fires up the grill for this tasty steak while my mom heads to the kitchen to prepare the rest of the meal.
—Sue Gronholz
Columbus, Wisconsin

1/3 cup spicy brown mustard
1/4 cup honey
1/2 teaspoon grated orange peel
1 fully cooked ham steak (about 2 pounds)

In a small bowl, combine mustard, honey and orange peel. Brush over one side of ham. Broil or grill, uncovered, over medium-hot heat for 7 minutes. Turn; brush with mustard mixture. Cook until well glazed and heated through, about 7 minutes. **Yield:** 6-8 servings.

Saucy Beef Casserole

I rely on canned soups and crunchy chow mein noodles to flavor this hearty ground beef bake. My family gobbles it up!
—*Ferne Spielvogel, Fairwater, Wisconsin*

1 pound ground beef
1 medium onion, chopped
1 can (10-3/4 ounces) condensed cream of chicken soup, undiluted
1 can (10-3/4 ounces) condensed vegetable soup, undiluted
3/4 cup chow mein noodles

In a skillet, cook beef and onion over medium heat until meat is no longer pink; drain. Stir in soups. Transfer to a greased 8-in. square baking dish.

Cover and bake at 350° for 25-30 minutes or until heated through. Uncover; sprinkle with chow mein noodles. Bake 5 minutes longer or until chow mein noodles are crisp. **Yield:** 4 servings.

Italian Pineapple Chicken

I created this one night when I was in a particular hurry. There is hardly any preparation involved, and everyone who tries it asks for the recipe. The tender five-ingredient entree features skillet-browned chicken breasts and pineapple slices seasoned with bottled salad dressing.
—*Becky Lohmiller, Monticello, Indiana*

4 boneless skinless chicken breast halves
1/2 cup Italian salad dressing
2 tablespoons olive oil
1 can (8 ounces) sliced pineapple, drained
1/3 cup shredded Swiss cheese, optional

Flatten chicken to 1/2-in. thickness. Pour salad dressing into a shallow bowl; dip chicken in dressing. In a large skillet, heat oil. Add chicken; cook over medium-high heat for 5-7 minutes on each side or until juices run clear. Remove and keep warm.

Add pineapple slices to the skillet; cook for 30 seconds on each side or until lightly browned. Place a slice on each chicken breast half. Sprinkle with cheese if desired. **Yield:** 4 servings.

Fast Baked Fish

I enjoy fixing hearty, home-style meals whenever I can. Time is often tight, though. Our son is a world-record-holding fisherman who keeps us supplied with fresh fish. So I make my Fast Baked Fish often. It's moist, tender and flavorful.

—*Judie Anglen*
Riverton, Wyoming

1-1/4 **pounds fish fillets**
   1 **teaspoon seasoned salt**
Pepper to taste
Paprika, optional
   3 **tablespoons butter,**
      melted

Place fish fillets in a greased 11-in. x 7-in. x 2-in. baking dish. Sprinkle with seasoned salt, pepper and paprika if desired. Drizzle with butter. Cover and bake at 400° for 15-20 minutes or until the fish flakes easily with a fork. **Yield:** 4 servings.

   Editor's Note: Orange roughy, haddock, trout or walleye may be used in this recipe.

Colorful Kabobs

We cook out all year long. These kabobs cook up in a snap and taste wonderful. My son likes to help assemble them.

—*Janell Aguda, Joelton, Tennessee*

  12 **cherry tomatoes**
   1 **pound fully cooked**
      smoked turkey sausage,
      cut into 1/2-inch chunks
   2 **medium green peppers,**
      cut into 1-inch pieces
   1 **medium onion, cut into**
      wedges
Hot cooked rice

Thread a cherry tomato onto six metal or soaked wooden skewers. Alternate the sausage, green pepper and onion pieces on skewers, ending with another tomato.

   Grill, uncovered, over medium-hot heat for 10-15 minutes or until meat is heated through and vegetables are tender. Remove meat and vegetables from skewers and serve over rice. **Yield:** 6 servings.

|SOAKING SKEWERS| To help prevent wooden skewers from burning or splintering while grilling, soak them in water for 15-30 minutes. Remove them from the water and then thread on the ingredients of your choice.

Maple Barbecued Chicken

This tender glazed chicken is so delicious, it will disappear very quickly. The sweet maple sauce is used to baste the chicken while grilling, with additional sauce served alongside for dipping. —*Ruth Lowen Hythe, Alberta*

✓ **Uses less fat, sugar or salt. Includes Nutritional Analysis and Diabetic Exchanges.**

3/4 cup barbecue sauce
3/4 cup maple pancake syrup
1/2 teaspoon salt
1/2 teaspoon maple flavoring
8 boneless skinless chicken breast halves (2 pounds)

In a bowl, combine the first four ingredients and mix well. Remove 3/4 cup to a small bowl for serving; cover and refrigerate.

Grill chicken, uncovered, over medium heat for 3 minutes on each side. Grill 6-8 minutes longer or until juices run clear, basting with remaining sauce and turning occasionally. Serve with reserved sauce. **Yield:** 8 servings.

Nutritional Analysis: One serving (one chicken breast with 1-1/2 tablespoons sauce) equals 228 calories, 2 g fat (trace saturated fat), 66 mg cholesterol, 436 mg sodium, 26 g carbohydrate, trace fiber, 27 g protein. **Diabetic Exchanges:** 3 lean meat, 1-1/2 fruit.

Fiesta Macaroni

When time is short, I rely on this family-pleasing main dish. It's so easy to fix, and everyone loves the zesty flavor that the salsa and chili beans provide. —*Sandra Castillo, Sun Prairie, Wisconsin*

1 package (16 ounces) elbow macaroni
1 pound ground beef
1 jar (16 ounces) salsa
10 ounces process cheese (Velveeta), cubed
1 can (15 ounces) chili-style beans

Cook macaroni according to package directions. Meanwhile, in a skillet, cook beef over medium heat until no longer pink; drain. Drain macaroni; set aside.

In a microwave-safe bowl, combine salsa and cheese. Microwave, uncovered, on high for 3-4 minutes or until cheese is melted. Stir into the skillet; add the macaroni and beans.

Transfer to a greased 13-in. x 9-in. x 2-in. baking dish. Bake, uncovered, at 350° for 30-35 minutes or until heated through. **Yield:** 6-8 servings.

Quick 'n' Easy Lasagna

I never have leftovers when I prepare this hearty crowd-pleaser. It's my son's favorite, and my husband and I like to make it on nights we have friends over to play cards.
—Brenda Richardson
Rison, Arkansas

16 lasagna noodles
2 pounds ground beef
1 jar (28 ounces) spaghetti sauce
1 pound process cheese (Velveeta), cubed

Cook noodles according to package directions. Meanwhile, in a large skillet, cook beef over medium heat until no longer pink; drain. Add the spaghetti sauce; heat through. Rinse and drain the noodles.

In a greased 13-in. x 9-in. x 2-in. baking dish, layer a third of the meat sauce and half of the noodles and cheese. Repeat the layers. Top with the remaining meat sauce. Cover and bake at 350° for 35 minutes or until bubbly. **Yield:** 6-8 servings.

Tomato Bacon Pie

This simple but savory pie makes a tasty addition to brunch buffets and leisurely luncheons. I rely on a cheesy mixture for the pie's golden topping and a refrigerated pastry shell for easy preparation.
—Gladys Gibson, Hodgenville, Kentucky

1 unbaked deep-dish pastry shell (9 inches)
3 medium tomatoes, cut into 1/4-inch slices
10 bacon strips, cooked and crumbled
1 cup (4 ounces) shredded cheddar cheese
1 cup mayonnaise

Bake pastry shell according to package directions; cool. Place tomatoes in the crust; sprinkle with bacon. In a bowl, combine the cheese and mayonnaise. Spoon over bacon in the center of pie, leaving 1 in. around edge.

Bake at 350° for 30-40 minutes or until golden brown (cover edges with foil if necessary to prevent overbrowning). **Yield:** 6 servings.

Editor's Note: Reduced-fat or fat-free mayonnaise may not be substituted for regular mayonnaise in this recipe.

Angel Hair Tuna

This recipe came from a dear friend, and it quickly became a favorite standby. Simply toss together a green salad and toast some garlic bread for a complete meal. —*Collette Burch, Edinburg, Texas*

2 packages (5.1 ounces *each*) angel hair pasta with Parmesan cheese dinner mix
1 can (12 ounces) tuna, drained and flaked
1/2 teaspoon Italian seasoning
3/4 cup crushed butter-flavored crackers (about 15)
1/4 cup butter, melted

Prepare pasta dinner mixes according to package directions. Stir in the tuna and Italian seasoning. Transfer to a serving bowl; cover and let stand for 5 minutes to thicken. Toss cracker crumbs and butter; sprinkle over the top. Serve immediately. **Yield:** 4 servings.

|TUNA TIDBITS| Canned tuna is precooked and can be water- or oil-packed. It comes in three grades, the best being solid or fancy (large pieces), followed by chunk (smaller pieces) and flaked (bits and pieces). Water-packed tuna not only contains fewer calories, but it also has a fresher flavor.

Pork Chops with Apples and Stuffing

The heartwarming blend of cinnamon and apples is the perfect accompaniment to these tender pork chops. This dish is always a winner with my family. It's a main course I can serve with little preparation.
—*Joan Hamilton*
Worcester, Massachusetts

6 boneless pork loin chops (1 inch thick)
1 tablespoon vegetable oil
1 package (6 ounces) crushed stuffing mix
1 can (21 ounces) apple pie filling with cinnamon

In a skillet, brown pork chops in oil over medium-high heat. Meanwhile, prepare stuffing according to package directions. Spread pie filling into a greased 13-in. x 9-in. x 2-in. baking dish. Place the pork chops on top; spoon stuffing over chops.

Cover and bake at 350° for 35 minutes. Uncover; bake 10 minutes longer or until a meat thermometer reads 160°. **Yield:** 6 servings.

Beef in Onion Gravy

I double this super recipe to feed our family of four so I'm sure to have leftovers to send with my husband to work for lunch. His co-workers tell him he's lucky to have someone who fixes him such special meals. It's our secret that it's an easy slow-cooker dinner!

—*Denise Albers*
Freeburg, Illinois

1 can (10-3/4 ounces) condensed cream of mushroom soup, undiluted
2 tablespoons onion soup mix
2 tablespoons beef broth
1 tablespoon quick-cooking tapioca
1 pound beef stew meat, cut into 1-inch cubes
Hot cooked noodles *or* mashed potatoes, optional

In a slow cooker, combine the soup, soup mix, broth and tapioca; let stand for 15 minutes. Stir in the beef. Cover and cook on low for 6-8 hours or until meat is tender. Serve over noodles or mashed potatoes if desired. **Yield:** 3 servings.

|NO PEEKING!| Refrain from lifting the lid while the slow cooker is cooking unless you're instructed in a recipe to stir or add ingredients. The loss of steam can mean an additional 15 to 30 minutes of cooking time each time you lift the lid. Be sure the lid is seated properly, not tilted or askew. The steam during cooking creates a seal.

Chicken Fried Rice

I rely on a fried rice mix to start this speedy skillet supper. It makes the most of leftover cooked chicken and a can of crunchy water chestnuts.
—*Kathy Hoyt, Maplecrest, New York*

1 package (6.2 ounces) fried rice mix
2 cups cubed cooked chicken
1-1/2 cups cooked broccoli florets
1 can (8 ounces) sliced water chestnuts, drained
1 cup (4 ounces) shredded mozzarella cheese

Cook rice according to package directions. Stir in chicken, broccoli and water chestnuts; heat through. Sprinkle with cheese. **Yield:** 4 servings.

Tangy Pork Tenderloin

A simple marinade adds sweet flavor and tangy zip to juicy pork tenderloin. No one will ever guess there are only four ingredients in this sauce. For a spicier version, I like to add more chili powder.

—Christopher Bingham
Lansing, Michigan

2 pork tenderloins
   (1 pound *each*)
2/3 cup honey
1/2 cup Dijon mustard
1/4 to 1/2 teaspoon chili
   powder
1/4 teaspoon salt

Place pork tenderloins in a large resealable plastic bag or shallow glass container. In a bowl, combine the remaining ingredients; set aside 2/3 cup. Pour remaining marinade over pork; turn to coat. Seal or cover and refrigerate for at least 4 hours, turning occasionally.

Drain and discard marinade. Grill pork, covered, over indirect medium heat for 8-9 minutes on each side or until meat juices run clear and a meat thermometer reads 160°-170°. In a saucepan, warm the reserved sauce; serve with the pork. **Yield:** 6 servings.

Swiss Tuna Bake

My husband enjoys cooking just as much as I do. One night he tossed together this comforting casserole from meager ingredients we had in our cupboard. It turned out to be the best-tasting tuna casserole I have ever had! Swiss cheese flavors the noodles nicely.

—Joanne Callahan
Far Hills, New Jersey

4 cups cooked medium
   egg noodles
1-1/2 cups (6 ounces) shredded
   Swiss cheese
1 cup mayonnaise
1 can (6 ounces) tuna,
   drained and flaked
1 cup seasoned bread
   crumbs, *divided*

In a large bowl, combine the noodles, cheese, mayonnaise and tuna. Sprinkle 1/2 cup bread crumbs into a greased 9-in. square baking dish. Spread noodle mixture over crumbs. Sprinkle with the remaining crumbs. Bake, uncovered, at 350° for 20 minutes or until heated through. **Yield:** 4 servings.

Editor's Note: Reduced-fat or fat-free mayonnaise may not be substituted for regular mayonnaise in this recipe.

Artichoke Chicken

A friend agreed to repair some plumbing in exchange for a home-cooked dinner, but he showed up before I could shop for groceries. A can of artichokes in the pantry inspired me to combine a favorite hot dip recipe with a chicken bake. The results were so delicious, he said he'd rush over anytime.

—*Lisa Robisch, Cincinnati, Ohio*

1 can (14 ounces) water-packed artichoke hearts, well drained and chopped
3/4 cup grated Parmesan cheese
3/4 cup mayonnaise
Dash garlic powder
4 boneless skinless chicken breast halves

In a bowl, combine the artichokes, cheese, mayonnaise and garlic powder. Place chicken in a greased 11-in. x 7-in. x 2-in. baking dish. Spread with artichoke mixture. Bake, uncovered, at 375° for 30-35 minutes or until chicken juices run clear. **Yield:** 4 servings.

Editor's Note: Reduced-fat or fat-free mayonnaise may not be substituted for regular mayonnaise in this recipe.

Sweet and Savory Brisket

I like this recipe not only because it makes such tender and flavorful beef, but because it takes advantage of a slow cooker. It's wonderful to come home from work and have this mouth-watering main dish waiting for you. The beef doubles as a warm sandwich filling, too. —*Chris Snyder, Boulder, Colorado*

1 beef brisket (3 to 3-1/2 pounds), cut in half
1 cup ketchup
1/4 cup grape jelly
1 envelope onion soup mix
1/2 teaspoon pepper

Place half of the brisket in a slow cooker. In a bowl, combine the ketchup, jelly, soup mix and pepper; spread half over meat. Top with the remaining meat and ketchup mixture.

Cover and cook on low for 8-10 hours or until meat is tender. Slice brisket; serve with cooking juices. **Yield:** 8-10 servings.

Editor's Note: This is a fresh beef brisket, not corned beef.

Seasoned Cube Steaks

Soy sauce really wakes up the flavor of these nicely browned cube steaks. I serve this meaty main dish with mixed vegetables and rice or baked potatoes. My family loves this meal.

—*Cathee Bethel, Lebanon, Oregon*

1 cup soy sauce
1 teaspoon dried minced garlic
1 teaspoon dried minced onion
4 cube steaks (about 1-1/4 pounds)

In a large resealable plastic bag, combine the soy sauce, garlic and onion; add cube steaks. Seal bag; turn to coat. Refrigerate for 30-45 minutes, turning once.

Drain and discard marinade. Place steaks on a greased broiler pan. Broil 4 in. from the heat for about 4 minutes on each side or until meat reaches desired doneness. **Yield:** 4 servings.

Broiled Chicken Cordon Bleu

I serve this meal at least monthly. For variety, I sometimes use different types of cheese, such as Monterey Jack or cheddar. I even replace the ham with other favorite cold cuts.　　—*Hope Meece Fowler, Indiana*

4 boneless skinless chicken breast halves
1/4 cup butter, melted
4 thin slices fully cooked ham
4 tablespoons honey mustard salad dressing
4 thin slices Swiss *or* mozzarella cheese

Place chicken on the rack of a broiler pan. Broil 4 in. from the heat for 3 minutes; turn and broil 3 minutes on the other side. Brush with butter. Continue turning and basting until juices run clear, about 4 minutes.

Place a ham slice on each chicken breast; broil for 1-2 minutes. Spread 1 tablespoon dressing over each; top with cheese. Broil for 30 seconds or until cheese is melted. **Yield:** 4 servings.

Honey-Dijon Ham

Your family will think you took hours to prepare dinner when you slice servings of this delicious ham. Really, you just put it in the oven and baste it once! The glaze combines honey, brown sugar and mustard for tasty results. —*Karin Young Carlsbad, California*

1 boneless fully cooked
   ham (about 3 pounds)
1/3 cup honey
2 tablespoons Dijon
   mustard
2 tablespoons brown sugar
1 tablespoon water

Place ham on a greased rack in a shallow roasting pan. Bake, uncovered, at 325° for 50-60 minutes. Combine honey, mustard and sugar; brush about 3 tablespoonfuls over ham.

Bake 10-15 minutes longer or until a meat thermometer reads 140° and ham is heated through. Stir water into remaining glaze; heat through and serve with the ham. **Yield:** 8-10 servings.

Easy Meat Loaf

My mother-in-law invented this recipe by mistake, but it was so well received, it became the most popular way for her to make meat loaf. It couldn't be any easier. —*Pat Jensen, Oak Harbor, Ohio*

1 egg, lightly beaten
1 can (10-1/2 ounces)
   condensed French onion
   soup, undiluted
1-1/3 cups crushed
   butter-flavored crackers
   (about 33 crackers)
1 pound lean ground beef
1 can (10-3/4 ounces)
   condensed golden
   mushroom soup,
   undiluted

In a bowl, combine the egg, onion soup and cracker crumbs. Crumble beef over mixture and mix well. Shape into a loaf. Place in a greased 11-in. x 7-in. x 2-in. baking dish. Bake, uncovered, at 350° for 30 minutes.

Pour mushroom soup over loaf. Bake 1 hour longer or until meat is no longer pink and a meat thermometer reads 160°; drain. Let stand for 10 minutes before slicing. **Yield:** 4 servings.

|MMM..MEAT LOAF| When shaping meat loaves, handle the mixture as little as possible to keep the final product light in texture. Combine all of the ingredients except for the ground beef. Then crumble the beef over the mixture and mix well.

Fisherman's Specialty

A friend at work shared some of his fresh catch prepared in this simple way. After one bite, I knew it was the best fried fish I'd ever tasted. Whenever I catch bass, crappie or bluegill, my wife uses this recipe. The fillets come out moist and not fishy-tasting. Our family won't eat fish any other way.

—Bruce Headley, Greenwood, Missouri

2 eggs
1 to 2 teaspoons lemon-pepper seasoning, *divided*
6 bluegill *or* perch fillets (2 to 3 ounces *each*)
1 cup crushed saltines (about 30 crackers)
Vegetable oil

In a shallow bowl, beat eggs and 1 teaspoon lemon-pepper. Dip fillets in egg mixture, then coat with cracker crumbs. Sprinkle with remaining lemon-pepper.

In a skillet, heat 1/4 in. of oil. Fry fillets for 3-4 minutes on each side or until fish flakes easily with a fork. **Yield:** 3 servings.

Turkey Broccoli Hollandaise

This delectable dish is a great way to use extra turkey. The original recipe called for Thanksgiving leftovers, but my family loves it so much that I prepare this version all year long.

—Pamela Yoder, Elkhart, Indiana

1 cup fresh broccoli florets
1 package (6 ounces) stuffing mix
1 envelope hollandaise sauce mix
2 cups cubed cooked turkey *or* chicken
1 can (2.8 ounces) french-fried onions

Place 1 in. of water and broccoli in a saucepan. Bring to a boil. Reduce heat; cover and simmer for 5-8 minutes or until crisp-tender. Meanwhile, prepare stuffing and sauce mixes according to package directions.

Spoon stuffing into a greased 11-in. x 7-in. x 2-in. baking dish. Top with turkey. Drain broccoli; arrange over turkey. Spoon sauce over the top; sprinkle with onions. Bake, uncovered, at 325° for 25-30 minutes or until heated through. **Yield:** 6 servings.

Chicken Potato Bake

On evenings I'm busy helping our two kids with homework and don't have time to spend in the kitchen, I rely on this easy recipe. Bottled Italian salad dressing, Italian seasoning and Parmesan cheese give fast flavor to the juicy chicken and tender potatoes in this satisfying supper.

—*Debbi Mullins, Canoga Park, California*

1 broiler/fryer chicken (about 3 pounds), cut up
1 pound red potatoes, cut into chunks
1/2 to 3/4 cup prepared Italian salad dressing
1 tablespoon Italian seasoning
1/2 to 3/4 cup grated Parmesan cheese

Place chicken in a greased 13-in. x 9-in. x 2-in. baking dish. Arrange potatoes around chicken. Drizzle with dressing; sprinkle with Italian seasoning and Parmesan cheese.

Cover and bake at 400° for 20 minutes. Uncover; bake 20-30 minutes longer or until potatoes are tender and chicken juices run clear. **Yield:** 4 servings.

Peachy Pork

Who says you can't make a hearty dinner when you're racing against the clock? This unique combination of peach preserves and salsa makes a heartwarming main dish your family will ask for time and time again. —*Marilyn Monroe, Erie, Michigan*

1 pound pork tenderloin, cut into 1/8- to 1/4-inch slices
1 to 2 tablespoons vegetable oil
3 to 4 garlic cloves, minced
1 jar (16 ounces) salsa
1/4 cup peach preserves
Hot cooked rice, optional

In a large skillet, saute pork in oil for 4 minutes. Add garlic; cook and stir 1 minute longer. Stir in salsa and preserves; bring to a boil. Reduce heat; cover and simmer for 2 minutes or until meat is no longer pink. Serve over rice if desired. **Yield:** 3-4 servings.

Hearty Hamburger Casserole

I love to invent my own recipes. I used convenient stuffing mix and canned vegetable soup to come up with this tasty and satisfying supper. —*Regan Delp, Independence, Virginia*

1 pound ground beef
1 can (19 ounces) ready-to-serve chunky vegetable soup
1 package (6 ounces) instant stuffing mix
1/2 cup shredded cheddar cheese

In a skillet, cook beef over medium heat until no longer pink; drain. Stir in soup and set aside. Prepare stuffing mix according to package directions; spoon half into a greased 2-qt. baking dish. Top with beef mixture, cheese and remaining stuffing. Bake, uncovered, at 350° for 30-35 minutes or until heated through. **Yield:** 4 servings.

|BUY IN BULK| Ground beef is often sold in large economy sizes. These packages are a bargain because you can use some of the meat now and freeze the rest for future use. Ground beef can be frozen for up to 2 weeks in its original packaging.

Tortilla Beef Bake

My family loves Mexican food, so I came up with this simple, satisfying casserole that gets its spark from salsa. We like it so much that there are rarely leftovers. —*Kim Osburn, Ligonier, Indiana*

1-1/2 pounds ground beef
1 can (10-3/4 ounces) condensed cream of chicken soup, undiluted
2-1/2 cups crushed tortilla chips, *divided*
1 jar (16 ounces) salsa
1-1/2 cups (6 ounces) shredded cheddar cheese

In a skillet, cook beef over medium heat until no longer pink; drain. Stir in soup. Sprinkle 1-1/2 cups tortilla chips in a greased shallow 2-1/2-qt. baking dish. Top with beef mixture, salsa and cheese.

Bake, uncovered, at 350° for 25-30 minutes or until bubbly. Sprinkle with the remaining chips. Bake 3 minutes longer or until chips are lightly toasted. **Yield:** 6 servings.

Breaded Ranch Chicken

A coating containing corn-flakes, Parmesan cheese and ranch dressing mix adds delectable flavor to the chicken pieces in this recipe and bakes to a pretty golden color. It's a mainstay I can always count on.
—Launa Shoemaker
Midland City, Alabama

3/4 cup crushed cornflakes
3/4 cup grated Parmesan cheese
1 envelope ranch salad dressing mix
8 boneless skinless chicken breast halves (2 pounds)
1/2 cup butter, melted

In a shallow bowl, combine the cornflakes, Parmesan cheese and salad dressing mix. Dip chicken in butter, then roll in cornflake mixture to coat.

Place in a greased 13-in. x 9-in. x 2-in. baking dish. Bake, uncovered, at 350° for 45 minutes or until chicken juices run clear. **Yield:** 8 servings.

Tuna Delight

A handful of ingredients is all it takes to put a meal on the table. This recipe makes a speedy dinner on busy weeknights or a tasty lunch when unexpected guests drop by.
—Marie Green
Belle Fourche, South Dakota

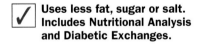 **Uses less fat, sugar or salt. Includes Nutritional Analysis and Diabetic Exchanges.**

1-3/4 cups frozen mixed vegetables, thawed
1 can (12 ounces) tuna, drained and flaked
1 can (10-3/4 ounces) condensed cream of chicken or celery soup, undiluted
Hot cooked rice or noodles

In a large saucepan, combine the vegetables, tuna and soup. Cook and stir until heated through. Serve over rice or noodles. **Yield:** 3 servings.

Nutritional Analysis: One 1-cup serving (prepared with water-packed tuna and reduced-fat cream of chicken soup; calculated without rice) equals 260 calories, 4 g fat (1 g saturated fat), 42 mg cholesterol, 1,166 mg sodium, 21 g carbohydrate, 5 g fiber, 34 g protein. **Diabetic Exchanges:** 3 lean meat, 1 starch, 1 vegetable.

Bubble Pizza

A top-ranked food with teens, pizza can quickly quell a growling tummy! This recipe has a no-fuss crust made from refrigerated biscuits. For a jazzed-up version, add any of your favorite toppings such as green pepper, mushrooms, black olives or fresh tomatoes. Anything goes with this easy entree! —*Jo Groth*
Plainfield, Iowa

1-1/2 pounds ground beef
1 can (15 ounces) pizza sauce
2 tubes (12 ounces *each*) refrigerated buttermilk biscuits
1-1/2 cups (6 ounces) shredded mozzarella cheese
1 cup (4 ounces) shredded cheddar cheese

In a skillet, cook the beef over medium heat until no longer pink; drain. Stir in pizza sauce. Quarter the biscuits; place in a greased 13-in. x 9-in. x 2-in. baking dish. Top with the beef mixture.

Bake, uncovered, at 400° for 20-25 minutes. Sprinkle with cheeses. Bake 5-10 minutes longer or until cheese is melted. Let stand for 5-10 minutes before serving. **Yield:** 6-8 servings.

Chow Mein Chicken

This basic recipe can be expanded many ways, but it's quite a success by itself. Sometimes I add sliced water chestnuts for extra crunch or a green vegetable for a burst of color.   —*Roberta Fall*
Paw Paw, Michigan

1 can (10-3/4 ounces) condensed cream of chicken soup, undiluted
1 can (10-1/2 ounces) condensed chicken with rice soup, undiluted
1 can (5 ounces) evaporated milk
2 cups cubed cooked chicken
1 can (3 ounces) chow mein noodles

In a bowl, combine soups and milk. Stir in chicken. Transfer to a greased 8-in. square baking dish. Bake, uncovered, at 350° for 40 minutes; stir. Sprinkle with chow mein noodles. Bake 5-10 minutes longer or until bubbly and noodles are crisp. **Yield:** 4 servings.

Turkey and Stuffing Pie

For a fast and flavorful way to use up Thanksgiving leftovers, try this main-dish pie. This is such a handy recipe during the holidays.
—*Debbi Baker, Green Springs, Ohio*

 ✓ **Uses less fat, sugar or salt. Includes Nutritional Analysis and Diabetic Exchanges.**

> 3 cups prepared stuffing
> 2 cups cubed cooked turkey
> 1 cup (4 ounces) shredded Swiss cheese
> 3 eggs
> 1/2 cup milk

Press stuffing onto the bottom and up the sides of a well-greased 9-in. pie plate. Top with turkey and cheese. Beat eggs and milk; pour over cheese. Bake at 350° for 35-40 minutes or until a knife inserted near the center comes out clean. Let stand 5-10 minutes before serving. **Yield:** 8 servings.

Nutritional Analysis: One serving (prepared with reduced-fat Swiss cheese, fat-free milk and egg substitute equivalent to 3 eggs) equals 327 calories, 1,065 mg sodium, 46 mg cholesterol, 39 g carbohydrate, 28 g protein, 6 g fat, 2 g fiber. **Diabetic Exchanges:** 3 lean meat, 2 starch.

Ravioli Casserole

The whole family will love the fun, cheesy flavor of this main dish that tastes like lasagna without all the fuss. Time-saving ingredients, including prepared spaghetti sauce and frozen ravioli, hurry the preparation along. —*Mary Ann Rothert, Austin, Texas*

> 1 jar (28 ounces) spaghetti sauce
> 1 package (25 ounces) frozen cheese ravioli, cooked and drained
> 2 cups (16 ounces) small-curd cottage cheese
> 4 cups (16 ounces) shredded mozzarella cheese
> 1/4 cup grated Parmesan cheese

Spread 1/2 cup of spaghetti sauce in an ungreased 13-in. x 9-in. x 2-in. baking dish. Layer with half of the ravioli, 1-1/4 cups of sauce, 1 cup of cottage cheese and 2 cups of mozzarella cheese. Repeat layers. Sprinkle with the Parmesan cheese.

Bake, uncovered, at 350° for 30-40 minutes or until bubbly. Let stand 5-10 minutes before serving. **Yield:** 6-8 servings.

Editor's Note: 4-5 cups of any style cooked ravioli may be substituted for the frozen cheese ravioli.

Cheesy Beef Macaroni

Little ones will light up the room with smiles when you bring this supper to the table. Crunchy canned corn is an appealing addition to the mild and cheesy combination of ground beef and pasta.

—Dena Evetts, Sentinel, Oklahoma

1 pound ground beef
1 can (15-1/4 ounces) whole kernel corn, drained
1 can (10-3/4 ounces) condensed cream of chicken soup, undiluted
8 ounces process cheese (Velveeta), shredded
2-1/2 cups cooked elbow macaroni

In a large skillet, cook beef over medium heat until no longer pink; drain. Add the corn and soup. Set aside 1/2 cup cheese for topping; stir remaining cheese into meat mixture until melted. Gently stir in macaroni until coated.

Transfer to a greased 8-in. square baking dish. Top with reserved cheese. Bake, uncovered, at 350° for 20-25 minutes or until heated through. **Yield:** 4-6 servings.

Crispy Chicken Strips

This is an easy method for dressing up chicken. Roll strips in a quick coating made with potato flakes and bread crumbs, then cook them for a couple minutes in a skillet.

—Dawn Hart
Lake Havasu City, Arizona

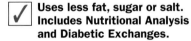 **Uses less fat, sugar or salt. Includes Nutritional Analysis and Diabetic Exchanges.**

3/4 pound boneless skinless chicken breasts
1/2 cup mashed potato flakes
1/2 cup seasoned bread crumbs
Egg substitute equivalent to 1 egg
2 tablespoons olive oil

Flatten chicken to 1/2-in. thickness; cut into 1-in. strips. In a shallow bowl, combine the potato flakes and bread crumbs. Dip chicken in egg substitute, then in potato mixture. In a skillet, cook chicken in oil for 4-5 minutes or until golden. **Yield:** 3 servings.

Nutritional Analysis: One serving equals 327 calories, 629 mg sodium, 63 mg cholesterol, 19 g carbohydrate, 28 g protein, 14 g fat. **Diabetic Exchanges:** 3 meat, 1-1/2 starch.

Bean and Beef Skillet

The mix of ground beef, beans and barbecue sauce in this skillet dish is a mainstay for us. I'll often brown the meat with the sauce and freeze it in a resealable bag. Later, I thaw it, add the beans, cook and serve.

—Rose Purrington
Windom, Minnesota

1 pound ground beef
1 medium onion, chopped
1 can (28 ounces) baked beans
1/4 cup barbecue sauce *or* ketchup
1 cup (4 ounces) shredded cheddar cheese

In a large skillet, cook beef and onion over medium heat until meat is no longer pink; drain. Stir in beans and barbecue sauce; heat through. Sprinkle with cheese; cover and cook on low until cheese is melted. **Yield:** 4 servings.

|SERVING ALTERNATIVES| Use this recipe as a dip by scooping it up with tortilla chips. Or you could crumble corn chips over the top. You might even mix the meat and beans with taco sauce, spoon it onto tortillas and roll them up like a burrito.

Mac and Cheese Tuna Casserole

This dish is so easy to fix, and the flavor is better than any tuna helper I've ever tried. It was a staple when I was in college since a box of macaroni and cheese and a can of tuna cost so little.

—Suzanne Zick, Osceola, Arkansas

1 package (7-1/4 ounces) macaroni and cheese
1 can (10-3/4 ounces) condensed cream of celery soup, undiluted
1 can (6 ounces) tuna, drained and flaked
1/2 cup milk
1 cup (4 ounces) shredded cheddar cheese
Minced fresh parsley, optional

Prepare macaroni and cheese according to package directions. Stir in soup, tuna and milk. Pour into a greased 2-qt. baking dish. Sprinkle with cheese and parsley if desired. Bake, uncovered, at 350° for 20 minutes or until cheese is melted. **Yield:** 4 servings.

Sausage Spaghetti Spirals

My family loves this flavorful casserole with hearty chunks of sausage and green pepper. The recipe makes a big pan, so it's nicely sized for a potluck.
—Carol Carlton
Wheaton, Illinois

✓ **Uses less fat, sugar or salt. Includes Nutritional Analysis and Diabetic Exchanges.**

- **1 pound bulk Italian sausage**
- **1 medium green pepper, chopped**
- **5 cups spiral pasta, cooked and drained**
- **1 jar (28 ounces) meatless spaghetti sauce**
- **1-1/2 cups (6 ounces) shredded mozzarella cheese**

In a skillet, cook sausage and green pepper over medium heat until meat is no longer pink; drain. Stir in pasta and spaghetti sauce; mix well.

Transfer to a greased 13-in. x 9-in. x 2-in. baking dish. Cover and bake at 350° for 25 minutes. Uncover; sprinkle with cheese. Bake 5-10 minutes longer or until the cheese is melted. **Yield:** 10 servings.

Nutritional Analysis: One 1-cup serving (prepared with turkey Italian sausage and reduced-fat mozzarella) equals 249 calories, 8 g fat (3 g saturated fat), 34 mg cholesterol, 710 mg sodium, 28 g carbohydrate, 2 g fiber, 16 g protein. **Diabetic Exchanges:** 2 starch, 1-1/2 lean meat.

Savory Roast Chicken

Brushing the bird with a savory-seasoned butter makes the meat nice and moist. This roasted chicken is so easy to make and tastes so delicious!
—Connie Moore, Medway, Ohio

- **1 broiler/fryer chicken (2-1/2 to 3 pounds)**
- **2 tablespoons butter, melted**
- **3 tablespoons lemon juice**
- **1 tablespoon minced fresh savory *or* 1 teaspoon dried savory**

Place chicken, breast side up, on a rack in a shallow roasting pan. Combine butter, lemon juice and savory; brush over chicken. Bake, uncovered, at 375° for 1-1/2 hours or until juices run clear, basting occasionally with the pan drippings. **Yield:** 4 servings.

|"SPRING" CHICKEN| As with any poultry, the younger the chicken, the more tender it is. Younger chickens, including broiler/fryers, are best cooked with dry-heat methods like baking, frying, roasting and grilling.

Breakfast Skewers

These brown 'n' serve sausage kabobs are fun, different and delicious. Plus, any egg dish goes well with them.
—*Bobi Raab, St. Paul, Minnesota*

1 package (7 ounces) brown 'n' serve sausage links
1 can (20 ounces) pineapple chunks, drained
10 medium fresh mushrooms
2 tablespoons butter, melted
Maple syrup

Cut sausages in half; alternately thread sausages, pineapple and mushrooms onto metal or soaked bamboo skewers. Brush with butter and syrup.

Grill, uncovered, over medium-hot heat, turning and basting with syrup, for 8 minutes or until sausages are lightly browned and fruit is heated through. **Yield:** 5 servings.

|ANOTHER EYE-OPENER| Turn plain smoked sausage into a breakfast treat by wrapping each slice with half of a bacon strip. Secure it with a toothpick, then place in a baking dish and sprinkle with brown sugar. Bake at 350° for 1 hour.

Salsa Fish

My family loves outdoor activities, especially fishing. I give their catch of the day some unexpected zip with salsa. It dresses up these golden crumb-coated fillets and keeps them moist and tender.
—*Diane Grajewski, North Branch, Michigan*

2 pounds fish fillets (walleye, bass *or* perch)
1 cup seasoned bread crumbs
1 tablespoon vegetable oil
1-1/2 cups salsa
8 ounces shredded *or* sliced mozzarella *or* provolone cheese

Coat fish fillets in bread crumbs. In a skillet, brown fillets in oil. Arrange in a greased 13-in. x 9-in. x 2-in. baking dish. Top with salsa and cheese.

Bake, uncovered, at 400° for 7-10 minutes or until the fish flakes easily with a fork and the cheese is melted. **Yield:** 6 servings.

Turkey Asparagus Casserole

It takes just minutes to assemble this creamy casserole filled with tender turkey. Convenient frozen asparagus lends bright color and garden flavor while a sprinkling of french-fried onion rings provides a yummy crunch.
—*Cheryl Schut, Grand Rapids, Michigan*

1 package (8 ounces) frozen chopped asparagus
2 cups cubed cooked turkey
1 can (10-3/4 ounces) condensed cream of chicken soup, undiluted
1/4 cup water
1 can (2.8 ounces) french-fried onions

In a small saucepan, cook asparagus in a small amount of water for 2 minutes; drain. Place in a greased 11-in. x 7-in. x 2-in. baking dish. Top with turkey. Combine soup and water; spoon over turkey.

Bake, uncovered, at 350° for 25-30 minutes. Sprinkle with onions. Bake 5 minutes longer or until golden brown. **Yield:** 4 servings.

Editor's Note: Out of turkey? Cooked chicken can be substituted measure-for-measure in this recipe.

French Bread Pizza

This pizza is a great change of pace. It's soft...easy to chew...and just plain fun to eat—the kids feel like they are each getting their own personal pizza. For a garden pizza, cover it with your favorite vegetables in place of the ground beef.
—*Sue McLaughlin, Onawa, Iowa*

1/2 pound ground beef
1 can (16 ounces) pizza sauce
1 jar (8 ounces) sliced mushrooms, drained
1 loaf (1 pound) French bread
2 cups (8 ounces) shredded mozzarella cheese

In a medium skillet, cook beef over medium heat until no longer pink; drain. Stir in pizza sauce and mushrooms; set aside. Cut bread in half lengthwise, then into eight pieces.

Spread meat sauce on bread; place on a greased baking sheet. Sprinkle with mozzarella. Bake, uncovered, at 400° for 10 minutes or until cheese is melted and bubbly. **Yield:** 6-8 servings.

Sesame Ginger Chicken

Why grill plain chicken breasts when a simple ginger-honey basting sauce can make them extra special? This tempting chicken is a wonderful summer main dish since it's quick and light. We love it.

—Nancy Johnson
Connersville, Indiana

2 tablespoons soy sauce
2 tablespoons honey
1 tablespoon sesame seeds, toasted
1/2 teaspoon ground ginger
4 boneless skinless chicken breast halves
2 green onions with tops, cut into thin strips, optional

In a small bowl, combine the first four ingredients; set aside. Pound the chicken breasts to 1/4-in. thickness. Grill over medium-hot heat, turning and basting frequently with soy sauce mixture, for 8 minutes or until juices run clear. Garnish with onions if desired. **Yield:** 4 servings.

Saucy Spareribs

My husband likes spareribs, so when my mom gave me this stovetop recipe, I knew I had to try it. He loves the tender ribs and barbecue sauce.

—Melanie Sanders, Kaysville, Utah

2 pounds pork spareribs
2 cans (12 ounces *each*) cola
1 cup ketchup
2 tablespoons cornstarch
2 tablespoons cold water

In a large nonstick skillet, brown the ribs; drain. Add the cola and ketchup; cover and simmer for 1 hour or until the meat is tender.

Remove ribs and keep warm. Transfer 2 cups of sauce to a saucepan. Bring to a boil. In a small bowl, combine the cornstarch and cold water; stir into sauce. Bring to a boil; cook for 1-2 minutes or until thickened. Serve over the ribs. **Yield:** 2 servings.

|TAKE IT SLOW| Saucy Spareribs also could be prepared in the slow cooker. Just combine all of the ingredients, set the slow cooker to low and let the ribs cook for 4 to 6 hours.

Honey–Mustard Chicken

I get bored with the same old chicken, so I came up with this simple recipe. The coating adds fast flavor to tender chicken cooked on the stovetop.
—*Laura Theofilis*
Leonardtown, Maryland

✓ **Uses less fat, sugar or salt. Includes Nutritional Analysis and Diabetic Exchanges.**

4 boneless skinless chicken breast halves (1 pound)
1 cup dry bread crumbs
1 teaspoon plus 2 tablespoons Dijon mustard, *divided*
3 tablespoons honey
2 tablespoons butter

Flatten chicken to 1/4-in. thickness. In a shallow bowl, combine bread crumbs and 1 teaspoon of mustard. In another shallow bowl, combine honey and remaining mustard. Dip chicken in honey-mustard mixture, then coat with crumbs.

In a nonstick skillet over medium heat, cook chicken in butter on both sides until juices run clear, about 8 minutes. **Yield:** 4 servings.

Nutritional Analysis: One serving (prepared with reduced-fat margarine) equals 338 calories, 583 mg sodium, 73 mg cholesterol, 34 g carbohydrate, 31 g protein, 9 g fat, 1 g fiber. **Diabetic Exchanges:** 4 very lean meat, 2 starch, 1 fat.

Pineapple Ham Bake

Brunch is a great meal to mark special occasions. At our house, we've celebrated birthdays, confirmations and graduations with a favorite mid-morning menu. I found Pineapple Ham Bake in a church cookbook from my grandfather's hometown. It's simple to fix, and the tangy pineapple flavor goes well with the casserole.
—*Patricia Throlson, Hawick, Minnesota*

2 cans (8 ounces *each*) crushed pineapple, undrained
2/3 cup packed brown sugar
1 tablespoon vinegar
2 teaspoons ground mustard
1 pound fully cooked ham, cut into bite-size pieces

Combine the first four ingredients in an ungreased 2-qt. baking dish; mix well. Stir in ham. Bake, uncovered, at 350° for 30-40 minutes or until heated through. Serve with a slotted spoon. **Yield:** 8 servings.

Mini Sausage Pizzas

I dress up English muffins with sausage and cheese to make these handheld breakfast pizzas. My husband and son really enjoy them in the morning. —*Janice Garvert, Plainville, Kansas*

1 pound bulk pork sausage
2 jars (5 ounces *each*) sharp American cheese spread
1/4 cup butter, softened
1/8 to 1/4 teaspoon cayenne pepper
12 English muffins, split

In a large skillet, cook sausage over medium heat until no longer pink; drain well. In a small mixing bowl, beat the cheese, butter and pepper. Stir in the sausage. Spread on cut sides of muffins.

Wrap individually and freeze for up to 2 months. Or place on a baking sheet and bake at 425° for 8-10 minutes or until golden brown.

To use frozen pizzas: Unwrap and place on a baking sheet. Bake at 425° for 10-15 minutes or until golden brown. **Yield:** 2 dozen.

Italian Flank Steak

Savory and satisfying, this flank steak is nice for entertaining or busy days since it marinates overnight and grills in minutes. Leftovers, if there are any, make super sandwiches the next day.
—*Walajean Saglett, Canandaiqua, New York*

 Uses less fat, sugar or salt. Includes Nutritional Analysis and Diabetic Exchanges.

2 envelopes (.7 ounce *each*) fat-free Italian salad dressing mix
2 tablespoons vegetable oil
1 tablespoon lemon juice
1 flank steak (1 pound)

Combine salad dressing mix, oil and lemon juice. Brush onto both sides of steak; place in a shallow dish. Cover and refrigerate several hours or overnight.

Grill over hot heat for 4 minutes per side for medium, 5 minutes per side for medium-well or until desired doneness is reached (for rare, a meat thermometer should read 140°; medium, 160°; well-done 170°). **Yield:** 4 servings.

Nutritional Analysis: One serving equals 267 calories, 793 mg sodium, 59 mg cholesterol, 8 g carbohydrate, 24 g protein, 16 g fat. **Diabetic Exchanges:** 3 meat, 1/2 starch.

Dijon Chicken Kabobs

People are always asking for the recipe for these tangy, juicy chicken kabobs. They're a fun and festive way to bake chicken.

—*Earleen Lillegard, Prescott, Arizona*

✓ **Uses less fat, sugar or salt. Includes Nutritional Analysis and Diabetic Exchanges.**

1/2 cup Dijon mustard
1 tablespoon finely chopped green onion
2 cups fresh bread crumbs
1/4 cup minced fresh parsley
1-1/4 pounds boneless skinless chicken breasts, cut into 3/4-inch chunks

In a bowl, combine mustard and onion. In another bowl, combine bread crumbs and parsley. Toss chicken in mustard mixture, then coat evenly with crumb mixture. Line a baking sheet with foil; coat the foil with nonstick cooking spray.

Thread chicken onto metal or soaked wooden skewers, leaving a small space between chunks. Place on the prepared baking sheet. Bake, uncovered, at 450° for 6-8 minutes or until juices run clear. **Yield:** 5 servings.

Nutritional Analysis: One serving equals 222 calories, 762 mg sodium, 73 mg cholesterol, 12 g carbohydrate, 30 g protein, 6 g fat. **Diabetic Exchanges:** 4 very lean meat, 1 starch.

Ribs with Plum Sauce

I found the recipe for this tangy-sweet basting sauce when a surplus of plums sent me searching for new ideas to use all the fruit. In summer, I like to finish the ribs on the grill, brushing on the sauce, after first baking them in the oven.

—*Marie Hoyer*
Hodgenville, Kentucky

5 to 6 pounds pork spareribs
3/4 cup soy sauce
3/4 cup plum jam *or* apricot preserves
3/4 cup honey
2 to 3 garlic cloves, minced

Cut ribs into serving-size pieces; place with bone side down on a rack in a shallow roasting pan. Cover and bake at 350° for 1 hour or until ribs are tender; drain.

Combine remaining ingredients; brush some of the sauce over ribs. Bake at 350° or grill over medium heat, uncovered, for 30 minutes, brushing occasionally with sauce. **Yield:** 6 servings.

Green Chili Burritos

My husband and I love Mexican food, so I usually have the ingredients for these tasy burritos on hand. A woman in our congregation shared the recipe. They soon became a fast favorite in our home, and when I serve them at church potlucks, they disappear quickly.

—Kathy Ybarra
Rock Springs, Wyoming

1 can (16 ounces) refried beans
8 flour tortillas (6 inches)
1/2 pound ground beef, cooked and drained
1 cup (4 ounces) shredded sharp cheddar cheese, *divided*
1 can (4-1/2 ounces) chopped green chilies

Spread refried beans over tortillas. Top each with beef and 2 tablespoons of cheese. Fold ends and sides over filling and roll up; place seam side down in a greased 13-in. x 9-in. x 2-in. baking dish.

Sprinkle with chilies and remaining cheese. Bake, uncovered, at 350° for 20 minutes or until heated through. **Yield:** 4 servings.

Oven Swiss Steak

There's no need to brown the steak first, so you can get this main course into the oven in short order. The fork-tender results are sure to remind you of Swiss steak Grandma used to make, with lots of sauce left over for dipping.
—Sue Call, Beech Grove, Indiana

 Uses less fat, sugar or salt. Includes Nutritional Analysis and Diabetic Exchanges.

2 pounds boneless round steak (1/2 inch thick)
1/4 teaspoon pepper
1 medium onion, thinly sliced
1 can (4 ounces) mushroom stems and pieces, drained
1 can (8 ounces) no-salt-added tomato sauce
Hot cooked noodles, optional

Trim beef; cut into serving-size pieces. Place in a greased 13-in. x 9-in. x 2-in. baking dish. Sprinkle with pepper. Top with the onion, mushrooms and tomato sauce.

Cover and bake at 325° for 1-3/4 to 2 hours or until meat is tender. Serve over noodles if desired. **Yield:** 8 servings.

Nutritional Analysis: One serving (calculated without noodles) equals 209 calories, 112 mg sodium, 68 mg cholesterol, 4 g carbohydrate, 26 g protein, 10 g fat. **Diabetic Exchanges:** 3 lean meat, 1 vegetable.

Sunday Chicken and Stuffing

This hearty entree is a surefire family pleaser. It's easy to prepare because you don't have to brown the chicken. Plus, it looks so nice you can serve it to company. —*Charlotte Kidd, Lagrange, Ohio*

1 package (6 ounces) instant chicken stuffing mix
6 boneless skinless chicken breast halves
1 can (10-3/4 ounces) condensed cream of chicken soup, undiluted
1/3 cup milk
1 tablespoon dried parsley flakes

Prepare stuffing according to package directions; spoon down the center of a greased 13-in. x 9-in. x 2-in. baking dish. Place chicken around stuffing. Combine soup, milk and parsley; pour over chicken.

Cover and bake at 400° for 20 minutes. Uncover and bake 10-15 minutes longer or until chicken juices run clear. **Yield:** 6 servings.

Turkey Tenderloin Supreme

We're a busy hockey and figure skating family, so we're always on the go. Served over rice, this fast skillet supper makes a good home-cooked meal when there's little time.
—*Nancy Levin*
Chesterfield, Missouri

✓ **Uses less fat, sugar or salt. Includes Nutritional Analysis and Diabetic Exchanges.**

6 turkey breast tenderloin slices (3/4 inch thick and 4 ounces *each*)
1 tablespoon butter
3 green onions, thinly sliced
1 can (10-3/4 ounces) condensed cream of chicken soup, undiluted
1/4 cup water

In a large skillet, brown turkey in butter. Add onions; cook for 1-2 minutes. Combine soup and water; pour over turkey. Bring to a boil. Reduce heat; cover and simmer for 8-10 minutes or until meat juices run clear. **Yield:** 6 servings.

Nutritional Analysis: One serving (prepared with reduced-fat margarine and reduced-fat soup) equals 175 calories, 264 mg sodium, 81 mg cholesterol, 5 g carbohydrate, 26 g protein, 5 g fat. **Diabetic Exchanges:** 3 very lean meat, 1 vegetable, 1 fruit.

Duck with Cherry Sauce

My mom prepared this golden tender roast duck often for Sunday dinner when I was growing up. It was one of my dad's favorite meals. The cheery cherry sauce stirs up easily and makes this main dish doubly delightful.
—*Sandy Jenkins*
Elkhorn, Wisconsin

1 domestic duckling (4 to 5 pounds)
1 jar (12 ounces) cherry preserves
1 to 2 tablespoons red wine vinegar
Bing cherries, star fruit and kale, optional

Prick skin of duckling and place, breast side up, on a rack in a shallow roasting pan. Tie drumsticks together. Bake, uncovered, at 325° for 2 hours or until juices run clear and a meat thermometer reads 180°. (Drain fat from pan as it accumulates.) Cover; let stand for 20 minutes before carving.

Meanwhile, for sauce, combine preserves and vinegar in a small saucepan. Cook and stir over medium heat until heated through. Serve with duck. Garnish platter with fruit and kale if desired. **Yield:** 4-5 servings.

Easy and Elegant Ham

I fix this moist, tender ham to serve my large family. It can be readied quickly in the morning, frees up my oven, tastes outstanding and can feed a crowd. Covered with colorful pineapple slices, cherries and orange glaze, its showstopping appearance appeals to all. —*Denise DiPace, Medford, New Jersey*

2 cans (20 ounces *each*) sliced pineapple
1 fully cooked boneless ham (about 6 pounds), halved
1 jar (6 ounces) maraschino cherries, well drained
1 jar (12 ounces) orange marmalade

Drain pineapple, reserving juice; set juice aside. Place half of the pineapple in an ungreased 5-qt. slow cooker. Top with the ham. Add cherries, remaining pineapple and reserved pineapple juice. Spoon marmalade over ham. Cover and cook on low for 6-7 hours or until heated through.

Remove to a warm serving platter. Let stand for 10-15 minutes before slicing. Serve pineapple and cherries with sliced ham. **Yield:** 18-20 servings.

Spaghetti Carbonara

This is a swift and yummy recipe that I received from a dear friend. My family asks for it often and I'm always happy to oblige.

—Roni Goodell, Spanish Fork, Utah

- **1 package (7 ounces) thin spaghetti**
- **10 bacon strips, diced**
- **1/3 cup butter**
- **2 eggs, lightly beaten**
- **3/4 cup grated Parmesan cheese**

Cook spaghetti according to package directions. Meanwhile, in a skillet, cook bacon over medium heat until crisp; drain on paper towels. Add butter to drippings; heat until melted.

Drain spaghetti; toss with eggs and Parmesan cheese. Add to skillet; cook and stir over medium heat for 3-4 minutes or until eggs are set. Sprinkle with bacon. **Yield:** 3-4 servings.

Green 'n' Gold Egg Bake

I need just five ingredients to assemble this pretty casserole. The firm squares have a delicious spinach flavor that's welcome at breakfast or dinner.

—Muriel Paceleo Montgomery, New York

✓ Uses less fat, sugar or salt. Includes Nutritional Analysis and Diabetic Exchanges.

- **1 cup seasoned bread crumbs, *divided***
- **2 packages (10 ounces *each*) frozen chopped spinach, thawed and squeezed dry**
- **3 cups (24 ounces) small-curd cottage cheese**
- **1/2 cup grated Romano *or* Parmesan cheese**
- **5 eggs**

Sprinkle 1/4 cup bread crumbs into a greased 8-in. square baking dish. Bake at 350° for 3-5 minutes or until golden brown. In a bowl, combine the spinach, cottage cheese, Romano cheese, three eggs and remaining crumbs. Spread over the baked crumbs. Beat remaining eggs; pour over spinach mixture.

Bake, uncovered, at 350° for 45 minutes or until a knife inserted near the center comes out clean. Let stand for 5-10 minutes before serving. **Yield:** 9 servings.

Nutritional Analysis: One 1/2-cup serving (prepared with fat-free cottage cheese and egg substitute) equals 181 calories, 6 g fat (2 g saturated fat), 127 mg cholesterol, 808 mg sodium, 15 g carbohydrate, 2 g fiber, 18 g protein. **Diabetic Exchanges:** 2 lean meat, 1 starch.

Breaded Pork Chops

No matter how busy the day becomes, I strongly believe everyone should sit down together at least once around a meal. My brother-in-law invented this recipe, which is a family favorite. Sometimes I'll make the pork chops Italian-style by adding red sauce and more Parmesan cheese.

—*Ann Ingalls*
Gladstone, Missouri

1 cup Italian-seasoned dry bread crumbs
2 tablespoons grated Parmesan cheese
1/3 cup bottled ranch salad dressing
6 pork chops (1/2 inch thick)

Combine bread crumbs and Parmesan cheese in a shallow dish. Place dressing in another shallow dish. Dip pork chops in dressing, then coat in crumb mixture.

Place in an ungreased 13-in. x 9-in. x 2-in. baking pan. Bake, uncovered, at 375° for 25 minutes or until pork is no longer pink. **Yield:** 4-6 servings.

|PICKING OUT PORK| When buying pork, look for meat that's pale pink with a small amount of marbeling and white fat. If you want succulent chops, choose those that are about 1/2 to 1 inch thick.

Cheeseburger 'n' Fries Casserole

There are only four ingredients in this quick recipe—and you're likely to have them all on hand. Kids love it because, as the name suggests, it combines two of their favorite fast foods.

—*Karen Owen, Rising Sun, Indiana*

2 pounds lean ground beef
1 can (10-3/4 ounces) condensed golden mushroom soup, undiluted
1 can (10-3/4 ounces) condensed cheddar cheese soup, undiluted
1 package (20 ounces) frozen crinkle-cut French fries

In a skillet, cook the beef over medium heat until no longer pink; drain. Stir in soups. Pour into a greased 13-in. x 9-in. x 2-in. baking dish. Arrange French fries on top. Bake, uncovered, at 350° for 50-55 minutes or until the fries are golden brown. **Yield:** 6-8 servings.

Barbecued Chicken Pizza

My pizza starts with a prepared bread shell and barbecue sauce, plus leftover cooked chicken. Then I simply assemble and bake. My daughter, Haley, loves creating smiling pizza "faces" with shredded cheese and fresh veggie toppings.

—*Patricia Richardson*
Verona, Ontario

1 **prebaked Italian bread shell crust (14 ounces)**
2/3 **cup honey garlic barbecue sauce**
1 **small red onion, chopped**
1 **cup cubed cooked chicken**
2 **cups (8 ounces) shredded mozzarella cheese**

Place the crust on a pizza pan. Spread with barbecue sauce; sprinkle with onion, chicken and cheese. Bake at 350° for 10 minutes or until cheese is melted. **Yield:** 4 servings.

|SERVING ALTERNATIVES| Cut the pizza into small bite-size pieces and serve it as an appetizer. Or use any thick flat bread for the crust and replace the chicken with round steak.

Pasta with Sausage and Tomatoes

I reach for this recipe whenever I crave spaghetti sauce but don't have the time to make my usual spaghetti and meatballs recipe. This sausage and diced tomatoes blend is fast and very flavorful.

—*Michelle Fryer Dommel, Quakertown, Pennsylvania*

1 **pound bulk Italian sausage**
2 **cans (16 ounces *each*) diced tomatoes, undrained**
1-1/2 **teaspoons chopped fresh basil *or* 1/2 teaspoon dried basil**
1 **package (12 ounces) pasta, cooked and drained**

In a skillet, cook sausage over medium heat until no longer pink; drain. Add tomatoes and basil. Simmer, uncovered, for 10 minutes. Serve immediately over pasta. **Yield:** 4 servings.

Editor's Note: For even more flavor, use cans of diced tomatoes with garlic and onion.

Cheesy Crab Burritos

Everyone who tries this elegant variation on the standard burrito loves it. I'm always asked for the recipe. Serve them with a green salad for a lighter lunch or with traditional rice and beans for supper.

—*Karen Dye, Tempe, Arizona*

1 package (8 ounces)
   cream cheese, softened
2 cups (8 ounces) shredded
   cheddar cheese
1 package (8 ounces)
   imitation crabmeat,
   flaked
8 flour tortillas (10 inches)
Salsa

In a mixing bowl, combine the cream cheese and cheddar cheese. Stir in the crab. Spoon down the center of each tortilla; roll up tightly and place on an ungreased baking sheet. Bake at 350° for 20 minutes or until heated through. Serve with salsa. **Yield:** 4 servings.

Broiled Orange Roughy

The fillets are flaky, moist and mildly flavored. They can be broiled in the oven, but I often cook them on our outdoor grill instead to reduce kitchen cleanup.

—*Judy Bernacki, Las Vegas, Nevada*

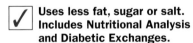

✓ **Uses less fat, sugar or salt. Includes Nutritional Analysis and Diabetic Exchanges.**

1-1/2 pounds fresh *or* frozen
   orange roughy, red
   snapper *or* haddock
   fillets, thawed
1 teaspoon garlic powder
1/4 cup butter, melted
1/4 cup lemon juice
1/4 cup soy sauce
Paprika, optional

Place fillets in a shallow dish; sprinkle with garlic powder. Combine butter, lemon juice and soy sauce; pour over fish and turn. Marinate for 10 minutes.

Drain and discard marinade. Place fillets on a broiler pan. Broil 3-4 in. from the heat for 10 minutes or until fish flakes easily with a fork, turning once. Sprinkle with paprika. **Yield:** 4 servings.

Nutritional Analysis: One serving (prepared with orange roughy and reduced-sodium soy sauce) equals 189 calories, 7 g fat (4 g saturated fat), 50 mg cholesterol, 489 mg sodium, 5 g carbohydrate, trace fiber, 26 g protein. **Diabetic Exchanges:** 4 very lean meat, 1 fat.

Pesto Chicken Penne

A convenient pesto sauce mix provides the pleasant basil flavor in this simple chicken and pasta combination. This entree requires little effort, yet seems elegant.

—Beth Martin Sine
Faulkner, Maryland

8 ounces penne *or any* medium pasta
1 envelope pesto sauce mix
3/4 cup milk
1/4 cup olive oil
2 cups cubed cooked chicken *or turkey*
Shredded Parmesan cheese, optional

Cook the pasta according to package directions. Meanwhile, in a large saucepan, whisk together the pesto mix, milk and oil. Bring to a boil. Reduce heat; simmer, uncovered, for 5 minutes.

Add chicken; heat through. Drain pasta. Add to the sauce and toss to coat. Sprinkle with Parmesan cheese if desired. **Yield:** 4-6 servings.

Mock Lobster

My family loves when I serve Mock Lobster with macaroni and cheese or coleslaw. For a change of taste, you can substitute your favorite seafood sauce for the melted butter.

—Gloria Jarrett, Loveland, Ohio

1-1/2 to 2 pounds frozen cod *or* haddock fillets, partially thawed
1-1/2 teaspoons salt
2 teaspoons seafood seasoning *or* paprika
3 tablespoons vinegar
Melted butter

Cut fillets into 2-in. x 2-in. pieces; place in a skillet. Cover with water. Add salt and seafood seasoning; bring to a boil. Reduce heat; simmer, uncovered, for 10 minutes. Drain.

Cover with cold water. Add vinegar and bring to a boil. Reduce heat; simmer, uncovered, for 10 minutes. Drain. Serve with melted butter. **Yield:** 4-6 servings.

Garlic Rosemary Turkey

The house smells so good while this turkey is cooking that my family can hardly wait until it's done! This is a beautiful, succulent main dish that deliciously serves a crowd.

—*Cathy Dobbins*
Rio Rancho, New Mexico

✓ **Uses less fat, sugar or salt. Includes Nutritional Analysis and Diabetic Exchanges.**

1 whole turkey (10 to 12 pounds)
6 to 8 garlic cloves
2 large lemons, halved
2 teaspoons dried rosemary, crushed
1 teaspoon rubbed sage
Gravy, optional

Cut six to eight small slits in turkey skin; insert garlic between the skin and meat. Squeeze two lemon halves inside the turkey and leave them inside. Squeeze remaining lemon over outside of turkey. Spray the turkey with nonstick cooking spray; sprinkle with rosemary and sage.

Place on a rack in a roasting pan. Bake, uncovered, at 325° for 1 hour. Cover and bake 2-1/2 to 3-1/2 hours longer or until a meat thermometer reads 185°. Serve with gravy if desired. **Yield:** 8-10 servings.

Nutritional Analysis: One serving (4 ounces of white meat without skin; calculated without gravy) equals 144 calories, 57 mg sodium, 88 mg cholesterol, trace carbohydrate, 31 g protein, 1 g fat. **Diabetic Exchange:** 4 very lean meat.

Tender Pork Roast

This is a melt-in-your-mouth, fall-apart-tender pork roast. It's wonderful to serve to company because it never fails to please.
—*LuVerne Peterson, Minneapolis, Minnesota*

1 boneless pork roast (about 3 pounds)
1 can (8 ounces) tomato sauce
3/4 cup soy sauce
1/2 cup sugar
2 teaspoons ground mustard

Cut roast in half; place in a 5-qt. slow cooker. Combine remaining ingredients; pour over roast. Cover and cook on low for 8-9 hours or until a meat thermometer reads 160°-170°. Remove roast to a serving platter and keep warm. If desired, skim fat from pan juices and thicken for gravy. **Yield:** 8 servings.

|TESTING FOR DONENESS| The best way to test a pork roast's doneness is with a meat thermometer. Cutting into it to see if it's still pink lets too many of the juices run out.

Taco Dogs

A taco shell makes a good holder for a hot dog dressed up with a tasty combination of baked beans and cheese...and holds up better than a plain bun. When our children were young, they asked for this meal at least once a week. I was always happy to make it for them because it goes from start to the supper table in less than 30 minutes.

—*Kat Thompson, Prineville, Oregon*

1 package (1 pound) hot dogs
10 slices process American cheese
10 hard taco shells, warmed
1 can (16 ounces) baked beans, warmed

Prepare hot dogs according to package directions. Place a cheese slice and hot dog in each taco shell; top with beans. **Yield:** 10 tacos.

Sweet-Sour Chicken Casserole

Apricot preserves give a different twist to this saucy sweet-and-sour chicken. It's a snap to stir up and serve over rice.

—*Melanie May, Fishers, Indiana*

 Uses less fat, sugar or salt. Includes Nutritional Analysis and Diabetic Exchanges.

2 cups cubed cooked chicken
1 can (20 ounces) unsweetened pineapple chunks, drained
1 jar (12 ounces) apricot preserves *or* spreadable fruit
1 can (10-3/4 ounces) condensed cream of chicken soup, undiluted
1 can (8 ounces) water chestnuts, drained
Hot cooked rice, optional

In a bowl, combine the first five ingredients. Transfer to a greased 2-qt. baking dish. Bake, uncovered, at 350° for 30 minutes or until heated through. Serve over rice if desired. **Yield:** 6 servings.

Nutritional Analysis: One serving (prepared with reduced-fat soup and spreadable fruit; calculated without rice) equals 259 calories, 413 mg sodium, 44 mg cholesterol, 41 g carbohydrate, 16 g protein, 3 g fat, 3 g fiber. **Diabetic Exchanges:** 2 lean meat, 2 fruit, 1/2 vegetable.

Golden Game Hens

I served game hens at a diplomatic dinner when my wife, Ruth, was the defense attaché at the American Embassy in Budapest, Hungary. They were an appealing choice because they filled a plate and garnered many fine comments.
—*Andy Anderson, Graham, Washington*

6 **Cornish game hens (20 ounces** *each***)**
1 **medium tart apple, sliced**
1 **medium onion, sliced**
1/4 **cup butter, melted**
1/4 **cup soy sauce**

Loosely stuff hens with apple and onion. Place on a rack in a shallow baking pan. Combine butter and soy sauce; brush over hens.

Bake, uncovered, at 350° for 50-60 minutes or until a meat thermometer reads 165° and juices run clear, basting occasionally. **Yield:** 6 servings.

|GAME HEN FACTS| Cornish game hens are a cross between Cornish and White Rock chickens and typically weigh 1-1/2 pounds or less. They look elegant, have tender white meat and take less time to prepare than a whole chicken.

Mexicali Pork Chops

These fast and tender pork chops are ready to serve in about 10 minutes! They get their zippy flavor from a packet of taco seasoning. Spoon salsa over the top for even more flavor.
—*Laura Cohen*
Eau Claire, Wisconsin

1 **envelope taco seasoning**
4 **boneless pork loin chops (1/2 inch thick)**
1 **tablespoon vegetable oil**
Salsa

Rub taco seasoning over pork chops. In a skillet, cook chops in oil over medium-high heat until meat is no longer pink and juices run clear, about 9 minutes. Serve with salsa. **Yield:** 4 servings.

Barbecue Beef Patties

I frequently fix these family-pleasing patties that taste like individual meat loaves. Barbecue sauce brushed on top gives them fast flavor.
—*Marlene Harguth, Maynard, Minnesota*

1 egg
1/2 cup barbecue sauce,
divided
3/4 cup crushed cornflakes
1/2 to 1 teaspoon salt
1 pound ground beef

In a bowl, combine egg, 1/4 cup barbecue sauce, cornflake crumbs and salt. Add beef and mix well. Shape into four oval patties, about 3/4 in. thick. Place in a greased 11-in. x 7-in. x 2-in. baking pan. Spread with remaining barbecue sauce.

Bake, uncovered, at 375° for 25-30 minutes or until meat is no longer pink and a meat thermometer reads 160°; drain. **Yield:** 4 servings.

Chicken Nugget Casserole

Youngsters will need just five ingredients to help prepare this easy entree. Our kids love to eat chicken nuggets this way. It's a satisfying supper with spaghetti and a salad.
—*Tylene Loar, Mesa, Arizona*

1 package (13-1/2 ounces) frozen chicken nuggets
1/3 cup grated Parmesan cheese
1 can (26-1/2 ounces) spaghetti sauce
1 cup (4 ounces) shredded mozzarella cheese
1 teaspoon Italian seasoning

Place chicken nuggets in a greased 11-in. x 7-in. x 2-in. baking dish. Sprinkle with Parmesan cheese. Top with spaghetti sauce, mozzarella cheese and Italian seasoning.

Cover and bake at 350° for 30-35 minutes or until chicken is heated through and cheese is melted. **Yield:** 4-6 servings.

Bean Burritos

My husband and I have two sons. With our demanding careers, main dishes like this one that can be prepared in a flash are essential for us. I always have the ingredients for this recipe on hand. Cooking the rice and shredding the cheese the night before save precious minutes at dinnertime.

—Beth Osborne Skinner
Bristol, Tennessee

1 can (16 ounces) refried beans
1 cup salsa
1 cup cooked long grain rice
2 cups (8 ounces) shredded cheddar cheese, *divided*
12 flour tortillas (6 to 7 inches)

In a bowl, combine the beans, salsa, rice and 1 cup cheese. Spoon about 1/3 cup off-center on each tortilla. Fold the sides and ends over filling and roll up.

Arrange burritos in a greased 13-in. x 9-in. x 2-in. baking dish. Sprinkle with the remaining cheese. Cover and bake at 375° for 20-25 minutes or until heated through. **Yield:** 1 dozen.

Potato Sloppy Joe Bake

I created this speedy sensation while racing against the clock one day. I needed a quick meal that was low on ingredients but high on taste, so I came up with this hearty casserole.

—Ruth Chiarenza, Cumberland, Maryland

1 pound ground beef
1 can (15-1/2 ounces) sloppy joe sauce
1 can (10-3/4 ounces) condensed cream of potato soup, undiluted
1 package (32 ounces) frozen cubed hash brown potatoes, thawed
1 cup (4 ounces) shredded cheddar cheese

In a skillet, cook beef over medium heat until no longer pink; drain. Add sloppy joe sauce and soup. Place hash browns in a greased 13-in. x 9-in. x 2-in. baking dish. Top with beef mixture.

Cover and bake at 450° for 20 minutes. Uncover; bake 10 minutes longer or until heated through. Sprinkle with cheese. **Yield:** 6-8 servings.

Soups & Sandwiches

Fast Fiesta Soup, p. 124

Chuck Wagon Burgers, p. 129

|SANDWICHES|

Cucumber Sandwiches

I was introduced to a similar sandwich by a friend many years ago. I sometimes add thinly sliced onions for a change of pace. Along with fruit salad, it makes a light summer lunch.

—Karen Schriefer, Stevensville, Maryland

1 carton (8 ounces) cream cheese spread
2 teaspoons ranch salad dressing mix
12 slices pumpernickel rye bread
2 to 3 medium cucumbers

In a bowl, combine cream cheese and dressing mix. Spread on one side of each slice of bread. Peel cucumbers if desired; thinly slice and place on six slices of bread. Top with remaining bread. Serve immediately. **Yield:** 6 servings.

Cran-Orange Turkey Bagel

I adapted the recipe for this tasty turkey sandwich from a deli where I worked. To make it easier to eat, we often dip each bite into the cranberry mixture instead of spreading it inside. *—Tanya Smeins Kalamazoo, Michigan*

1 can (11 ounces) mandarin oranges, drained
1 can (16 ounces) whole-berry cranberry sauce
6 tablespoons cream cheese, softened
6 onion bagels *or* flavor of your choice, split and toasted
1 pound thinly sliced cooked turkey

In a bowl, mash mandarin oranges with a fork. Stir in cranberry sauce. Spread cream cheese over the bottom of each bagel; top with turkey and cran-orange sauce. Replace bagel tops. **Yield:** 6 servings.

Editor's Note: Poppy, sesame and wheat bagels are also good choices for these sandwiches.

Cheesy Wild Rice Soup

We often eat easy-to-make soups when there's not a lot of time to cook. I replaced the wild rice requested in the original recipe with a boxed rice mix. This creamy concoction is now a family favorite.

—Lisa Hofer
Hitchcock, South Dakota

1 package (6 ounces) quick-cooking long grain and wild rice mix
4 cups milk
1 can (10-3/4 ounces) condensed cream of potato soup, undiluted
8 ounces process cheese (Velveeta), cubed
1/2 pound sliced bacon, cooked and crumbled

In a large saucepan, prepare rice according to package directions. Stir in milk, soup and cheese; mix well. Cook and stir until cheese is melted. Garnish with bacon. **Yield:** 6-8 servings.

Buffalo Chicken Wing Soup

My husband and I love buffalo chicken wings, so we created a soup with the same zippy flavor. It's very popular with guests. Start with a small amount of hot sauce, then add more if needed to suit your family's tastes.

—Pat Farmer, Falconer, New York

6 cups milk
3 cans (10-3/4 ounces *each*) condensed cream of chicken soup, undiluted
3 cups shredded cooked chicken (about 1 pound)
1 cup (8 ounces) sour cream
1/4 to 1/2 cup hot pepper sauce

Combine all ingredients in a slow cooker. Cover and cook on low for 4-5 hours. **Yield:** 8 servings (2 quarts).

|SHREDDING MEAT| To shred beef, pork or chicken for sandwiches or soups, place it in a shallow pan. Then simply pull the meat into thin shreds using two forks.

Oven-Baked Burgers

A seasoned coating mix and steak sauce dress up these hamburgers that cook in the oven rather than on the grill. I like to use a sweet and spicy steak sauce for the best flavor.
—*Mike Goldman*
Arden Hills, Minnesota

1/4 cup steak sauce
2 tablespoons plus 1/3 cup Shake'n Bake seasoned coating mix, *divided*
1 pound ground beef
4 hamburger buns, split
4 lettuce leaves

In a bowl, combine the steak sauce and 2 tablespoons of coating mix. Crumble beef over mixture and mix until combined. Shape into four 3-1/2-in. patties. Dip both sides of patties in remaining coating.

Place on an ungreased baking sheet. Bake at 350° for 20 minutes or until no longer pink, turning once. Serve on buns with lettuce. **Yield:** 4 servings.

|SHAPING HAMBURGER PATTIES| Use a 1/2-cup measuring cup or ice cream scoop to make equal size patties. Gently form each portion into a patty. For moist light-textured burgers, be careful not to over-mix or over-handle the meat mixture.

Quick Pea Soup

This brightly colored, fresh-tasting soup is one of our daughter's favorites. She purees it in the blender in just seconds, then "zaps" a mugful in the microwave until heated through.
—*Paula Zsiray*
Logan, Utah

 Uses less fat, sugar or salt. Includes Nutritional Analysis and Diabetic Exchanges.

1-1/2 cups frozen peas, thawed
1-1/4 cups milk, *divided*
1/4 teaspoon salt, optional
1/8 teaspoon pepper

Place the peas and 1/4 cup of milk in a blender; cover and process until pureed. Pour into a saucepan; add salt if desired, pepper and remaining milk. Cook and stir for 5 minutes or until heated through. **Yield:** 2 servings.

Nutritional Analysis: One 1-cup serving (prepared with fat-free milk and without salt) equals 137 calories, 200 mg sodium, 3 mg cholesterol, 22 g carbohydrate, 11 g protein, 1 g fat. **Diabetic Exchanges:** 1 starch, 1 skim milk.

Hot Ham 'n' Swiss

I've been preparing these versatile open-faced sandwiches for more than 20 years for different occasions and mealtimes. They're a special beginning to a cozy Sunday brunch.   —Debbie Petrun
Smithfield, Pennsylvania

5 eggs
8 slices Italian bread
(3/4 inch thick)
1 pound thinly sliced deli
ham
8 slices Swiss cheese

In a shallow bowl, beat the eggs. Dip both sides of bread in eggs. Cook on a greased hot griddle until lightly browned on both sides. Transfer to a baking sheet; top each slice with ham and cheese. Broil 4 in. from the heat for 5 minutes or until the cheese is melted. **Yield:** 8 servings.

|BROILING BASICS| When a recipe says to "broil 4 inches from the heat", it's referring to the food's surface, not the bottom of the pan. If you measure from the rack on which the pan sits, the food will be too close to the heat and could burn before it cooks through.

Beef Noodle Soup

I take advantage of convenience items to prepare this hearty soup in a hurry. Bowls of the chunky mixture are chock-full of ground beef, ramen noodles and mixed vegetables. —Arlene Lynn, Lincoln, Nebraska

1 pound ground beef
1 can (46 ounces) V8 juice
1 envelope onion soup mix
1 package (3 ounces) beef
ramen noodles
1 package (16 ounces)
frozen mixed vegetables

In a large saucepan, cook beef over medium heat until no longer pink; drain. Stir in the V8 juice, soup mix, contents of noodle seasoning packet and mixed vegetables.

Bring to a boil. Reduce heat; simmer, uncovered, for 6 minutes or until vegetables are tender. Return to a boil; stir in noodles. Cook for 3 minutes or until noodles are tender. **Yield:** 8 servings.

Cheesy Beef Buns

These satisfying sandwiches would be great to put together ahead of time and wrap in foil until ready to bake. Warm from the oven, the crispy buns are piled with cheesy slices of roast beef.
—*Marlene Harguth, Maynard, Minnesota*

1 medium onion, chopped
2 tablespoons butter
1 jar (8 ounces) process cheese sauce
1 pound thinly sliced cooked roast beef
6 French *or* Italian sandwich buns, split

In a skillet, saute onion in butter until tender. Stir in cheese sauce until melted. Cook and stir until heated through. Stir in beef until evenly coated.

Spoon onto buns; wrap each in aluminum foil. Bake at 350° for 8-10 minutes or until bread is crispy. **Yield:** 6 servings.

Triple-Decker Salmon Club

You're in for a tasty treat with these deliciously different triple-deckers. Guests love the short-on-time sandwiches. Even those who don't ordinarily like salmon or cottage cheese enjoy them. —*Jane Bone Cape Coral, Florida*

3/4 cup small-curd cottage cheese
1/4 cup dill pickle relish
1 can (6 ounces) salmon, drained, bones and skin removed
1 celery rib, chopped
6 slices bread, toasted
2 lettuce leaves, optional

In a small bowl, combine cottage cheese and pickle relish. In another bowl, combine salmon and celery.

For each sandwich, top one piece of toast with lettuce if desired and half of the cottage cheese mixture. Top with a second piece of toast; spread with half of the salmon mixture. Top with a third piece of toast. Serve immediately. **Yield:** 2 servings.

Applesauce Sandwiches

Cinnamon and sugar spice up these fun sandwiches for breakfast or a snack. Since we have plenty of apple trees, I often use homemade applesauce. But the store-bought kind tastes almost as good. —*Eunice Bralley*
Thornville, Ohio

1 cup applesauce
8 slices bread
1/4 cup butter, softened
1 tablespoon sugar
1/4 teaspoon ground cinnamon

Spread the applesauce on four slices of bread; top with remaining bread. Lightly butter the outsides of sandwiches. Toast on a hot griddle for 3-4 minutes on each side or until golden brown. Combine sugar and cinnamon; sprinkle over hot sandwiches. Serve immediately. **Yield:** 4 servings.

|FROM–SCRATCH APPLESAUCE| Quickly make homemade applesauce by combining chunks of apple with a little orange juice, cinnamon and nutmeg in a blender or food processor. Process until mixture reaches the desired texture.

Corny Clam Chowder

Cream gives richness to the canned items that make up this satisfying chowder. I sometimes make it in the slow cooker, so it can simmer while I finish work around the house. —*Karen Johnston*
Syracuse, Nebraska

1 can (14-3/4 ounces) cream-style corn
1 can (10-3/4 ounces) condensed cream of potato soup, undiluted
1-1/2 cups half-and-half cream
1 can (6-1/2 ounces) minced clams, drained
6 bacon strips, cooked and crumbled

In a saucepan, combine corn, soup and cream; heat through. Stir in clams; heat through. Garnish with bacon. **Yield:** 4 servings.

Open-Faced Sandwich Supreme

My husband and I first sampled this delicious open-faced sandwich at a restaurant. It seemed so easy, I duplicated it at home. It's also tasty with cheese sauce in place of the hollandaise sauce or asparagus instead of broccoli. —*Phyllis Smith*
Mariposa, California

3 cups small broccoli florets
1 envelope hollandaise sauce mix
8 ounces sliced deli turkey
8 ounces sliced deli ham
4 slices sourdough bread, toasted

In a saucepan, cook the broccoli in a small amount of water until tender; drain. Prepare the hollandaise sauce according to package directions. Warm the turkey and ham if desired; layer over the toast. Top with the broccoli and sauce. **Yield:** 4 servings.

Tortellini Soup

This soup is fast to fix, flavorful and good for you. Packaged cheese tortellini meets colorful summer squash, fresh spinach and shredded carrots in every eye-appealing bowl. —*Chris Snyder*
Boulder, Colorado

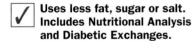 **Uses less fat, sugar or salt. Includes Nutritional Analysis and Diabetic Exchanges.**

5 cups chicken broth
3-1/2 cups shredded carrots (about 10 ounces)
1 cup chopped yellow summer squash
3 cups torn fresh spinach
1 package (9 ounces) refrigerated cheese tortellini

In a large saucepan, combine the broth, carrots and squash. Bring to a boil. Reduce heat; simmer, uncovered, for 3 minutes. Stir in spinach and tortellini. Cover and cook for 5 minutes or until the tortellini is heated through. **Yield:** 7 servings.

Nutritional Analysis: One serving (1 cup) equals 160 calories, 3 g fat (2 g saturated fat), 14 mg cholesterol, 806 mg sodium, 24 g carbohydrate, 3 g fiber, 8 g protein. **Diabetic Exchanges:** 2 vegetable, 1 starch.

Creamy Cauliflower Soup

My aunt always made this smooth, rich-tasting soup for me when I came to visit. I could smell it simmering as soon as I arrived. I think of her whenever I have a bowlful.
—*Heather Kasprick*
Keewatin, Ontario

1 **medium head cauliflower, broken into florets**
2 **cans (10-3/4 ounces *each*) condensed cream of chicken soup, undiluted**
1 **can (10-3/4 ounces) condensed cheddar cheese soup, undiluted**
1 **can (14-1/2 ounces) chicken broth**
2 **cups milk**

Place cauliflower in a saucepan with 1 in. of water; bring to a boil. Reduce heat; cover and simmer for 5-10 minutes or until crisp-tender.

Meanwhile, in another saucepan, combine soups, broth and milk; heat through. Drain the cauliflower; stir into soup. **Yield:** 9 servings.

Taco Puffs

I got this recipe from a friend years ago and still make these cheesy sandwiches regularly. I serve them for dinner along with a steaming bowl of soup or fresh green salad. Any leftovers taste even better the next day for lunch. A helpful hint: Plain refrigerated biscuits seal together better than buttermilk types.
—*Jan Schmid, Hibbing, Minnesota*

1 **pound ground beef**
1/2 **cup chopped onion**
1 **envelope taco seasoning**
2 **tubes (16.3 ounces *each*) large refrigerated biscuits**
8 **ounces cheddar cheese slices *or* 2 cups (8 ounces) shredded cheddar cheese**

In a skillet, cook beef and onion over medium heat until beef is no longer pink; drain. Add the taco seasoning and prepare according to package directions. Cool slightly.

Flatten half of the biscuits into 4-in. circles; place in greased 15-in. x 10-in. x 1-in. baking pans. Spoon 1/4 cup meat mixture onto each; top with two cheese slices or 1/4 cup shredded cheese. Flatten the remaining biscuits; place on top and pinch edges to seal tightly. Bake at 400° for 15 minutes or until golden brown. **Yield:** 8 servings.

Hot Dog Sandwiches

These kid-pleasing sandwiches taste just like hot dogs smothered in mustard and relish. Drop the frozen sandwiches in lunch bags before school in the morning. By noon, they'll be thawed and ready to eat.

—*Iola Egle, McCook, Nebraska*

  6 **hot dogs, minced**
1/2 **cup dill pickle relish**
1/4 **cup chili sauce**
  2 **tablespoons prepared mustard**
 12 **slices bread**

In a small bowl, combine hot dogs, relish, chili sauce and mustard; mix well. Spread on six slices of bread; top with the remaining bread. Freeze for up to 2 months. Remove sandwiches from the freezer at least 4 hours before serving. **Yield:** 6 servings.

Baked Bean Chili

Who says a good chili has to simmer all day? This zippy chili—with a touch of sweetness from the baked beans—can be made on the spur of the moment. It's an excellent standby when unexpected guests drop in. Served with bread and a salad, it's a hearty dinner everyone raves about.

—*Nancy Wall*
Bakersfield, California

2 **pounds ground beef**
3 **cans (28 ounces** *each***) baked beans**
1 **can (46 ounces) tomato juice**
1 **can (11-1/2 ounces) V8 juice**
1 **envelope chili seasoning**

In a Dutch oven, cook beef over medium heat until no longer pink; drain. Stir in the remaining ingredients. Bring to a boil. Reduce heat; simmer, uncovered, for 10 minutes. **Yield:** 24 servings.

Zesty Tomato Soup

When some friends stopped by unexpectedly, my husband, Phil, came up with this fast-to-fix soup that tastes home-made. Two easy ingredients give canned soup just the right amount of zip. —*JoAnn Gunio Franklin, North Carolina*

2 cans (10-3/4 ounces *each*) condensed tomato soup, undiluted
2-2/3 cups water
2 teaspoons chili powder
Oyster crackers *or* shredded Monterey Jack cheese, optional

In a saucepan, combine the first three ingredients; heat through. Garnish with crackers or cheese if desired. **Yield:** 4-5 servings.

|SPEEDY SOUP| Create instant soup by combining leftover vegetables with chicken or beef broth in a blender and processing until smooth. For soup in minutes, add chicken or beef broth to leftover rice and stir in some lightly sauteed vegetables. Heat just until warmed through.

Apple Sausage Pitas

This is such a simple recipe, but it's my favorite breakfast for family or company. Filled with sausage and apple slices, the meal-in-hand sandwiches are great to munch on the way to work or school.
—*Michelle Komaroski, Pueblo, Colorado*

1 package (8 ounces) brown-and-serve sausage links, sliced
4 medium tart apples, peeled and thinly sliced
1/4 cup maple syrup
4 pita breads (6 inches), halved

In a skillet, cook sausage and apples until sausage is heated through and apples are tender. Add syrup; heat through. In a microwave, warm pitas on high for 20 seconds. Fill with the sausage mixture. **Yield:** 4 servings.

Wagon Wheel Chili

Youngsters are sure to love the fun shape of the wagon wheel pasta in this zippy chili. It's easy to whip up with canned chili and tomato sauce, so it's great for a hot lunch or quick dinner.
—*Lora Scroggins*
El Dorado, Arkansas

2 cups uncooked wagon
 wheel *or* spiral pasta
1 can (15 ounces) chili
1 can (8 ounces) tomato
 sauce
3 tablespoons ketchup
1/2 teaspoon chili powder
Shredded cheddar cheese,
 optional

Cook pasta according to package directions. Meanwhile, in a large saucepan, combine the chili, tomato sauce, ketchup and chili powder. Mix well; heat through. Drain and rinse pasta; stir into chili. Garnish with cheese if desired. **Yield:** 3-4 servings.

Low-Fat Broccoli Soup

This delicious soup is a great way to eat a nutritious vegetable. It has a wonderful garden-fresh flavor and pretty green color.
—*Kay Fairley, Charleston, Illinois*

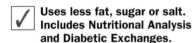
✓ Uses less fat, sugar or salt.
 Includes Nutritional Analysis
 and Diabetic Exchanges.

2 cups chopped fresh *or*
 frozen broccoli
1/2 cup chopped onion
1 can (14-1/2 ounces)
 reduced-sodium chicken
 broth
2 tablespoons cornstarch
1 can (12 ounces) fat-free
 evaporated milk

In a saucepan, combine broccoli, onion and broth; simmer for 10-15 minutes or until vegetables are tender. Puree half of the mixture in a blender; return to the saucepan.

In a small bowl, whisk cornstarch and 3 tablespoons of milk until smooth. Gradually add remaining milk. Stir into the broccoli mixture. Bring to a boil; boil and stir for 2 minutes. **Yield:** 4 servings.

Nutritional Analysis: One 3/4-cup serving equals 112 calories, 157 mg sodium, 5 mg cholesterol, 18 g carbohydrate, 9 g protein, 1 g fat. **Diabetic Exchanges:** 2 vegetable, 1/2 skim milk.

Vegetable Noodle Soup

This creamy soup is great on a cold winter day. I created it when I didn't have all the ingredients for broccoli soup. I like this combo even better.
—*Judie Peters, Camden, Indiana*

3-1/2 cups milk
1 package (16 ounces) frozen California-blend vegetables
1/2 cup cubed process cheese (Velveeta)
1 envelope chicken noodle soup mix

In a large saucepan, bring milk to a boil. Stir in vegetables and return to a boil. Reduce heat; cover and simmer for 6 minutes.

Stir in cheese and soup mix. Return to a boil. Reduce heat. Simmer, uncovered, for 5-7 minutes or until the noodles are tender and the cheese is melted, stirring occasionally. **Yield:** 5-6 servings.

Bacon–Tomato Bagel Melts

My husband introduced me to this open-faced sandwich shortly after we got married, and it quickly became an all-time favorite. It's good made with plain or onion bagels. Have fun experimenting with various toppings and dressings, too.
—*Lindsay Orwig, Grand Terrace, California*

2 bagels, split and toasted
8 tomato slices
8 bacon strips, cooked
1 cup (4 ounces) shredded mozzarella cheese
Prepared ranch salad dressing

Place bagel halves cut side up on a baking sheet. Top each with two tomato slices and two bacon strips. Sprinkle with cheese. Broil 5 in. from the heat for 1-2 minutes or until cheese begins to brown. Serve with ranch dressing. **Yield:** 4 sandwiches.

|BACON TIDBITS| If you roll a package of bacon into a tube and secure it with a rubber band before refrigerating, the slices will come apart more easily. Pricking bacon with a fork reduces excess curling and helps it lie flat in the pan.

Cream of Carrot Soup

I came up with this rich yummy soup when I was in a hurry one day and we needed something hot to eat. It's versatile, too. You can substitute most any vegetable with excellent results.

—Ruth Andrewson, Leavenworth, Washington

4 cups chicken broth
4 large carrots, cut into chunks
1/2 cup heavy whipping cream
1 teaspoon sugar

In a saucepan, bring broth and carrots to a boil. Reduce heat; simmer, uncovered, until carrots are tender, about 15 minutes. Cool slightly.

In a blender, cover and process soup in small batches until smooth; return to the pan. Stir in cream and sugar; heat through. **Yield:** 5 servings.

Quick Chili

I've made this mild-tasting and hearty main-dish chili for over 40 years, much to the delight of my family and friends. I can serve up a steaming bowlful in minutes to take the chill out of a cold winter day.

—Jean Ward, Montgomery, Texas

 Uses less fat, sugar or salt. Includes Nutritional Analysis and Diabetic Exchanges.

1 pound ground beef
1 can (10-3/4 ounces) condensed tomato soup, undiluted
1 can (15 ounces) chili beans in gravy, undrained
2 to 3 teaspoons chili powder
1/2 cup water, optional

In a saucepan, cook beef over medium heat until no longer pink; drain. Add soup, beans and chili powder. Reduce heat. Cover and simmer for 20 minutes. Add water if a thinner soup is desired. **Yield:** 4 servings.

Nutritional Analysis: One serving (prepared with lean ground beef and reduced-sodium, reduced-fat tomato soup) equals 344 calories, 341 mg sodium, 108 mg cholesterol, 24 g carbohydrate, 31 g protein, 5 g fat. **Diabetic Exchanges:** 3 meat, 1-1/2 starch.

Italian Beef Hoagies

You'll need just five ingredients to feed a crowd these tender and tangy sandwiches. On weekends, I start the roast the night before, so I can shred it in the morning. —*Lori Piatt* *Danville, Illinois*

1 boneless sirloin tip roast (about 4 pounds), halved
2 envelopes Italian salad dressing mix
2 cups water
1 jar (16 ounces) mild pepper rings, undrained
18 hoagie buns, split

Place roast in a 5-qt. slow cooker. Combine the salad dressing mix and water; pour over roast. Cover and cook on low for 8 hours or until meat is tender.

Remove meat; shred with a fork and return to slow cooker. Add pepper rings; heat through. Spoon 1/2 cup meat mixture onto each bun. **Yield:** 18 servings.

Strawberry Soup

This refreshing chilled soup is a lovely addition to a special brunch or luncheon. With its fruity flavor and thick frothy texture, you could even serve it as a punch! —*Lucia Johnson, Massena, New York*

1 pint fresh strawberries, hulled
1/2 cup white wine *or* apple juice
1/2 cup sugar
2 tablespoons lemon juice
1 teaspoon grated lemon peel

In a blender, combine all ingredients. Cover and process until smooth. Pour into two bowls; cover and refrigerate until thoroughly chilled, about 1-2 hours. **Yield:** 2 servings.

|COLD SOUP CLUE| When making cold soups, remember that chilling food mutes its flavor, so be sure to taste just before serving and adjust the seasoning if necessary. Keep in mind that most cold soups will be thicker than when they were at room temperature.

Spinach Cheese Swirls

My family loves dividing up this super-easy sandwich that's brimming with great spinach and onion flavor. Refrigerated pizza dough shaves minutes off prep time and creates a golden brown crust. The cheesy slices taste terrific warm or cold, so they're great for lunches, picnics or trips.
—*Mary Nichols*
Dover, New Hampshire

1 package (10 ounces) frozen chopped spinach, thawed and drained
2 cups (8 ounces) shredded mozzarella cheese
1 cup finely chopped onion
1 garlic clove, minced
1 tube (10 ounces) refrigerated pizza crust

In a bowl, combine the first four ingredients and mix well. On a greased baking sheet, roll pizza dough into a 14-in. x 10-in. rectangle; seal any holes. Spoon filling over crust to within 1 in. of edge.

Roll up jelly-roll style, starting with a long side; seal the ends and place seam side down. Bake at 400° for 25-27 minutes or until golden brown. Cut into slices to serve. **Yield:** 4 servings.

Chicken Dumpling Soup

Although we were on a tight budget when I was a youngster, we always had good food. This comforting soup with soft dumplings was one of Mom's mainstays. —*Brenda Risser, Willard, Ohio*

 Uses less fat, sugar or salt. Includes Nutritional Analysis and Diabetic Exchanges.

2 cans (10-3/4 ounces *each*) condensed cream of chicken soup, undiluted
3-1/3 cups milk, *divided*
1-2/3 cups biscuit/baking mix

In a 3-qt. saucepan, combine soup and 2-2/3 cups of milk. Bring to a boil over medium heat; reduce heat. In a bowl, combine biscuit mix with remaining milk just until blended.

Drop by rounded tablespoons onto simmering soup. Cook, uncovered, for 10 minutes. Cover and simmer 10-12 minutes longer or until dumplings test done (do not lift lid while simmering). Serve immediately. **Yield:** 4 servings.

Nutritional Analysis: One serving (prepared with reduced-fat cream of chicken soup, fat-free milk and reduced-fat biscuit mix) equals 359 calories, 1,276 mg sodium, 16 mg cholesterol, 60 g carbohydrate, 13 g protein, 6 g fat, 1 g fiber. **Diabetic Exchanges:** 3 starch, 1 skim milk, 1 fat.

Meal on a Bun

Looking for a break from the usual peanut butter and jelly sandwich? This easy concoction is sure to be a hit with kids of all ages. I've replaced the jelly with a juicy slice of pineapple and topped it off with cheddar cheese.

—Lavina Taylor, Moline, Illinois

4 hamburger buns, split
1/2 cup peanut butter
1 can (8 ounces) pineapple
    slices, drained
4 slices cheddar cheese

Place buns, cut side up, on a baking sheet. Spread with peanut butter. Place a pineapple slice on each bun bottom and a cheese slice on each bun top. Bake at 350° for 5-7 minutes or until cheese is melted. Place cheese-topped buns over pineapple. **Yield:** 4 servings.

Chilled Cantaloupe Soup

A friend in New York shared the recipe for this chilled melon soup that's pleasantly spiced with cinnamon. Most people are skeptical when I describe it, but after one spoonful, they're hooked. It's easy to prepare, pretty to serve and so refreshing.

—Margaret McNeil, Memphis, Tennessee

 Uses less fat, sugar or salt.
Includes Nutritional Analysis
and Diabetic Exchanges.

1 medium cantaloupe,
    peeled, seeded and
    cubed
2 cups orange juice,
    divided
1 tablespoon lime juice
1/4 to 1/2 teaspoon ground
    cinnamon
Fresh mint, optional

Place cantaloupe and 1/2 cup orange juice in a blender or food processor; cover and process until smooth. Transfer to a large bowl; stir in lime juice, cinnamon and remaining orange juice. Cover and refrigerate for at least 1 hour. Garnish with mint if desired. **Yield:** 6 servings.

Nutritional Analysis: One 3/4-cup serving equals 70 calories, 9 mg sodium, 0 cholesterol, 17 g carbohydrate, 1 g protein, trace fat. **Diabetic Exchange:** 1 fruit.

Spinach Potato Soup

I first made this fresh-tasting soup for a school potluck on St. Patrick's Day. It was a hit, and now I make it throughout the year.

—*Lois McAtee, Oceanside, California*

3 cups milk
1 can (15 ounces) sliced potatoes, drained
1 package (10 ounces) frozen creamed spinach, thawed
1/2 teaspoon dried basil
1/2 to 3/4 teaspoon garlic salt

Combine all ingredients in a saucepan. Bring to a boil. Reduce heat; cover and simmer for 15 minutes. Cool slightly.

Transfer mixture to a blender; cover and process until small pieces of potato remain. Return to the pan and heat through. **Yield:** 4-6 servings.

Dogs in a Sweater

For a new twist on an old favorite, try these skewered hot dogs wrapped with breadstick dough and baked. They're fun to dip in ketchup, mustard or ranch dressing. The dressed-up dog recipe comes kid-tested from the National Hot Dog and Sausage Council.

1 package (11 ounces) refrigerated breadstick dough
8 hot dogs
8 Popsicle sticks
Ketchup, mustard *and/or* ranch dressing

Separate dough; roll each piece into a 15-in. rope. Insert sticks into hot dogs lengthwise. Starting at one end, wrap dough in a spiral around hot dog; pinch ends to seal.

Place 1 in. apart on a baking sheet that has been coated with nonstick cooking spray. Bake at 350° for 18-20 minutes. Serve with the toppings of your choice. **Yield:** 8 servings.

Pizza Grilled Cheese

Combine two all-time lunch favorites into one, and you've got this recipe. My teenage son, Tim, created the sandwich with dipping sauce to satisfy his love for pizza. —*Robin Kettering Newville, Pennsylvania*

1 tablespoon butter, softened
2 slices bread
1 slice provolone *or* mozzarella cheese
6 slices pepperoni
3 tablespoons pizza sauce
Additional pizza sauce, optional

Butter one side of each slice of bread. Place one slice in a skillet, butter side down. Top with the cheese, pepperoni, pizza sauce and second bread slice, butter side up.

Cook over medium heat until golden brown, turning once. Serve sandwich with additional pizza sauce if desired. **Yield:** 1 serving.

|GET A GRIDDLE| If you enjoy grilled sandwiches, you may want to invest in an electric or stove-top griddle, which will allow you to grill four to six sandwiches at a time.

Bacon Bean Sandwiches

My mother-in-law first shared this scrumptious open-faced sandwich with us, and it's now a favorite around our house. The flavors of the bacon, beans, onion and cheese complement each other wonderfully!
—*Dorothy Klass, Tabor City, North Carolina*

5 slices bread, lightly toasted
1 can (16 ounces) pork and beans
10 bacon strips, cooked and drained
4 slices onion, separated into rings
5 slices process American cheese

Place toast on an ungreased baking sheet. Spread each slice with 3 tablespoons beans. Top each with two bacon strips, a few onion rings and a cheese slice. Bake at 350° for 15-20 minutes or until cheese is melted and lightly browned. **Yield:** 5 servings.

Fast Fiesta Soup

This spicy soup was served at a very elegant lunch, and the hostess was deluged with requests for the recipe. The colorful combination is a snap to throw together...just open the cans and heat.
—*Patricia White*
Monrovia, California

✓ Uses less fat, sugar or salt. Includes Nutritional Analysis and Diabetic Exchanges.

2 cans (10 ounces *each*) diced tomatoes and green chilies
1 can (15-1/4 ounces) whole kernel corn, drained
1 can (15 ounces) black beans, rinsed and drained
Shredded cheddar cheese and sour cream, optional

In a saucepan, combine tomatoes, corn and beans; heat through. Garnish servings with cheese and sour cream if desired. **Yield:** 4 servings.

Nutritional Analysis: One serving (prepared with no-salt-added diced tomatoes and without cheese and sour cream) equals 210 calories, 576 mg sodium, 0 cholesterol, 42 g carbohydrate, 10 g protein, 2 g fat, 10 g fiber. **Diabetic Exchanges:** 2-1/2 starch, 1 vegetable.

Tangy Beef Turnovers

My mom's recipe for these flavorful pockets called for dough made from scratch, but I streamlined it by using crescent rolls. My children love them plain or dipped in ketchup.
—*Claudia Bodeker*
Ash Flat, Arkansas

1 pound ground beef
1 medium onion, chopped
1 jar (16 ounces) sauerkraut, rinsed, drained and chopped
1 cup (4 ounces) shredded Swiss cheese
3 tubes (8 ounces *each*) refrigerated crescent rolls

In a skillet, cook beef and onion over medium heat until meat is no longer pink; drain. Add sauerkraut and cheese; mix well. Unroll crescent roll dough and separate into rectangles. Place on greased baking sheets; pinch seams to seal.

Place 1/2 cup beef mixture in the center of each rectangle. Bring corners to the center and pinch to seal. Bake at 375° for 15-18 minutes or until golden brown. **Yield:** 1 dozen.

Chicken Chili

My aunt gave me the recipe for this thick "instant" chili. To save time, I usually cook and cube the chicken the night before or use leftovers. The next day, it's simple to simmer the ingredients on the stovetop. I serve the hearty results with crunchy corn chips or warm bread.　　—Yvonne Morgan
Grand Rapids, Michigan

2 cans (15 ounces *each*) great northern beans, rinsed and drained
2 jars (16 ounces *each*) picante sauce
4 cups cubed cooked chicken
1 to 2 teaspoons ground cumin
Shredded Monterey Jack cheese

In a saucepan, combine beans, picante sauce, chicken and cumin. Bring to a boil. Reduce heat; cover and simmer for 20 minutes. Sprinkle individual servings with cheese. **Yield:** 6 servings.

Dilly Beef Sandwiches

My younger sister, Jean, shared this recipe, which puts a twist on the traditional barbecue sandwich. As a busy mother of four, Jean never has much time to cook, but she does like to entertain. This crowd-pleaser, made in a convenient slow cooker, is perfect for our large family gatherings.
　　—*Donna Blankenheim, Madison, Wisconsin*

1 boneless beef chuck roast (3 to 4 pounds)
1 jar (16 ounces) whole dill pickles, undrained
1/2 cup chili sauce
2 garlic cloves, minced
10 to 12 hamburger buns, split

Cut roast in half and place in a slow cooker. Add pickles with juice, chili sauce and garlic. Cover and cook on low for 8-9 hours or until beef is tender.

Discard pickles. Remove roast. When cool enough to handle, shred the meat. Return to the sauce and heat through. Using a slotted spoon, fill each bun with about 1/2 cup meat mixture. **Yield:** 10-12 servings.

Raisin Finger Sandwiches

As a registered nurse and mother of four, I'm very busy. That's why I like these sweet sandwiches. They're simple to assemble but look and taste like you put a lot of effort into them.

—Jeannie Dobbs, Bartlesville, Oklahoma

1 package (8 ounces)
  cream cheese, softened
1/4 cup mayonnaise
1/2 cup chopped pecans
 10 slices raisin bread

In a mixing bowl, beat cream cheese and mayonnaise until smooth. Stir in pecans. Spread over five slices of bread; top with remaining bread. Cut each sandwich into three strips. Serve immediately. **Yield:** 5 servings.

Corny Chicken Wraps

My girls like these tortilla roll-ups very much—they'll ask for them practically every week. Tender chicken combines with canned corn and salsa for a fast-to-fix main dish.
—Sue Seymour
Valatie, New York

 Uses less fat, sugar or salt. Includes Nutritional Analysis and Diabetic Exchanges.

2 cups cubed cooked
  chicken breast
1 can (11 ounces) whole
  kernel corn, drained
1 cup salsa
1 cup (4 ounces) shredded
  cheddar cheese
8 flour tortillas (6 inches),
  warmed

In a saucepan or microwave-safe bowl, combine chicken, corn and salsa. Cook until heated through. Sprinkle cheese over tortillas. Place about 1/2 cup chicken mixture down the center of each tortilla; roll up. Secure with toothpicks. **Yield:** 4 servings.

Nutritional Analysis: One serving (prepared with reduced-fat cheese and tortillas) equals 374 calories, 1,088 mg sodium, 61 mg cholesterol, 50 g carbohydrate, 26 g protein, 8 g fat, 3 g fiber. **Diabetic Exchanges:** 3 starch, 2 lean meat, 1 vegetable.

Hot Hoagies

A convenient package of Italian salad dressing mix provides the yummy herb flavor in these broiled sandwiches that I assemble for my family of 10. I use their favorite combination of meats and cheeses, then serve the sandwiches with chips and pickles. They're a hit every time. —*Paula Hadley*
Forest Hill, Louisiana

3/4 cup butter, softened
1 envelope Italian salad dressing mix
6 hoagie buns, split
12 to 16 ounces sliced luncheon meat (salami, ham *and/or* turkey)
12 thin slices cheese (Swiss, cheddar *and/or* brick)

Combine butter and salad dressing mix; spread 1 tablespoonful inside each bun. On bottom of each bun, layer one slice of meat, two slices of cheese and another slice of meat; replace tops. Spread 1 tablespoon butter mixture over top of each bun.

Place on a baking sheet. Broil 6 in. from the heat for 2-3 minutes or until tops are lightly browned. **Yield:** 6 servings.

Thick 'n' Quick Clam Chowder

You'd never guess that this thick, rich soup is a blend of convenient canned ingredients. My husband and I love it during our busy harvest season...it's so simple to simmer up when time is tight.
—*Betty Sitzman, Wray, Colorado*

1 can (10-3/4 ounces) condensed cream of celery soup, undiluted
1 can (10-3/4 ounces) condensed cheddar cheese soup, undiluted
1 can (10-3/4 ounces) condensed cream of onion soup, undiluted
3 cups half-and-half cream
2 cans (6-1/2 ounces *each*) chopped clams, drained

In a saucepan, combine the soups and cream; cook over medium heat until heated through. Add clams and heat through (do not boil). **Yield:** 6-8 servings.

Editor's Note: Add chopped clams to soups and chowders at the last minute so they don't lose their texture.

Tomato Corn Chowder

Five common ingredients are all you'll need to prepare this hearty full-flavored chowder. This is a terrific soup, particularly as the cooler fall and winter seasons set in. It's economical as well. —Sue McMichael Redding, California

4 bacon strips, diced
1 large onion, chopped
2 cans (15-1/4 ounces each) whole kernel corn, undrained
2 cans (14-1/2 ounces each) diced tomatoes, undrained
4 medium potatoes, peeled and diced

In a large saucepan, cook bacon over medium heat until crisp. Remove to paper towels. Drain, reserving 1 tablespoon drippings.

In the drippings, saute onion until tender. Add the corn, tomatoes and potatoes. Cook over medium heat for 25-30 minutes or until potatoes are tender. Sprinkle with bacon. **Yield:** 9 servings.

Nutty Marmalade Sandwiches

I make batches of fun-filled sandwiches to freeze for a few weeks' worth of brown-bag lunches. They taste so fresh you would never know they were ever frozen. The marmalade flavor in this hearty combination really shines through.
—Iola Egle, McCook, Nebraska

1/2 cup peanut butter
1/4 cup orange marmalade
1/4 cup shredded sharp cheddar cheese
1 to 2 teaspoons lemon juice
6 slices bread

In a small bowl, combine peanut butter, marmalade, cheese and lemon juice; mix well. Spread over three slices of bread; top with remaining bread. Freeze for up to 4 months. Remove from the freezer at least 4 hours before serving. **Yield:** 3 servings.

Five-Can Chili

Who says a thick hearty chili has to simmer all day on the stove? With five canned goods and zero prep time, a warm pot of this zesty specialty is a snap to whip up.
—*Jo Mann*
Westover, Alabama

1 can (15 ounces) chili with beans
1 can (15 ounces) mixed vegetables, drained
1 can (11 ounces) whole kernel corn, drained
1 can (10-3/4 ounces) condensed tomato soup, undiluted
1 can (10 ounces) diced tomatoes and green chilies

In a saucepan, combine all ingredients; heat through. **Yield:** 6 servings.

|CHILI CHOICES| When making chili, always make a double batch, freezing half for a quick meal another week. Leftover chili is great when spooned over spaghetti, in tacos and burritos, as an omelet filling, as a topping for burgers or hot dogs, or spooned on top of a baked potato and topped with cheese.

Chuck Wagon Burgers

Howdy, pardner! When our son requested a cowboy theme for his birthday party, I planned a Western-style meal including these savory burgers. In the spirit of true chuck wagon fare, I served them on large biscuits rather than buns.
—*Sharon Thompson*
Oskaloosa, Iowa

2 pounds ground beef
1 envelope onion soup mix
1/2 cup water
1 tube (16.3 ounces) large refrigerated biscuits
1/8 teaspoon seasoned salt

In a bowl, combine the beef, soup mix and water; mix well. Shape into eight 3/4-in.-thick patties. Grill, uncovered, or broil 4 in. from the heat for 5-6 minutes on each side or until meat is no longer pink.

Meanwhile, place biscuits on an ungreased baking sheet; sprinkle with seasoned salt. Bake at 375° for 12-14 minutes or until golden brown. Split; top each biscuit with a hamburger. **Yield:** 8 servings.

Salads & Dressings

Sunshine Salad, p. 133

Cottage Cheese Veggie Salad, p. 137

|DRESSINGS|

Buttermilk Salad Dressing, p. 132

Pimiento Potato Salad

A neighbor shared the recipe for this easy overnight salad. Tender potatoes and crunchy celery get refreshing flavor from a bottle of Italian dressing. It's a delicious change of pace from potato salads made with mayonnaise.
—*Dora Ledford*
Rockwall, Texas

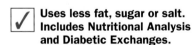 ✓ **Uses less fat, sugar or salt. Includes Nutritional Analysis and Diabetic Exchanges.**

2 pounds small red potatoes (about 12), cooked
4 green onions, thinly sliced
3 celery ribs, thinly sliced
1 jar (2 ounces) diced pimientos, drained
1 bottle (8 ounces) Italian salad dressing

Cut potatoes into 1/4-in. slices. In an ungreased 13-in. x 9-in. x 2-in. dish, layer half of the potatoes, onions, celery and pimientos. Repeat layers. Pour dressing over all. Cover and refrigerate overnight. Stir before serving. **Yield:** 12 servings.

Nutritional Analysis: One 3/4-cup serving (prepared with fat-free salad dressing) equals 65 calories, 202 mg sodium, 0 cholesterol, 13 g carbohydrate, 2 g protein, trace fat. **Diabetic Exchange:** 1 starch.

Buttermilk Salad Dressing

(Pictured on page 131)

This thick creamy mixture has the flavor of ranch dressing and is a breeze to blend together. Use it to top mixed greens or as a dip for raw vegetables.
—*Vicki Floden, Story City, Iowa*

✓ **Uses less fat, sugar or salt. Includes Nutritional Analysis and Diabetic Exchanges.**

3/4 cup 1% buttermilk
2 cups (16 ounces) 2% cottage cheese
1 envelope ranch salad dressing mix
Salad greens and vegetables of your choice

In a blender or food processor, combine the buttermilk, cottage cheese and salad dressing mix; cover and process for 20 seconds or until smooth. Pour into a small pitcher or bowl. Cover and refrigerate for 1 hour. Stir before serving with salad. **Yield:** 2-3/4 cups.

Nutritional Analysis: One serving (2 tablespoons dressing) equals 23 calories, 1 g fat (trace saturated fat), 3 mg cholesterol, 177 mg sodium, 2 g carbohydrate, 0 fiber, 3 g protein. **Diabetic Exchange:** 1/2 fat-free milk.

Sunshine Salad

(Pictured on page 130)

I found this recipe years ago and have made it many times since. When I prepare it for an evening meal, I call it "Sunset Salad".
—*Margaret Ulrich, Braidwood, Illinois*

1 can (20 ounces)
  pineapple tidbits
1 can (11 ounces)
  mandarin oranges
1 package (3.4 ounces)
  instant lemon pudding
1 cup quartered
  strawberries
1 cup sliced ripe bananas

Drain pineapple and oranges, reserving liquid. In a large bowl, combine pudding mix with reserved fruit juices. Fold in pineapple, oranges and strawberries. Chill for at least 2 hours. Add bananas just before serving. **Yield:** 8-10 servings.

Maple Cream Fruit Topping

Transform fruit salad into a special brunch treat with a dollop of this rich and creamy topping. The topping is also wonderful spooned over sliced melons.
—*Bethel Walters, Willow River, Minnesota*

1 tablespoon all-purpose
  flour
3/4 cup maple syrup
1 egg
1 tablespoon butter
1 cup heavy whipping
  cream, whipped

In a saucepan, combine flour, syrup and egg until smooth. Add butter. Bring to a boil; boil and stir for 2 minutes or until thickened and bubbly. Cover and refrigerate until completely cooled. Fold in whipped cream. **Yield:** about 2 cups.

Creamy Corn Salad

My daughter-in-law shared this fast five-ingredient recipe. It sounds too easy to be so good. Double the recipe if you're serving several people.

—June Mullins, Livonia, Missouri

✓ **Uses less fat, sugar or salt. Includes Nutritional Analysis and Diabetic Exchanges.**

1 can (15-1/4 ounces) whole kernel corn, drained
1 medium tomato, seeded and diced
2 tablespoons chopped onion
1/3 cup mayonnaise
1/4 teaspoon dill weed, optional

In a small bowl, combine the corn, tomato, onion, mayonnaise and dill weed if desired; mix well. Cover and refrigerate until serving. **Yield:** 4 servings.

Nutritional Analysis: One 1/2-cup serving (prepared with fat-free mayonnaise) equals 109 calories, 374 mg sodium, 0 cholesterol, 25 g carbohydrate, 3 g protein, 1 g fat. **Diabetic Exchanges:** 1 starch, 1 vegetable.

Orange Buttermilk Salad

I often serve this refreshing yet slightly sweet side dish. It goes great with a variety of main dishes, but I especially like it with ham.

—Carol Van Sickle
Versailles, Kentucky

1 can (20 ounces) crushed pineapple, undrained
1 package (6 ounces) orange gelatin
2 cups buttermilk
1 carton (8 ounces) frozen whipped topping, thawed

In a saucepan, bring pineapple to a boil. Remove from the heat; add gelatin and stir to dissolve. Add buttermilk and mix well. Cool to room temperature. Fold in whipped topping. Pour into an 11-in. x 7-in. x 2-in. dish. Refrigerate several hours or overnight. Cut into squares. **Yield:** 12 servings.

Snowball Peaches

Peach halves took on a festive look for a snowman-theme brunch I hosted when I mounded a fruity cream cheese mixture in them. You can put these simple individual salads together very quickly, and they're fun party fare.
—*Renae Moncur, Burley, Idaho*

2 packages (3 ounces *each*) cream cheese, softened
2 tablespoons apricot preserves
1 cup pineapple tidbits, drained
3 cans (15-1/4 ounces *each*) peach halves, drained
Leaf lettuce
Fresh mint, optional

In a small mixing bowl, beat the cream cheese and preserves until blended. Stir in pineapple. Place peaches cut side up on a lettuce-lined serving platter; fill with cream cheese mixture. Garnish with mint if desired. **Yield:** 15 servings.

|SOFTENING CREAM CHEESE| To quickly soften cream cheese, use the microwave. Simply remove the cream cheese from the foil package and place it on a microwave-safe plate. Microwave on medium power for 20 to 40 seconds, checking it at the minimum amount of time.

Balsamic Salad Dressing

My tomato juice-based dressing offers a nice combination of tangy and tart with only a trace of fat. We like our salad dressing tart, but you may want to add a little more sugar if that suits your family's tastes better.
—*Alice Coate, Bryan, Texas*

 Uses less fat, sugar or salt. Includes Nutritional Analysis and Diabetic Exchanges.

3/4 cup tomato juice
1/4 cup balsamic vinegar
1 envelope Italian salad dressing mix
2 teaspoons sugar

In a jar with a tight-fitting lid, combine all ingredients; shake well. Store in the refrigerator. **Yield:** 1 cup.

Nutritional Analysis: One serving (2 tablespoons) equals 18 calories, trace fat (0 saturated fat), 0 cholesterol, 397 mg sodium, 4 g carbohydrate, trace fiber, trace protein. **Diabetic Exchange:** Free food.

Frozen Cherry Salad

Pretty slices of this refreshing salad are dotted with colorful cherries for a festive look. The flavor is pleasant and not overly sweet. Prepared in advance and frozen, it's a treat that fits into many different menus. I serve it throughout the year.

—Gail Sykora
Menomonee Falls, Wisconsin

✓ Uses less fat, sugar or salt. Includes Nutritional Analysis and Diabetic Exchanges.

1 package (8 ounces) cream cheese, softened
1 carton (8 ounces) frozen whipped topping, thawed
1 can (21 ounces) cherry pie filling
2 cans (11 ounces *each*) mandarin oranges, drained
Maraschino cherries and orange wedges, optional

In a mixing bowl, combine the cream cheese and whipped topping. Stir in pie filling. Set aside 1/4 cup oranges for garnish. Fold remaining oranges into cream cheese mixture. Transfer to a 9-in. x 5-in. x 3-in. loaf pan. Cover and freeze overnight.

Remove from the freezer 15 minutes before cutting. Garnish with reserved mandarin oranges, and cherries and oranges if desired. **Yield:** 12 servings.

Nutritional Analysis: One serving (prepared with fat-free cream cheese, reduced-fat whipped topping and reduced-sugar pie filling and without maraschino cherries and oranges) equals 137 calories, 111 mg sodium, 2 mg cholesterol, 24 g carbohydrate, 3 g protein, 3 g fat. **Diabetic Exchanges:** 1 starch, 1/2 fruit, 1/2 fat.

After Thanksgiving Salad

This special salad tastes terrific made with either turkey or chicken. I serve it on a bed of lettuce, as a sandwich or in a croissant for a special occasion. It's a hit with my husband and our three kids.

—Ruthe Holmberg, Louisville, Kentucky

1 hard-cooked egg
4 cups shredded cooked turkey *or* chicken
3/4 cup mayonnaise
1 tablespoon sweet pickle relish
1/2 cup chopped pecans

In a bowl, mash the egg with a fork. Add turkey, mayonnaise and relish. Cover and refrigerate until serving. Stir in pecans just before serving. **Yield:** 4 servings.

Cottage Cheese Veggie Salad

(Pictured on page 131)

Just four ingredients mixed into regular cottage cheese give surprising flavor to this incredibly easy salad. I came up with the idea when I needed a quick side dish for lunch one day. It's light, refreshing and flavorful.
—*Jerraine Barlow, Colorado City, Arizona*

3 cups (24 ounces)
small-curd cottage
cheese
1 large ripe avocado,
peeled, pitted and
chopped
1 medium tomato, chopped
1/4 cup sliced stuffed olives
2 tablespoons sliced green
onions

In a serving bowl, combine the first four ingredients. Sprinkle with onions. Serve immediately. **Yield:** 8 servings.

Artichoke Heart Salad

I put together this fast five-ingredient salad after sampling a similar mixture from a salad bar. Bottled Italian dressing gives robust flavor to this simple treatment for canned artichoke hearts. It is a snap to make as a last-minute side dish.
—*Elizabeth Birkenmaier, Gladstone, Missouri*

1 can (14 ounces)
artichoke hearts,
quartered and drained
1 can (2-1/4 ounces)
sliced ripe olives,
drained, optional
1/3 cup chopped green
pepper
1/3 cup thinly sliced green
onions
3/4 cup Italian salad dressing

In a bowl, combine artichokes, olives if desired, green pepper and onions. Add dressing and toss to coat. Cover and refrigerate for at least 30 minutes. Serve with a slotted spoon. **Yield:** 3-4 servings.

Tricolor Pasta Salad

Pretty pasta spirals and convenient frozen veggies are tossed with a light dressing to make this colorful medley. Vegetarians can add protein-rich chickpeas or beans to make it a main dish.

—*Lorraine Darocha, Berkshire, Massachusetts*

1 package (16 ounces) tricolor spiral pasta
1 package (16 ounces) frozen California-blend vegetables (broccoli, cauliflower and carrots)
1 can (2-1/4 ounces) sliced ripe olives, drained
1 to 1-1/3 cups Italian salad dressing
1/4 to 1/2 teaspoon garlic salt, optional

Cook the pasta according to package directions. Meanwhile, place vegetables in a microwave-safe dish. Cover and microwave at 50% power for 7-8 minutes or until thawed; drain. Drain pasta and rinse in cold water.

In a bowl, combine the pasta, vegetables and olives. Combine salad dressing and garlic salt if desired; pour over salad and toss to coat. Refrigerate until serving. **Yield:** 6-8 servings.

Editor's Note: This recipe was tested in an 850-watt microwave.

French Bean Salad

I jazz up frozen green beans with onion, bacon and bottled salad dressing for a cool dish that's as big on flavor as it is on convenience. I created this recipe after trying a similar salad at a restaurant.

—*Penni Barringer*
Rosalia, Washington

2 cups frozen French-style green beans, thawed
2 tablespoons chopped onion
3 bacon strips, cooked and crumbled
1/4 cup ranch salad dressing

In a serving bowl, combine the beans, onion and bacon; stir in dressing. Refrigerate until serving. **Yield:** 3 servings.

Watermelon Gelatin Cups

Let these delightful watermelon wannabes add a bit of fun to your next picnic spread. Limes are halved and hollowed to hold pretty pink gelatin while mini chocolate chips serve as seeds in the cute cups.

—*Taste of Home Test Kitchen*

1 package (3 ounces) watermelon gelatin
1 cup boiling water
1 cup cold water
4 large limes
1/4 cup miniature chocolate chips

In a bowl, dissolve gelatin in boiling water. Stir in cold water. Refrigerate for 1 hour or until slightly thickened.

Meanwhile, slice limes in half lengthwise. With a small scissors or sharp knife, cut the membrane at each end to loosen pulp from shell. Using fingertips, pull membrane and pulp away from shell (discard pulp or save for another use).

Fold the chocolate chips into the gelatin; spoon into lime shells. Refrigerate for 2 hours or until completely set. **Yield:** 8 servings.

Honey Poppy Seed Dressing

This dressing is a light, refreshing way to dress up a plain lettuce salad. We also like it over fresh fruit.
—*Michelle Bentley, Niceville, Florida*

1/3 cup vegetable oil
1/4 cup honey
2 tablespoons cider vinegar
2 teaspoons poppy seeds
1/2 teaspoon salt

In a small bowl or jar with tight-fitting lid, combine all ingredients; mix or shake well. Store in the refrigerator. **Yield:** about 2/3 cup.

Cherry Coke Salad

Since my sister and I grew up in the '50s, I decided to surprise her with a "Fabulous '50s Party" on her birthday. This refreshing salad, which really features cola, was part of the menu. The soda adds to the bright, sparkling taste.
—*Judy Nix*
Toccoa, Georgia

1 can (20 ounces) crushed pineapple
1/2 cup water
2 packages (3 ounces *each*) cherry gelatin
1 can (21 ounces) cherry pie filling
3/4 cup cola

Drain pineapple, reserving juice; set fruit aside. In a saucepan or microwave, bring pineapple juice and water to a boil. Add gelatin; stir until dissolved. Stir in pie filling and cola. Pour into a serving bowl. Refrigerate until slightly thickened. Fold in reserved pineapple. Refrigerate until firm. **Yield:** 10-12 servings.

Fruit Medley

Straight from the pantry comes a super-simple, colorful and pleasant-tasting fruit dish. Pie filling dresses up this combination of canned fruits.
—*Margaret Anders, Helena, Montana*

1 can (21 ounces) peach *or* apricot pie filling
2 cans (15 ounces *each*) fruit cocktail, drained
1 can (20 ounces) pineapple chunks, drained
1 can (15 ounces) mandarin oranges, drained
2 medium firm bananas, sliced

In a large bowl, combine pie filling and canned fruits. Cover and refrigerate. Stir in bananas just before serving. **Yield:** 12-14 servings.

|BANANA HELP| Because refrigeration discolors bananas that have been peeled, always add them to fruit salads and desserts just before serving. You can also toss sliced bananas with lemon or orange juice to keep them from browning.

French Salad Dressing

This simple dressing has served me for many years. Using this basic recipe, I can easily make simple variations, usually with ingredients I have on hand. As a result, I have always made my own salad dressings.

—*Carolyn Ozment, Gaylesville, Alabama*

> 1/4 cup vegetable oil
> 2 tablespoons vinegar
> 3/4 teaspoon salt
> 1 garlic clove, minced
> Dash pepper

In a jar with a tight-fitting lid, combine the oil, vinegar, salt, garlic and pepper; shake well. Store in the refrigerator. **Yield:** about 1/3 cup.

|MAKING HOMEMADE DRESSING| If you plan on serving a vinegar and oil dressing right away, you can combine all of the ingredients in a jar with a tight-fitting lid and shake well. Otherwise, combine all of the ingredients except for the oil in a small bowl. When ready to serve, slowly add oil while mixing vigorously with a wire whisk.

Broccoli Waldorf Salad

This salad is as easy to prepare as it is to eat! A colorful combination of apples, raisins and pecans jazzes up broccoli florets in this summery side dish. Its tangy-sweet flavor makes it a standout at company picnics and church potlucks.

—*Vicki Roehrick, Chubbuck, Idaho*

 Uses less fat, sugar or salt. Includes Nutritional Analysis and Diabetic Exchanges.

> 6 cups broccoli florets
> 1 large red apple, chopped
> 1/2 cup raisins
> 1/4 cup chopped pecans
> 1/2 cup prepared coleslaw dressing

In a large serving bowl, combine the first four ingredients. Drizzle with dressing; toss to coat. Refrigerate leftovers. **Yield:** 10 servings.

Nutritional Analysis: One 3/4-cup serving (prepared with reduced-fat coleslaw dressing) equals 87 calories, 4 g fat (trace saturated fat), 3 mg cholesterol, 133 mg sodium, 14 g carbohydrate, 2 g fiber, 2 g protein. **Diabetic Exchanges:** 1 vegetable, 1 fruit.

Thousand Island Dressing

It's almost unbelievable that a dressing so easy to fix can be so good. I got the recipe from my daughter, Debbi.

—Darlis Wilfer, Phelps, Wisconsin

2 cups mayonnaise
1/4 cup chili sauce
1/4 cup pickle relish

In a bowl, combine all ingredients. Store in the refrigerator. **Yield:** 2-1/2 cups.

Rainbow Gelatin Cubes

These perky gelatin cubes are fun to serve and to eat! I vary the colors to match the occasion—pink and blue for a baby shower, school colors for a graduation party, etc. Kids of all ages snap them up.

—Deanna Pietrowicz
Bridgeport, Connecticut

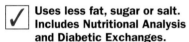
✓ Uses less fat, sugar or salt. Includes Nutritional Analysis and Diabetic Exchanges.

4 packages (3 ounces *each*) **assorted flavored gelatin**
6 envelopes unflavored gelatin, *divided*
5-3/4 cups boiling water, *divided*
1 can (14 ounces) sweetened condensed milk
1/4 cup cold water

In a bowl, combine one package flavored gelatin and one envelope unflavored gelatin. Stir in 1 cup boiling water until dissolved. Pour into a 13-in. x 9-in. x 2-in. dish coated with nonstick cooking spray; refrigerate until almost set but not firm, about 20 minutes.

In a bowl, combine the condensed milk and 1 cup boiling water. In another bowl, sprinkle two envelopes unflavored gelatin over cold water; let stand for 1 minute. Stir in 3/4 cup boiling water. Add to the milk mixture. Pour 1-1/4 cups of the creamy gelatin mixture over the first flavored gelatin layer. Refrigerate until set but not firm, about 25 minutes.

Repeat from beginning of recipe twice, alternating flavored gelatin with creamy gelatin layers. Chill each layer until set but not firm before pouring next layer on top. Make final flavored gelatin; spoon over top. Refrigerate for at least 1 hour after completing last layer before cutting into 1-in. squares. **Yield:** about 9 dozen.

Nutritional Analysis: One serving (two cubes, prepared with sugar-free gelatin and fat-free sweetened condensed milk) equals 26 calories, trace fat (0 saturated fat), 0 cholesterol, 27 mg sodium, 4 g carbohydrate, 0 fiber, 2 g protein. **Diabetic Exchange:** 1/2 fruit.

Tomato Avocado Salad

This salad is a family favorite. It's so colorful and very easy to make that I make it year-round, from summer barbecues to the winter holidays.
—*Vicky Rader*
Mullinville, Kansas

2 ripe avocados, peeled and sliced
2 large tomatoes, cut into wedges
1 medium onion, cut into wedges
1 cup Italian salad dressing
Lettuce leaves, optional

In a bowl, combine the avocados, tomatoes and onion; add dressing and stir to coat. Chill for 20-30 minutes. Serve over lettuce if desired. **Yield:** 6-8 servings.

|TOMATO TIPS| Buy tomatoes that are firm, well-shaped, richly colored and noticeably fragrant. They should be free from blemishes, heavy for their size and give slightly to palm pressure. Never refrigerate tomatoes—cold temperatures make the flesh pulpy and destroy the flavor. Instead, store them at room temperature away from direct sunlight.

Black Bean Salad

This salad goes wonderfully with chicken and Mexican main dishes and is great when you need something quick to make for a potluck dinner.
—*Peg Kenkel-Thomsen, Iowa City, Iowa*

 Uses less fat, sugar or salt. Includes Nutritional Analysis and Diabetic Exchanges.

2 cans (15 ounces *each*) black beans, rinsed and drained
1-1/2 cups salsa
2 tablespoons minced fresh parsley

Combine all ingredients in a bowl. Chill for 15 minutes. **Yield:** 8 servings.

Nutritional Analysis: One 1/2-cup serving equals 93 calories, 453 mg sodium, 0 cholesterol, 16 g carbohydrate, 6 g protein, 1 g fat. **Diabetic Exchange:** 1 starch.

Mom's Coleslaw

As the name says, this is my mom's recipe. You won't have to fuss with a lot of seasonings to fix this tangy coleslaw. This speedy salad is an old family favorite. We've shared the recipe with many friends over the years.
—Denise Augostine
Saxonburg, Pennsylvania

1 small head cabbage, shredded
3 medium carrots, shredded
1 cup mayonnaise
1/3 cup sugar
1/4 cup cider vinegar

In a large bowl, combine cabbage and carrots. In a small bowl, combine the mayonnaise, sugar and vinegar. Pour over cabbage mixture and toss to coat. Serve with a slotted spoon. **Yield:** 10-12 servings.

|SHREDDING CABBAGE| To shred cabbage by hand, cut it into wedges. Place cut side down on a cutting board. With a large sharp knife, cut into thin slices. For the crispest coleslaw, shred the cabbage, then immerse in ice water for an hour. Drain well and blot dry before refrigerating in a plastic bag until ready to use.

Three-Fruit Salad

Nothing could be easier than stirring up this refreshing salad. The tangy honey mustard salad dressing is a wonderful complement to the different fruit flavors.
—Ruth Andrewson
Leavenworth, Washington

 Uses less fat, sugar or salt. Includes Nutritional Analysis and Diabetic Exchanges.

2 medium ripe bananas, sliced
1 cup pineapple chunks
1 cup seedless grapes, halved
3 tablespoons honey mustard salad dressing

In a bowl, combine the fruit. Add dressing and toss to coat. Cover and refrigerate until serving. **Yield:** 4-6 servings.

Nutritional Analysis: One 1/2-cup serving (prepared with fat-free salad dressing) equals 79 calories, 39 mg sodium, 0 cholesterol, 20 g carbohydrate, 1 g protein, trace fat. **Diabetic Exchange:** 1 fruit.

Strawberry Asparagus Salad

This is my family's favorite springtime salad. The dressing is so light and refreshing, and the vivid combination of red berries and green asparagus is a real eye-catcher. —*Judi Francus*
Morristown, New Jersey

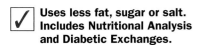 Uses less fat, sugar or salt. Includes Nutritional Analysis and Diabetic Exchanges.

1/4 cup lemon juice
2 tablespoons vegetable oil
2 tablespoons honey
2 cups cut fresh asparagus (1-inch pieces)
2 cups sliced fresh strawberries

In a small bowl, combine lemon juice, oil and honey; mix well. Cook asparagus in a small amount of water until crisp-tender, about 3-4 minutes; drain and cool. Arrange asparagus and strawberries on individual plates; drizzle with dressing. **Yield:** 8 servings.

Nutritional Analysis: One serving equals 68 calories, 1 mg sodium, 0 cholesterol, 9 g carbohydrate, 1 g protein, 4 g fat. **Diabetic Exchanges:** 1 fat, 1/2 fruit.

Olive Lover's Salad

Mom concocted this creative salad with a few simple ingredients. Chopped olives, celery and garlic are drizzled with oil, tossed and chilled for a cool and refreshing side dish that's perfect with any warm meal. —*Gina Mueller, Converse, Texas*

1 can (6 ounces) pitted ripe olives, drained and chopped
1 jar (5-3/4 ounces) stuffed olives, drained and chopped
2 celery ribs, chopped
2 garlic cloves, minced
2 tablespoons olive oil

In a bowl, combine olives, celery and garlic. Drizzle with oil; toss to coat. Cover and refrigerate for 4 hours or overnight. **Yield:** 3-1/2 cups.

|ABOUT OLIVES| The olive tree flourished in Spain, Tunisia, Morocco and Mediterranean countries for thousands of years, but it was not until the mid-16th century that there is a record of cuttings being carried to Peru by the Spaniards. In the 1700s, Franciscan monks brought the olive to Mexico and then north to California by way of the missions.

Green Pepper Salad Dressing

If you enjoy the flavor of green peppers, you'll love this salad dressing. Drizzle greens with the thick blend or serve it alongside a veggie tray for a pleasant change of pace.   —Elizabeth Montgomery
Taylorville, Illinois

1 cup mayonnaise
3 tablespoons finely chopped green pepper
2 tablespoons finely chopped onion
2 tablespoons minced fresh parsley
1 tablespoon lemon juice

In a bowl, combine all of the ingredients. Cover and refrigerate until serving. **Yield:** about 1-1/4 cups.

|PEPPER POINTER| Thoroughly wash bell peppers before seeding. Cut peppers in half by slicing vertically from one side of the stem all the way around to the other side of the stem. Break halves apart and the seed core should pop right out. Cut away the membranes, which can be bitter.

Strawberry-Glazed Fruit Salad

I first tasted this delightful salad at a friend's house when she served it with dinner. It tastes so good made with fresh strawberries. After sampling it, no one would ever believe how incredibly easy it is to prepare.
—Jeri Dobrowski
Beach, North Dakota

1 quart fresh strawberries, halved
1 can (20 ounces) pineapple chunks, drained
4 firm bananas, sliced
1 jar *or* pouch (16 ounces) strawberry glaze

In a large bowl, gently toss strawberries, pineapple and bananas; fold in the glaze. Chill for at least 1 hour. **Yield:** 6-8 servings.

Editor's Note: Strawberry glaze can often be found in the produce section of most grocery stores.

Lemonade Fruit Dressing

I like to dollop this tart yet rich dressing over an assortment of seasonal fruit. It makes a very colorful and refreshing salad that helps beat the summer heat.
—*Emma Magielda*
Amsterdam, New York

2 eggs
3/4 cup lemonade
concentrate
1/3 cup sugar
1 cup heavy whipping
cream, whipped
Assorted fresh fruit

In a heavy saucepan, combine eggs, lemonade concentrate and sugar. Cook and stir over low heat just until mixture comes to a boil. Cool to room temperature, stirring several times. Fold in the whipped cream. Serve over fruit. Refrigerate leftovers. **Yield:** about 3 cups.

Cucumber Shell Salad

Ranch dressing is the mild coating for this pleasant pasta salad chock-full of crunchy cucumber, onion and green peas. Wherever I take it, I'm always asked for the recipe. —*Paula Ishii, Ralston, Nebraska*

✓ **Uses less fat, sugar or salt.**
Includes Nutritional Analysis
and Diabetic Exchanges.

1 package (16 ounces)
medium shell pasta
1 package (16 ounces)
frozen peas, thawed
1 medium cucumber,
halved and sliced
1 small red onion, chopped
1 cup ranch salad dressing

Cook pasta according to package directions; drain and rinse in cold water. In a large bowl, combine the pasta, peas, cucumber and onion. Add dressing; toss to coat. Cover and chill at least 2 hours before serving. **Yield:** 16 servings.

Nutritional Analysis: One 3/4-cup serving (prepared with fat-free ranch dressing) equals 165 calories, 1 g fat (trace saturated fat), trace cholesterol, 210 mg sodium, 33 g carbohydrate, 3 g fiber, 6 g protein. **Diabetic Exchange:** 2 starch.

Crunchy Coleslaw

This crunchy cabbage salad is so easy to put together that we often have it for spur-of-the-moment picnics or when unexpected company stops by. It gets its nutty flavor from almonds and its crunch from ramen noodles.

—Julie Vavroch
Montezuma, Iowa

1/3 cup vegetable oil
1 package (3 ounces) beef-flavored ramen noodles
1/2 teaspoon garlic salt
1 package (16 ounces) shredded coleslaw mix
1 package (5 ounces) sliced almonds

In a small saucepan, heat oil. Stir in contents of noodle seasoning packet and garlic salt; cook for 3-4 minutes or until blended.

Meanwhile, crush the noodles and place in a bowl. Add coleslaw mix and almonds. Drizzle with oil mixture and toss to coat. Serve immediately. **Yield:** 6-8 servings.

Orange Pecan Salad

For a change of pace, replace the pecans with almonds, pistachios or sunflower kernels. Use sweet grapefruit, kiwi, apple slices or grapes in place of the oranges. And orange or plain yogurt with marmalade can be substituted for the peach yogurt. If you'd like to turn the salad into a meal in itself, lend it heartiness with chicken salad or grilled chicken. —Cheryl Mutch, Edmonton, Alberta

2 oranges, peeled and sectioned *or* 1 can (11 ounces) mandarin oranges, drained
1 small bunch leaf lettuce, torn
1/4 cup pecan halves, toasted
1/2 cup peach yogurt
3 tablespoons mayonnaise

Toss oranges, lettuce and pecans in a large salad bowl; set aside. Combine yogurt and mayonnaise; pour over salad just before serving. **Yield:** 4 servings.

|WASHING GREENS| Wash greens thoroughly in cool water. Pat them dry with a clean towel or paper towel to remove water. Store in a covered container or plastic bag, and refrigerate at least 1 hour before serving to crisp the greens. Place a piece of paper towel in the bottom of the container or bag to absorb excess moisture.

Walking Salad

This speedy stuffed apple is a great snack for a family hike. In a brown-bag lunch, it's a nice change from the usual peanut butter and jelly sandwich.
—*Mrs. John Crawford, Barnesville, Georgia*

2 tablespoons peanut butter
1 tablespoon raisins
1 teaspoon honey
1 medium apple, cored

In a small bowl, combine peanut butter, raisins and honey. Spoon into center of apple. **Yield:** 1 serving.

Editor's Note: Gala, Golden Delicious and Red Delicious apples are great for eating raw.

Cucumbers With Dressing

It wouldn't be summer if Mom didn't make lots of these creamy cucumbers. Just a few simple ingredients—mayonnaise, sugar, vinegar and salt—dress up slices of this crisp garden vegetable.
—*Michelle Beran, Claflin, Kansas*

1 cup mayonnaise
1/4 cup sugar
1/4 cup vinegar
1/4 teaspoon salt
4 cups sliced cucumbers

In a bowl, combine mayonnaise, sugar, vinegar and salt. Add cucumbers; stir to coat. Cover and refrigerate for 2 hours. **Yield:** 6-8 servings.

Low-Fat Blue Cheese Dressing

You'll never miss the fat in my full-flavored blue cheese dressing. I got the recipe from a chef at a California resort while on vacation a number of years ago. —*Tracey Baysinger, Salem, Missouri*

 Uses less fat, sugar or salt. Includes Nutritional Analysis and Diabetic Exchanges.

1 cup (8 ounces) fat-free cottage cheese
1 cup (8 ounces) fat-free plain yogurt
2 tablespoons chopped onion
1 garlic clove, minced
1 tablespoon crumbled blue cheese

In a blender or food processor, combine cottage cheese, yogurt, onion and garlic; cover and process until smooth. Stir in blue cheese. Store, covered, in the refrigerator. **Yield:** 1-3/4 cups.

  Nutritional Analysis: One serving (1 tablespoon) equals 11 calories, 34 mg sodium, 1 mg cholesterol, 1 g carbohydrate, 2 g protein, trace fat. **Diabetic Exchange:** Free food.

Cran-Apple Salad

This tart and tasty salad goes so wonderfully with lots of different meals. Folks will think you spent hours on it, but with less than five ingredients, preparation takes only minutes! Crunchy walnuts, celery and apples are a special way to dress up canned cranberry sauce.
—*Lucille Foster, Grant, Nebraska*

1 can (16 ounces) whole-berry cranberry sauce
1 medium unpeeled tart apple, diced
1 celery rib, thinly sliced
1/2 cup chopped walnuts

In a bowl, combine the cranberry sauce, apple and celery. Cover and refrigerate. Stir in walnuts just before serving. **Yield:** 4-6 servings.

Crab and Pea Salad

From picnics to potlucks, this fast-to-fix combination receives rave reviews. I like to garnish it with paprika, sliced hard-cooked eggs, tomatoes and croutons. —Janine Gillespie Milwaukie, Oregon

1 package (10 ounces) frozen peas, thawed
1 package (8 ounces) imitation crabmeat, flaked
6 to 8 bacon strips, cooked and crumbled
1/2 cup mayonnaise
1/4 teaspoon onion powder

In a bowl, combine peas, crab and bacon. Combine mayonnaise and onion powder; fold into the crab mixture. Cover and refrigerate until serving. **Yield:** 4-6 servings.

|PEA POINTER| For pea salads, simply pour cold water over the frozen peas and let stand about 5 minutes or until the peas are defrosted. Drain well before adding to the salad.

Mallow Fruit Cups

Instead of serving plain fruit cocktail, I toss in a few of my family's favorite ingredients to make this colorful concoction. I created this quick salad when our boys were younger, and it's been around ever since as a good hurry-up fill-in at meals. —Karen Coffman, Delphi, Indiana

 Uses less fat, sugar or salt. Includes Nutritional Analysis and Diabetic Exchanges.

1 can (15 ounces) fruit cocktail, drained
1 medium tart apple, diced
1/2 cup miniature marshmallows
1/2 cup whipped topping

In a bowl, combine all ingredients. Cover and refrigerate until serving. **Yield:** 4-6 servings.

Nutritional Analysis: One 1/2-cup serving (prepared with reduced-fat whipped topping) equals 91 calories, 6 mg sodium, 0 cholesterol, 21 g carbohydrate, trace protein, 1 g fat. **Diabetic Exchange:** 1-1/2 fruit.

Fourth of July Jell-O

With six children, I'm always looking for wholesome quick recipes. This colorful salad can be fixed by school-age children and looks so pretty served in a glass bowl.
—*Mabel Yoder, Bonduel, Wisconsin*

1 package (3 ounces) berry blue gelatin
2 cups boiling water, *divided*
1/2 cup cold water, *divided*
1 package (3 ounces) strawberry gelatin
1 can (15 ounces) pear halves, drained and cubed

In a bowl, dissolve blue gelatin in 1 cup boiling water. Stir in 1/4 cup cold water. Pour into an ungreased 9-in. x 5-in. x 3-in. loaf pan. Refrigerate until firm. Repeat with strawberry gelatin and remaining boiling and cold water.

When gelatin is set, cut into cubes. Just before serving, gently combine gelatin cubes and pears in a large glass bowl or individual dishes. **Yield:** 6-8 servings.

Greens with Herb Vinaigrette

Dijon mustard adds tanginess to the light vinaigrette that coats this salad. For variety, I sometimes add minced garlic or a tablespoon of whipping cream. You can even use flavored vinegars or different types of oil for a change of pace.
—*Sally Hook, Houston, Texas*

6 to 8 cups torn salad greens
3 tablespoons olive oil
1 tablespoon red wine vinegar
1/2 to 1 teaspoon Dijon mustard
1/2 teaspoon Italian seasoning

Place greens in a salad bowl. Combine remaining ingredients in a jar with tight-fitting lid; shake well. Pour over greens and toss to coat. **Yield:** 6-8 servings.

|TEARING SALAD GREENS| Just before serving, tear—don't cut—the greens into bite-size pieces. Cutting greens with a knife will turn the edges brown with time. Allow greens to stand at room temperature no longer than 15 minutes before serving.

Strawberry Spinach Salad

This is an especially good salad to take to summer potluck dinners. Folks always come back for second helpings of the pretty and refreshing salad.
—*Pat Brune, Ridgecrest, California*

3 tablespoons lemon juice
1/4 cup sugar
6 tablespoons vegetable oil
1 package (10 ounces) fresh spinach
2 cups sliced fresh strawberries

Place the lemon juice and sugar in a blender. With blender running, add oil in a slow steady stream; process until slightly thickened.

Just before serving, combine spinach and strawberries in a large salad bowl or individual bowls or plates; drizzle with dressing. **Yield:** 6-8 servings.

Raspberry Congealed Salad

My sisters and I especially enjoyed this cool tangy side dish our mom used to make. Now we make it often ourselves. It looks so lovely on the table. The pineapple and raspberries are a delectable duo, and pecans add a hearty crunch.
—*Nancy Duty*
Jacksonville, Florida

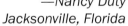

1 can (8 ounces) crushed pineapple
1 package (10 ounces) frozen unsweetened raspberries, thawed
1 package (3 ounces) raspberry gelatin
1 cup applesauce
1/4 cup coarsely chopped pecans
Mayonnaise, optional

Drain pineapple and raspberries, reserving juices. Place fruit in a large bowl; set aside. Add enough water to the juice to measure 1 cup. Pour into a saucepan; bring to a boil. Remove from the heat; stir in gelatin until dissolved.

Pour over fruit mixture. Add the applesauce and pecans. Pour into a 1-qt. bowl. Chill until set. Spoon into individual dessert dishes; top with a dollop of mayonnaise if desired. **Yield:** 6 servings.

Strawberry Rhubarb Gelatin

Rhubarb lends a hint of natural tartness to this sweet salad. As a fruity side dish, its vibrant color is sure to add eye-opening appeal to almost any meal. —*Opal Schmidt, Battle Creek, Iowa*

2 cups diced fresh *or* frozen rhubarb
1/2 to 3/4 cup sugar
1/4 cup water
1 package (3 ounces) strawberry gelatin
1-1/2 cups whipped topping

In a saucepan, bring rhubarb, sugar and water to a boil. Reduce heat; simmer, uncovered, for 3-5 minutes or until the rhubarb is softened.

Remove from the heat; stir in gelatin until dissolved. Pour into a bowl. Refrigerate for 20 minutes or until partially set. Fold in whipped topping. Chill until firm. **Yield:** 4 servings.

|A "GEL" OF A TIP| If your gelatin mixture sets too fast and you've passed the partially set step, place the bowl of gelatin in a pan of warm water and stir until the gelatin has softened. Chill again until the mixture is the consistency of unbeaten raw egg whites. Then fold in the whipped topping.

Tomato Tossed Salad

I stir chives and thyme into a pleasant dressing to drizzle over this simple salad. It's especially good with sun-ripened tomatoes right out of the garden. —*Edna Hoffman Hebron, Indiana*

6 cups shredded lettuce
2 medium tomatoes, cut into wedges
1/4 cup oil and vinegar salad dressing
1 teaspoon snipped chives
1/4 teaspoon dried thyme

Place lettuce and tomatoes in a salad bowl. Combine salad dressing, chives and thyme; drizzle over salad and toss gently. **Yield:** 4 servings.

Three-Pepper Salad

This salad is a five-ingredient time-saver that serves as an attractive and welcome variation on veggies. After topping the peppers and onion with bottled vinaigrette, I focus on my entree.
—*Marilou Robinson, Portland, Oregon*

 Uses less fat, sugar or salt. Includes Nutritional Analysis and Diabetic Exchanges.

1 *each* medium sweet red, yellow and green pepper, thinly sliced
1 small onion, cut into 1/4-inch wedges
1/3 cup prepared vinaigrette salad dressing

In a bowl, combine the red, yellow and green peppers and onion. Add salad dressing and toss to coat. Refrigerate until serving. **Yield:** 4 servings.

Nutritional Analysis: One 3/4-cup serving (prepared with fat-free Italian salad dressing) equals 58 calories, trace fat (trace saturated fat), 0 cholesterol, 187 mg sodium, 14 g carbohydrate, 2 g fiber, 1 g protein. **Diabetic Exchange:** 2 vegetable.

Simple Caesar Salad

In summer, I'll mix fresh tomato slices and vegetables from our garden in with the salad. I also experiment with different kinds of lettuce than romaine.
—*Carolene Esayenko, Calgary, Alberta*

6 cups torn romaine
1/2 cup Caesar croutons
2 bacon strips, cooked and crumbled
1/4 cup grated *or* shredded Parmesan cheese
1/3 cup Caesar salad dressing

In a large bowl, combine romaine, croutons, bacon and cheese. Add the salad dressing and toss to coat. **Yield:** 4-6 servings.

Golden Pumpkin Salad

This delicious salad is the result of a bumper crop of pumpkins. I had so many on hand, I started experimenting with different ways of preparing them. The sweet dish I'm sharing here is one we all enjoy.

—*Janell Burrell, Cornelia, Georgia*

2 cups shredded uncooked
  fresh pie pumpkin
1 can (8 ounces) crushed
  pineapple, undrained
1/2 cup raisins
1 tablespoon mayonnaise
1/2 teaspoon sugar
Leaf lettuce, optional

Place pumpkin in a 1-qt. microwave-safe bowl. Cover and microwave on high for 3 minutes; cool. Stir in pineapple, raisins, mayonnaise and sugar. Refrigerate overnight. Serve on lettuce if desired. **Yield:** 4 servings.

Editor's Note: This recipe was tested in an 850-watt microwave.

|TRADING PLACES| Pumpkin can be prepared in almost any way suitable for winter squash. Likewise, winter squash, such as acorn or hubbard, can be substituted for pumpkin in recipes.

Hash Brown Potato Salad

I've used this recipe for over 20 years, and it's still a family favorite. It stirs up and cooks in a jiffy, and it tastes just as good as a German potato salad that you fussed all day to make.

—*Joan Hallford, North Richland Hills, Texas*

5 bacon strips, diced
6 green onions, sliced
1 package (1 pound)
  frozen cubed hash brown
  potatoes
1/4 cup white wine vinegar
1/2 teaspoon celery salt

Place bacon in a 1-1/2-qt. microwave-safe bowl. Cover and microwave on high for 5-6 minutes or until bacon is crisp. Remove with a slotted spoon to paper towels to drain. Add onions to the drippings; cover and microwave on high for 1 minute.

Add the potatoes; cover and cook on high for 10 minutes, stirring several times. Add vinegar, celery salt and bacon; toss. **Yield:** 4 servings.

Editor's Note: This recipe was tested in an 850-watt microwave.

Red-Hot Candy Fluff

A friend at work gave me the recipe for this fluffy pink pineapple salad a few years ago, and I've been preparing it ever since. My two young children really enjoy it, especially when I tell them it has candy in it. —*Shelley Vickrey, Strafford, Missouri*

1 can (20 ounces) crushed pineapple, drained
1/4 cup red-hot candies
2 cups miniature marshmallows
1 carton (8 ounces) frozen whipped topping, thawed

In a bowl, combine the pineapple and candies. Cover and refrigerate for 8 hours or overnight. Stir in the marshmallows and whipped topping. Cover and refrigerate until serving. **Yield:** 6-8 servings.

Hawaiian Salad

To add a refreshing spark to any meal, try this tempting salad with tropical flair. A few simple ingredients are easily combined to make a memorable salad. We always empty the bowl. —*Lisa Andis Morristown, Indiana*

1 can (8 ounces) pineapple tidbits
6 to 8 cups torn salad greens
1 cup (4 ounces) shredded cheddar cheese
1/2 cup mayonnaise
1 tablespoon sugar

Drain pineapple, reserving 1 tablespoon juice. In a large bowl, combine greens, pineapple and cheese. In a small bowl, combine the mayonnaise, sugar and reserved pineapple juice; mix well. Pour over salad; toss to coat. Serve immediately. **Yield:** 6 servings.

Honey Mustard Salad Dressing

From the first time I tasted this salad dressing, it has been a favorite at our house, served almost exclusively. It's quick to prepare, and it's easily made "light" by using fat-free or reduced-fat mayo.

—*Patty Brewer, Kansas City, Missouri*

6 tablespoons mayonnaise
2 tablespoons Dijon mustard
2 tablespoons honey

In a bowl, combine the mayonnaise, mustard and honey; mix well. Store in refrigerator. **Yield:** about 1/2 cup dressing.

Pear Lime Gelatin

Packed with pears, this jolly gelatin salad is a light and refreshing treat for the holidays. My mom knew that fruit served in this fun form would get gobbled right up. She also liked it because the bowl looked like a sparkling jewel on our dinner table.

—*Sandy Jenkins*
Elkhorn, Wisconsin

 Uses less fat, sugar or salt. Includes Nutritional Analysis and Diabetic Exchanges.

1 can (29 ounces) pear halves, undrained
1 package (3 ounces) lime gelatin
1 package (3 ounces) cream cheese, cubed
1 cup whipped topping

Drain pears, reserving juice; set pears aside. Measure the juice; add water if needed to equal 1-1/2 cups. Pour into a saucepan; bring to a boil. Add gelatin; stir until dissolved. Gradually add cream cheese, whisking until smooth. Cover and refrigerate until cool.

Mash reserved pears; fold into gelatin mixture. Fold in whipped topping. Pour into a 6-cup serving bowl. Refrigerate until set. **Yield:** 6 servings.

Nutritional Analysis: One serving (prepared with sugar-free gelatin and reduced-fat cream cheese and whipped topping) equals 172 calories, 3 g fat (2 g saturated fat), 5 mg cholesterol, 398 mg sodium, 21 g carbohydrate, 2 g fiber, 8 g protein. **Diabetic Exchanges:** 2 fruit, 1 fat.

Applesauce Gelatin Squares

I make this attractive soft-set salad during the holidays and garnish it with ranch dressing that's tinted green. Or spoon on a dollop of whipped topping for a light sweet dessert anytime.
—*Judy Ernst*
Montague, Michigan

 Uses less fat, sugar or salt. Includes Nutritional Analysis and Diabetic Exchanges.

- **4 packages (.3 ounce *each*) sugar-free raspberry gelatin *or* flavor of your choice**
- **4 cups boiling water**
- **2 cups cold water**
- **1 jar (46 ounces) unsweetened applesauce**

In a bowl, dissolve gelatin in boiling water. Stir in cold water and applesauce. Pour into a 13-in. x 9-in. x 2-in. dish coated with nonstick cooking spray. Refrigerate for 8 hours or overnight. Cut into squares. **Yield:** 16 servings.

Nutritional Analysis: One serving equals 42 calories, 48 mg sodium, 0 cholesterol, 10 g carbohydrate, 1 g protein, trace fat. **Diabetic Exchange:** 1/2 fruit.

Zesty Vegetable Salad

This fresh-tasting medley is a terrific way to use your garden bounty. When people rave about it, I'm almost embarrassed to tell them how easy it is to make. —*Dana Nemecek, Skiatook, Oklahoma*

 Uses less fat, sugar or salt. Includes Nutritional Analysis and Diabetic Exchanges.

- **10 fresh mushrooms, sliced**
- **2 medium tomatoes, chopped**
- **2 medium cucumbers, peeled and chopped**
- **1 small onion, chopped**
- **1 bottle (8 ounces) zesty Italian salad dressing**

In a bowl, combine mushrooms, tomatoes, cucumbers and onion. Add dressing; toss to coat. Cover and chill at least 2 hours. Serve with a slotted spoon. **Yield:** 12 servings.

Nutritional Analysis: One 1/2-cup serving (prepared with fat-free salad dressing) equals 29 calories, 137 mg sodium, 0 cholesterol, 5 g carbohydrate, 1 g protein, trace fat. **Diabetic Exchange:** 1 vegetable.

Side Dishes & Condiments

Onion-Roasted Potatoes, p. 162

Green Beans Amandine, p. 167

| CONDIMENTS |

Zucchini Pancakes, p. 163

Onion-Roasted Potatoes

(Pictured on page 160 and on front cover)

Slightly crisp on the outside and tender on the inside, these potatoes are a hit with my family. This side dish is one of my favorites because the soup mix glazes the potatoes so nicely, and it's very simple to prepare.
—*Schelby Thompson, Winter Haven, Florida*

**2 pounds red potatoes,
   sliced 1/2 inch thick
1/3 cup vegetable oil
1 envelope dry onion soup
   mix**

Combine all ingredients in a large plastic bag; shake until well coated. Empty bag into an ungreased 13-in. x 9-in. x 2-in. baking pan.

Cover and bake at 350° for 35 minutes, stirring occasionally. Uncover and bake 15 minutes longer or until potatoes are tender. **Yield:** 6-8 servings.

Citrus Carrot Sticks

I frequently serve these julienned carrots that pick up a pleasant tang from orange juice and cumin. I like to tie up the carrots in little bundles with a cut green onion. But they also taste great from a serving bowl.
—*Amy Volk
Geneva, Illinois*

 **Uses less fat, sugar or salt.
Includes Nutritional Analysis
and Diabetic Exchanges.**

**3 tablespoons orange juice
1 teaspoon butter, melted
1/2 teaspoon ground cumin
1 pound carrots
6 cups water**

Combine orange juice, butter and cumin; set aside. Cut carrots into 3-in. chunks, then into matchstick strips. In a large saucepan, bring water to a boil. Add carrots; cook for about 2 minutes or until crisp-tender. Drain; place in a serving bowl. Drizzle with orange juice mixture. **Yield:** 6 servings.

Nutritional Analysis: One serving (prepared with margarine) equals 44 calories, 35 mg sodium, 0 cholesterol, 9 g carbohydrate, 1 g protein, 1 g fat. **Diabetic Exchange:** 1-1/2 vegetable.

Corn State Broccoli Bake

Since our state is known for growing corn, I planned a corn theme dinner for our grandson's first visit a number of years ago. A double dose of corn—whole kernel plus cream style—teams up with broccoli in this colorful side dish. —*Nadine Brimeyer*
Denver, Iowa

1 package (8 ounces) Chicken in a Biskit crackers, crushed
1/2 cup butter, melted
1 package (10 ounces) frozen chopped broccoli, thawed
1 can (15-1/4 ounces) whole kernel corn, drained
1 can (14-3/4 ounces) cream-style corn

Combine cracker crumbs and butter; reserve 1/2 cup for topping. In a bowl, combine broccoli, both cans of corn and remaining crumbs.

Transfer to a greased 2-qt. baking dish. Sprinkle with reserved crumb mixture. Bake, uncovered, at 375° for 25-30 minutes or until lightly browned. **Yield:** 6-8 servings.

|A KERNEL ON CORN| Corn was first grown in Mexico and Central America and was a staple of the Native Americans. Today, Americans annually consume about 25 pounds of corn per person. There are more than 200 varieties grown worldwide.

Zucchini Pancakes

(Pictured on page 161)

My Zucchini Pancakes are a delicious change of pace from the more common potato variety. They fry up golden brown, crispy on the outside and tender inside. —*Charlotte Goldberg*
Honey Grove, Pennsylvania

1-1/2 cups shredded zucchini
1 egg, lightly beaten
2 tablespoons biscuit/baking mix
3 tablespoons grated Parmesan cheese
1 tablespoon vegetable oil

In a bowl, combine zucchini, egg, baking mix and cheese. Heat oil in a skillet over medium heat; drop batter by 1/4 cupfuls and flatten. Fry until golden brown; turn and cook the other side. **Yield:** 4 servings.

Never-Fail Egg Noodles

Some 35 years ago, the small church I attended held a chicken and noodle fund-raiser supper. I was put in charge of noodles for 200 people! A dear lady shared this recipe and said it had been tried and tested by countless cooks. These noodles are just plain good eating!

—Kathryn Roach
Greers Ferry, Arkansas

1 egg plus 3 egg yolks
3 tablespoons cold water
1 teaspoon salt
2 cups all-purpose flour
Chopped fresh parsley, optional

In a mixing bowl, beat egg and yolks until light and fluffy. Add water and salt; mix well. Stir in flour. Turn onto a floured surface; knead until smooth. Divide into thirds.

Roll out each portion to 1/8-in. thickness. Cut noodles to desired width (noodles shown in the photo were cut 2 in. x 1/2 in.). Cook immediately in boiling salted water or chicken broth for 7-9 minutes or until tender. Drain; sprinkle with parsley if desired. **Yield:** about 5-1/2 cups.

Editor's Note: Uncooked noodles may be stored in the refrigerator for 2-3 days or frozen for up to 1 month. Unsalted water will reach a boil faster than salted water, so add salt to rapidly boiling water just before adding the pasta.

Blueberry Sauce Supreme

When we get "blue" here at SGB Farms, we're not sad—we're in the middle of our 5-week blueberry harvest, which starts in mid-June! We have 1,500 plants on 1.4 acres. Every day we eat blueberries on our cereal or enjoy them in muffins, pies and desserts. A favorite treat is Blueberry Sauce Supreme, which we love over pancakes and waffles.   —Clarence Scrivner, Hartsburg, Missouri

1/2 cup sugar
1/4 cup orange juice
   concentrate
2 tablespoons cornstarch
3 cups fresh *or* frozen
   blueberries

In a saucepan, combine sugar, orange juice concentrate and cornstarch; stir until smooth. Add blueberries and bring to a boil. Boil for 2 minutes, stirring constantly. **Yield:** 2-1/4 cups.

Sauteed Mushrooms

I frequently fix this speedy side dish for my hungry family. Spiced carrots would be a mouth-watering companion in the pan to the mushrooms.
                                                                    —*Hope Meece, Fowler, Indiana*

1/4 cup butter
  1 **pound fresh mushrooms, sliced**
  1 **tablespoon lemon juice**
  1 **tablespoon soy sauce**

In a skillet, melt butter. Add mushrooms, lemon juice and soy sauce. Saute for 6-8 minutes or until mushrooms are tender. **Yield:** 4 servings.

|SAUTEING SUGGESTIONS| Sauteing mushrooms brings out and concentrates their flavor. Make sure the pan and butter are hot and don't overcrowd—mushrooms exude a lot of moisture during cooking, and you want to be able to stir them around in the pan. Otherwise, they'll steam rather than saute.

Dilled Zucchini

These super squash couldn't be easier to prepare! Their mild flavor goes well with a variety of main dishes, but I especially like them alongside chicken. The recipe is a great way to put a bumper crop of zucchini to good use.
                                          —*Sundra Lewis*
                                       Bogalusa, Louisiana

 Uses less fat, sugar or salt. Includes Nutritional Analysis and Diabetic Exchanges.

  3 **medium zucchini, halved lengthwise**
  1 **tablespoon butter, melted**
1/4 **teaspoon dill weed**
Salt and pepper, optional

Place zucchini in a skillet and cover with water; bring to a boil over medium heat. Cook until tender, about 12-14 minutes. Drain; brush with butter. Sprinkle with dill and salt and pepper if desired. **Yield:** 6 servings.

Nutritional Analysis: One serving (prepared with margarine and without salt) equals 28 calories, 25 mg sodium, 0 cholesterol, 2 g carbohydrate, 1 g protein, 2 g fat. **Diabetic Exchanges:** 1/2 vegetable, 1/2 fat.

Easy Pasta Alfredo

Who would believe that five simple ingredients could taste so rich and delicious? This creamy, comforting sauce can be made in a matter of minutes. —*Karin DeCarlo, Milford, Pennsylvania*

1/2 cup butter
1 cup heavy whipping cream
1/8 teaspoon ground nutmeg
1 cup shredded Parmesan cheese
1 package (19 ounces) frozen cheese tortellini

In a saucepan, melt butter over medium-low heat. Add cream and nutmeg; heat through but do not boil. Stir in Parmesan cheese until melted.

Cook tortellini according to package directions; drain. Transfer to a large serving bowl. Add the cheese sauce and toss to coat. Serve immediately. **Yield:** 4 servings.

Mom's Carrot Casserole

Rich and cheesy, this casserole is the very best way to eat carrots. Pretty orange slices peek out from under a bed of buttery cracker crumbs. My mom loves to cook and share recipes. She picked this one up from a dear friend.
—*Gloria Grant, Sterling, Illinois*

2 pounds carrots, sliced
1/2 cup butter, *divided*
6 ounces process cheese (Velveeta), cubed
1/4 teaspoon dill weed
1/2 cup crushed saltines (about 15 crackers)

Place carrots in a saucepan and cover with water; bring to a boil. Reduce heat; cover and simmer until tender, about 10 minutes. Drain; place in a greased 1-1/2-qt. baking dish.

In a small saucepan, melt 1/4 cup butter and cheese, stirring often. Stir in dill. Pour over the carrots. Toss the saltines and remaining butter; sprinkle over carrots. Bake, uncovered, at 350° for 25-30 minutes or until lightly browned and bubbly. **Yield:** 8 servings.

Grilled Peppers and Zucchini

This versatile side dish is so simple and quick that I had to share it. Grilling the colorful veggies in a foil packet means one less dish to wash, but I often stir-fry the mixture on the stovetop instead.

—Karen Anderson
Fair Oaks, California

1 medium green pepper, julienned
1 medium sweet red pepper, julienned
2 medium zucchini, julienned
1 tablespoon butter
2 teaspoons soy sauce

Place the vegetables on a double layer of heavy-duty foil (about 18 in. x 15 in.). Dot with butter; drizzle with soy sauce. Fold foil around vegetables and seal tightly. Grill, covered, over medium heat for 10-15 minutes or until vegetables are crisp-tender. **Yield:** 3-4 servings.

Green Beans Amandine

(Pictured on page 161)

It's hard to improve on the taste Mother Nature gives to fresh green beans, but my own mom has for years using this recipe. I have always thought the crunchy almonds were a super addition.

—Brenda DuFresne, Midland, Michigan

✓ Uses less fat, sugar or salt. Includes Nutritional Analysis and Diabetic Exchanges.

1 pound fresh *or* frozen green beans, cut into 2-inch pieces
1/2 cup water
1/4 cup slivered almonds
2 tablespoons butter
1 teaspoon lemon juice
1/4 teaspoon seasoned salt, optional

In a saucepan, bring beans and water to a boil; reduce heat to medium. Cover and cook for 10-15 minutes or until the beans are crisp-tender; drain and set aside. In a large skillet, cook almonds in butter over low heat. Stir in lemon juice and seasoned salt if desired. Add beans and heat through. **Yield:** 6 servings.

Nutritional Analysis: One 1/2-cup serving (prepared with margarine and without seasoned salt) equals 92 calories, 50 mg sodium, 0 cholesterol, 7 g carbohydrate, 3 g protein, 7 g fat. **Diabetic Exchanges:** 1-1/2 fat, 1 vegetable.

Crumb-Topped Brussels Sprouts

This makes a flavorful side dish sure to dress up any meal. Even folks who normally don't care for brussels sprouts like them prepared this way. The bread crumb and Parmesan cheese coating is a delicious way to top them off. —*Ruth Peterson Jenison, Michigan*

1-1/2 **pounds fresh *or* frozen brussels sprouts**
3 **tablespoons butter, melted, *divided***
1/4 **cup Italian-seasoned dry bread crumbs**
2 **tablespoons grated Parmesan cheese**

Cut an X in the core of each brussels sprout. In a saucepan, cook brussels sprouts in salted water until crisp-tender, about 8-10 minutes; drain. Place in an ungreased shallow 1-1/2-qt. baking dish. Drizzle with 2 tablespoons butter.

Combine bread crumbs, Parmesan cheese and remaining butter; sprinkle over brussels sprouts. Cover and bake at 325° for 10 minutes. Uncover and bake 10 minutes longer. **Yield:** 4-6 servings.

Editor's Note: Brussels sprouts can be cooked, cooled, quartered and made into a cold salad, mixed with diced tomatoes and tossed with a vinaigrette. After cooking and cooling, they can also be cut into 1/4-inch slices and sauteed with scallions, garlic and minced ginger for a wonderful change of pace.

Cherry Sauce for Ham

I often whip up this simple topping to pour over ham at church dinners. It's long been a favored condiment there—and at home, too. The concoction's spicy zing comes from the dab of mustard I pour into the mix. —*Tess Krumm, Fargo, North Dakota*

1 **can (21 ounces) cherry pie filling**
1 **tablespoon brown sugar**
1/2 **teaspoon prepared mustard**

Combine all the ingredients in a small saucepan; bring to a boil. Reduce heat and simmer for 5-10 minutes. **Yield:** 2 cups.

Sweet-and-Sour Beets

With their lovely jewel tones and tangy glaze, these beets take center stage. They always earn rave reviews!

—*Emily Chaney, Penobscot, Maine*

 Uses less fat, sugar or salt. Includes Nutritional Analysis and Diabetic Exchanges.

1/2 cup water
1/4 cup vinegar
  2 teaspoons cornstarch
  4 teaspoons sugar
  2 cups sliced cooked beets

In a saucepan, combine water, vinegar and cornstarch; bring to a boil. Cook and stir for 1-2 minutes; remove from the heat. Add sugar and beets; let stand for 1 hour. Heat through just before serving. **Yield:** 4 servings.

Nutritional Analysis: One serving equals 49 calories, 37 mg sodium, 0 cholesterol, 12 g carbohydrate, 1 g protein, trace fat. **Diabetic Exchange:** 2 vegetable.

Chunky Cinnamon Applesauce

As a young girl, I was amazed when Mom transformed fresh apples into this delightful, lovely mixture. I'm not sure if I liked it so much because it was made with candies or because it tasted wonderful.

—*Barbara Hyatt, Folsom, California*

  8 medium tart apples,
    peeled and quartered
  1 cup water
  1 cup sugar
1/4 cup red-hot candies

Place apples and water in a 5-qt. saucepan. Cover and cook over medium-low heat for 20 minutes or until tender. Mash the apples. Add sugar and candies. Cook, uncovered, until sugar and candies are dissolved. Remove from the heat; cool. Refrigerate until serving. **Yield:** 6 cups.

Creamy Italian Noodles

This is an easy recipe for no-fail noodles that are a flavorful accompaniment to most any meat. Rich and creamy, they're special enough for company, too. —*Linda Hendrix, Moundville, Missouri*

1 package (8 ounces) wide egg noodles
1/4 cup butter, softened
1/2 cup heavy whipping cream, half-and-half cream *or* evaporated milk
1/4 cup grated Parmesan cheese
2-1/4 teaspoons Italian salad dressing mix

Cook noodles according to package directions; drain and place in a bowl. Toss with butter. Add the remaining ingredients and mix well. Serve immediately. Yield: 4-6 servings.

|CRASH COURSE IN CREAM| Cream is categorized according to the amount of milk fat it contains. Heavy whipping cream has a fat content of between 36% and 40%. Half-and-half is a mixture of equal parts milk and cream, and contains from 10% to 18% milk fat. Evaporated milk comes in whole, reduced-fat and fat-free versions, and has had 60% of the water removed.

Cheesy Squash

I'm a retired police officer and now a deputy sheriff who loves to cook. But with my busy schedule, I must rely on speedy side dishes like this one. The squash retains its fresh taste and cooks to a perfect tender-crispness. You can give this cheesy treatment to other fresh veggies, too. It's so quick that I make some variation of it a few times a week. Everyone loves it! —*Randy Lawrence Clinton, Mississippi*

1 small zucchini
1 small yellow summer squash
Salt and pepper to taste
1 cup (4 ounces) shredded mozzarella cheese
1/4 cup grated Parmesan cheese

Cut zucchini and yellow squash into 1/4-in. slices. Place in a greased shallow 1-qt. baking dish. Sprinkle with salt and pepper. Top with cheeses. Broil 4 in. from the heat for 7-10 minutes or until squash is crisp-tender and cheese is bubbly. Serve immediately. Yield: 2 servings.

Barbecue Butter Beans

Flavorful bacon and a sweet sauce spark the flavor of Barbecue Butter Beans. It takes only minutes to stir together this speedy side dish, making it perfect for potlucks.

—Linda Hartsell
Apple Creek, Ohio

2 cans (15 ounces *each*) butter beans, rinsed and drained
3/4 cup packed brown sugar
1/2 cup ketchup
1/2 cup chopped onion
3 bacon strips, diced

In a bowl, combine the beans, brown sugar, ketchup and onion. Transfer to a greased 1-1/2-qt. baking dish. Sprinkle with bacon. Bake, uncovered, at 350° for 1-1/2 hours. **Yield:** 4-6 servings.

Fried Green Tomatoes

My grandmother came up with her own version of fried green tomatoes years ago. Our family loves it. It's a traditional taste of the South that anyone anywhere can enjoy!

—Melanie Chism
Coker, Alabama

4 medium green tomatoes
1 teaspoon salt
1/4 teaspoon lemon-pepper seasoning
3/4 cup cornmeal
1/2 cup vegetable oil

Slice tomatoes 1/4 in. thick. Sprinkle both sides with salt and lemon-pepper. Let stand for 20-25 minutes. Coat with cornmeal. In a large skillet, heat oil over medium heat. Fry tomatoes for 3-4 minutes on each side or until tender and golden brown. Drain on paper towels. Serve immediately. **Yield:** 6-8 servings.

BAKED GREEN TOMATOES Cut 4 medium green tomatoes into 1/2-inch slices; arrange in a greased baking dish. Season with salt and pepper. Sprinkle 1/2 cup brown sugar and 3/4 cup buttery cracker crumbs over the top; dot with 4 tablespoons butter. Bake at 350° for 25-35 minutes or until tender but still firm.

Cheesy Broccoli Macaroni

You'll need just four ingredients to fix this macaroni and cheese that gets extra flavor from broccoli and bacon. It's a quick and easy dish, and it makes a nice lunch or side dish for supper.
—Dorothy Pritchett
Wills Point, Texas

1 cup frozen chopped broccoli
8 ounces process cheese (Velveeta), cubed
2-1/2 cups cooked elbow macaroni
3 bacon strips, cooked and crumbled

In a large saucepan, cook broccoli according to package directions until crisp-tender; drain. Add the cheese; cook and stir over medium-low heat until cheese is melted. Add macaroni; heat through. Sprinkle with bacon. **Yield:** 4 servings.

|PASTA POINTER| Cook the elbow macaroni for Cheesy Broccoli Macaroni ahead of time. It can be stored in the refrigerator up to 2 days in an airtight container. Warm the pasta by placing it in a colander and rinsing it with hot water. Drain well before adding to the recipe.

Cinnamon Cream Syrup

Looking for a change of pace from maple syrup? Try this special topping. It jazzes up pancakes, waffles or French toast.
—Mrs. Hamilton Myers Jr., Charlottesville, Virginia

1 cup sugar
1/2 cup light corn syrup
1/4 cup water
3/4 teaspoon ground cinnamon
1/2 cup evaporated milk

In a saucepan, combine the sugar, corn syrup, water and cinnamon; bring to a boil over medium heat. Boil for 2 minutes or until thickened. Remove from the heat; cool for 5 minutes. Stir in milk. **Yield:** 1-1/2 cups.

|SWEET SUGGESTION| Before measuring syrupy sweeteners such as honey and corn syrup, lightly coat the measuring cup with vegetable oil. Every drop of the syrup will easily slip out instead of clinging to the sides of the cup. Use clear measuring cups for syrups.

Green Bean Bundles

I like to bake green beans in little bundles secured with strips of bacon. A few minutes under the broiler makes the bacon crispy. This dish gets its tang from Italian dressing, which the beans are baked in.
—*Ame Andrews, Little Rock, Arkansas*

6 cups water
1/2 pound fresh green beans, trimmed
4 to 6 bacon strips
3/4 cup Italian salad dressing

In a saucepan, bring water to a boil. Add beans; cover and cook for 3 minutes. Drain and set aside. Cut bacon in half lengthwise; place on a microwave-safe plate. Microwave on high for 2-1/2 to 3 minutes or until edges curl. Place four or five beans on each bacon strip; wrap bacon around beans and tie in a knot.

Place bundles in an 8-in. square baking dish. Drizzle with salad dressing. Bake, uncovered, at 350° for 10-15 minutes or until beans are crisp-tender. Broil 4 in. from the heat for 2-3 minutes or until bacon is crisp. **Yield:** 4-6 servings.

Seafood Stuffing

For an easy and elegant side dish, I add canned crab and shrimp to boxed stuffing mix. When I served this to my mom as part of her birthday dinner, she said it was the best she had ever tasted...and next time she wanted just the stuffing for her meal!
—*Marcy Thrall, Haddam Neck, Connecticut*

1 package (6 ounces) instant chicken-flavored stuffing mix
1 can (6 ounces) crabmeat, drained and cartilage removed *or* 1 cup imitation crabmeat
1 can (6 ounces) small shrimp, rinsed and drained *or* 1 cup frozen small cooked shrimp
1 teaspoon lemon juice

Prepare stuffing according to package directions. Gently stir in crab, shrimp and lemon juice. Serve immediately. **Yield:** 4-6 servings.

Sweet 'n' Sour Rhubarb Sauce

The beauty of this easy sauce is its natural bright-red color and its versatility. It's so good served over chicken, turkey or pork.

—*Sharon Logan, Fort Atkinson, Wisconsin*

**4 cups diced fresh *or*
frozen rhubarb, thawed**
**2 cups fresh *or* frozen
cranberries**
1-1/4 cups sugar
1/2 cup orange juice
1/2 cup honey

In a large saucepan, combine all ingredients. Bring to a boil; reduce heat. Simmer, uncovered, for 15-20 minutes or until rhubarb is tender and sauce is thickened. **Yield:** 3-3/4 cups.

Fruited Sweet Potatoes

I dress up convenient canned sweet potatoes and apricot halves with brown sugar and cinnamon. This fast-to-fix side dish is delicious with a ham dinner.

—*Nancy Zimmerman*
Cape May Court House, New Jersey

✓ **Uses less fat, sugar or salt.
Includes Nutritional Analysis
and Diabetic Exchanges.**

**2 cans (15 ounces *each*)
cut sweet potatoes**
**1 can (15-1/4 ounces)
apricot halves**
3 tablespoons brown sugar
1 tablespoon cornstarch
**1/8 teaspoon ground
cinnamon**

Drain sweet potatoes and apricots, reserving 1/2 cup syrup from each. If desired, cut apricots into fourths. Place potatoes and apricots in a greased 1-1/2-qt. baking dish.

In a saucepan, combine brown sugar, cornstarch, cinnamon and reserved syrup; stir until smooth. Bring to a boil over medium-high heat. Remove from the heat; pour over potatoes and apricots. Bake, uncovered, at 350° for 25 minutes or until bubbly. **Yield:** 6 servings.

Nutritional Analysis: One 1/2-cup serving (prepared with light apricot halves) equals 192 calories, 68 mg sodium, 0 cholesterol, 46 g carbohydrate, 2 g protein, trace fat. **Diabetic Exchanges:** 2 starch, 1 fruit.

Bacon Cheese Fries

These tempting potatoes are one finger food I can make a meal of. Quick to fix, they're a hit with dinner guests. Ranch dressing is a tasty alternative to sour cream. —*Marilyn Dutkus*
Laguna Beach, California

1 package (32 ounces) frozen French fried potatoes
1 cup (4 ounces) shredded cheddar cheese
1/2 cup thinly sliced green onions
1/4 cup cooked crumbled bacon
Ranch salad dressing

Cook French fries according to package directions. Place fries on a broiler-proof dish or platter. Sprinkle with cheese, onions and bacon. Broil for 1-2 minutes or until cheese is melted. Serve with ranch dressing. **Yield:** 8-10 servings.

Green Chili Rice

With only five ingredients, this rich and creamy rice casserole mixes up in a snap. I always get requests for the recipe.
—*Sandra Hanson, Emery, South Dakota*

1 can (10-3/4 ounces) condensed cream of celery soup, undiluted
1 cup (8 ounces) sour cream
1 can (4 ounces) chopped green chilies
1 cup (4 ounces) shredded cheddar cheese
1-1/2 cups uncooked instant rice

In a bowl, combine the soup, sour cream, chilies and cheese. Stir in rice. Transfer to a greased shallow 1-1/2-qt. baking dish. Bake, uncovered, at 350° for 20 minutes or until rice is tender. **Yield:** 4-6 servings.

Creamy Sweet Corn

I like to use half-and-half cream to dress up both fresh and frozen corn. The simple side dish tastes rich and takes just minutes to simmer together on the stovetop.

—*Florence Jacoby*
Granite Falls, Minnesota

2 cups fresh *or* frozen corn
1/4 cup half-and-half cream
2 tablespoons butter
1 tablespoon sugar
1/2 teaspoon salt

In a saucepan, combine all ingredients. Bring to a boil over medium heat; reduce heat. Simmer, uncovered, for 6-8 minutes or until heated through. **Yield:** 4 servings.

Light Scalloped Potatoes

Even with lighter ingredients like reduced-sodium chicken bouillon and Parmesan cheese, this is a comforting potato dish.

—*Tamie Foley, Pasadena, California*

 Uses less fat, sugar or salt. Includes Nutritional Analysis and Diabetic Exchanges.

6 medium potatoes, peeled and thinly sliced
3 cups water
4 reduced-sodium chicken bouillon cubes
1 garlic clove, minced
1/2 cup grated Parmesan cheese
Minced fresh parsley, optional

Place potatoes in a greased 2-qt. baking dish that has been coated with nonstick cooking spray. In a saucepan, heat water, bouillon and garlic until bouillon is dissolved; pour over potatoes. Sprinkle with Parmesan cheese.

Bake, uncovered, at 350° for 1-1/4 to 1-1/2 hours or until tender. Let stand 10 minutes before serving. Sprinkle with parsley if desired. Serve with a slotted spoon. **Yield:** 6 servings.

Nutritional Analysis: One 1/2-cup serving equals 175 calories, 168 mg sodium, 7 mg cholesterol, 32 g carbohydrate, 3 g protein, 3 g fat. **Diabetic Exchanges:** 2 starch, 1/2 fat.

|HOT POTATO HINTS| Store potatoes in a basket, net bag or paper bag in a dry, dark, cool, well-ventilated area for up to 2 weeks; do not refrigerate. Refrigerating potatoes causes them to become overly sweet and to turn dark when cooked.

Crunchy Celery Casserole

I first sampled this tempting treatment for celery when a friend brought it to a 4-H covered dish dinner. We could not believe how good it tastes or how easy it is to prepare in the microwave.

—*Michelle Garretson, Newcomerstown, Ohio*

10 celery ribs, thinly sliced
2 cans (10-3/4 ounces *each*) condensed cream of celery soup, undiluted
1 can (8 ounces) sliced water chestnuts, drained
1 can (2.8 ounces) french-fried onions

In a bowl, combine the celery, soup and water chestnuts. Pour into a greased microwave-safe 8-in. square dish. Cover and microwave on high for 27 minutes or until the celery is tender, stirring every 5 minutes. Sprinkle with onions. Microwave, uncovered, 5 minutes longer. **Yield:** 8 servings.

Editor's Note: This recipe was tested in an 850-watt microwave.

Noodle Rice Pilaf

By adding a few fine egg noodles to a rice pilaf, you can have a deliciously different side dish. Terrific with fish, this dish also goes well with meat or poultry.

—*Kathy Schrecengost, Oswego, New York*

1/4 cup butter
1 cup long grain rice
1/2 cup uncooked fine egg noodles *or* vermicelli
2-3/4 cups chicken broth
2 tablespoons minced fresh parsley

In a saucepan, melt butter. Add the rice and noodles; cook and stir until lightly browned, about 3 minutes. Stir in broth; bring to a boil. Reduce heat; cover and simmer for 20-25 minutes or until broth is absorbed and rice is tender. Stir in parsley. **Yield:** 4 servings.

Tangy Barbecue Sauce

This sweet and tangy basting sauce came from my husband's family. With just four ingredients, it's simple to stir up. A speedy alternative to bottled sauce, it can be brushed on chicken, ribs, pork or even turkey.

—*Jenine Schmidt, Stoughton, Wisconsin*

1 cup ketchup
2/3 cup packed brown sugar
2 teaspoons prepared mustard
1/2 teaspoon ground nutmeg

In a bowl, combine all ingredients. Store in the refrigerator. **Yield:** 1-1/3 cups.

|BASTING BASICS| When grilling, brush on thick or sweet sauces during the last 10 to 15 minutes of cooking, basting and turning every few minutes to prevent burning. Use tongs to turn meat instead of a meat fork to avoid piercing and losing juices.

Glazed Carrot Coins

When I pull fresh carrots from the garden, my mouth waters just thinking about how this simple recipe enhances their flavor with brown sugar and a hint of lemon.

—*Pat Habiger, Spearville, Kansas*

12 medium carrots, cut into 1-inch pieces
1/2 cup packed brown sugar
3 tablespoons butter
1 tablespoon grated lemon peel
1/4 teaspoon vanilla extract

In a saucepan, cook carrots in a small amount of water until crisp-tender; drain. Remove and keep warm. In the same pan, heat brown sugar and butter until bubbly. Stir in lemon peel.

Return carrots to pan; cook and stir over low heat for 10-15 minutes or until glazed. Remove from the heat; stir in vanilla. **Yield:** 6 servings.

Asparagus With Pimientos

This lovely, simple-to-prepare spring dish highlights the asparagus rather than hiding it. The delicate topping of Parmesan cheese and bread crumbs complements the asparagus flavor and looks impressive.

—Adeline Piscitelli
Sayreville, New Jersey

1 pound fresh asparagus, trimmed
1/4 cup dry bread crumbs
3 tablespoons butter
2 tablespoons grated Parmesan cheese
2 tablespoons chopped pimientos

In a saucepan over medium heat, cook asparagus in boiling salted water until tender, about 8 minutes. Meanwhile, in a skillet, brown bread crumbs in butter. Drain asparagus; place in a serving dish. Sprinkle with crumbs, cheese and pimientos. **Yield:** 4-6 servings.

|ASPARAGUS TIPS| Choose firm, bright-green stalks with tight tips. Avoid limp, dry-looking spears. In general, the thinner the spear, the more tender it will be. If you pick asparagus stalks that are all approximately the same size and thickness, they'll cook more evenly.

Creamy Horseradish Sauce

My favorite way to use this sauce is on cold roast beef sandwiches. But it really complements a variety of foods.

—Florence Palmer, Marshall, Illinois

1 cup heavy whipping cream
1 cup mayonnaise
1/8 teaspoon salt
1/4 cup prepared horseradish

In a mixing bowl, whip cream until soft peaks form. Add mayonnaise and salt; blend thoroughly. Fold in horseradish. Store in the refrigerator. **Yield:** 3-1/2 cups.

|ABOUT HORSERADISH| Prepared horseradish is available white (preserved in vinegar) and red (preserved in beet juice). Store it in a tightly covered jar in the refrigerator; it will keep about 4 to 6 weeks. Stored in the freezer, it'll last 6 months. As prepared horseradish ages, it darkens and loses its pungency.

Savory Sprouts

Cream of chicken soup creates the easy sauce that coats these tender sprouts. Seasoned with thyme and sprinkled with sliced almonds, this side dish is special enough for guests.　*—Daphne Blandford Gander, Newfoundland*

1 package (16 ounces) frozen brussels sprouts
1 can (10-3/4 ounces) condensed cream of chicken soup, undiluted
3 tablespoons milk
1/4 teaspoon dried thyme
1/4 cup sliced almonds, toasted

Cut an X in the core of each brussels sprout. In a saucepan, cook brussels sprouts according to package directions; drain. Remove sprouts and set aside.

To the saucepan, add soup, milk and thyme; heat through. Return sprouts to pan; stir to coat. Transfer to a serving dish; sprinkle with almonds. **Yield:** 4-6 servings.

Breaded Eggplant Slices

These crisp golden rounds are a fun and different way to serve eggplant. Even folks who aren't fond of eggplant like it fixed this way.　*—Phyllis Schmalz, Kansas City, Kansas*

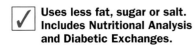 **Uses less fat, sugar or salt. Includes Nutritional Analysis and Diabetic Exchanges.**

1 medium eggplant (about 1 pound)
1/2 cup dry bread crumbs
1/4 cup grated Parmesan cheese
1 bottle (8 ounces) fat-free Italian salad dressing

Cut eggplant into 1/2-in. slices. In a shallow bowl, combine bread crumbs and Parmesan cheese. Place salad dressing in another bowl. Dip eggplant into salad dressing, then coat with crumb mixture.

Arrange in a single layer on baking sheets coated with non-stick cooking spray. Bake at 450° for 12-15 minutes or until golden brown, turning once. **Yield:** 4 servings.

Nutritional Analysis: One serving equals 153 calories, 3 g fat (2 g saturated fat), 7 mg cholesterol, 975 mg sodium, 25 g carbohydrate, 4 g fiber, 6 g protein. **Diabetic Exchanges:** 2 vegetable, 1 starch.

Stewed Tomato Pasta

I'm the mother of two very active boys, and this flavorful dish is one they'll always eat. Another reason I love it is because I usually have the ingredients on hand. —*Tracey Jones, Chesapeake, Virginia*

 ✓ Uses less fat, sugar or salt. Includes Nutritional Analysis and Diabetic Exchanges.

> 2 cans (14-1/2 ounces *each*) Italian stewed tomatoes, undrained
> 1 can (14-1/2 ounces) chicken broth
> 2 tablespoons vegetable oil
> 1 teaspoon Italian seasoning
> 1 package (12 ounces) spiral pasta

In a large saucepan or Dutch oven, combine the tomatoes, broth, oil and Italian seasoning; bring to a boil. Add pasta. Reduce heat; cover and simmer for 16-18 minutes or until pasta is tender, stirring occasionally. **Yield:** 8-10 servings.

Nutritional Analysis: One 3/4-cup serving (prepared with reduced-sodium broth) equals 217 calories, 243 mg sodium, 1 mg cholesterol, 37 g carbohydrate, 6 g protein, 5 g fat. **Diabetic Exchanges:** 2 starch, 1 vegetable, 1 fat.

Maple Apple Topping

I discovered this sweet topping when I had an abundance of apples to use up. It's a great alternative to bottled syrup. My family enjoys the tender apples and crunchy nuts over waffles, but the topping is also wonderful over slices of pound cake or scoops of vanilla ice cream.
—*Ruth Harrow*
Alexandria, New Hampshire

> 1/2 cup butter
> 3 large tart apples, peeled and sliced
> 1-1/2 cups maple syrup
> 1 teaspoon ground cinnamon
> 1/2 cup chopped nuts

In a large skillet, melt butter. Add the apples, syrup and cinnamon. Cook and stir over medium-low heat until apples are tender. Stir in nuts. **Yield:** 8 servings.

Peppered Corn

This peppy side dish is always the first to disappear whenever I take it to a potluck dinner. The jalapeno peppers add just the right amount of zip to the corn. —*Kim Garner, Batesville, Arkansas*

1 package (8 ounces)
  cream cheese, cubed
1/3 cup butter
2 cans (11 ounces *each*)
  Mexicorn, drained
2 to 4 medium jalapeno
  peppers, seeded and
  minced

In a saucepan over low heat, cook and stir the cream cheese and butter until smooth. Stir in corn and jalapenos. Pour into an ungreased 8-in. square baking dish. Bake, uncovered, at 350° for 15-20 minutes or until bubbly. **Yield:** 6-8 servings.

Editor's Note: When cutting or seeding hot peppers, use rubber or plastic gloves to protect your hands. Avoid touching your face.

Easy Berry Relish

This tart, flavorful relish will catch your eye and entice your taste buds. It captures the flavor of the holiday season and adds beautiful color to a meal. Plus, it only has five ingredients. Your guests will be impressed. —*Dorothy Anderson Ottawa, Kansas*

1 package (12 ounces)
  fresh *or* frozen
  cranberries
2-1/2 cups sugar
1-2/3 cups ginger ale
1/3 cup lemon juice
1 package (3 ounces)
  raspberry gelatin

In a saucepan, combine the first four ingredients. Cook over medium heat until the berries pop, about 15 minutes. Remove from the heat; stir in gelatin until dissolved. Pour into serving bowl. Chill overnight. **Yield:** 5 cups.

Golden Potatoes

Golden Potatoes make even canned potatoes taste terrific. I like to serve my fancy-looking side dish to company because it looks like I fussed to make it.
—Carla Cagle
Marceline, Missouri

2 cans (15 ounces *each*) whole white potatoes, drained
1/4 cup butter, melted
1/2 teaspoon seasoned salt
2 to 3 tablespoons grated Parmesan cheese
1 tablespoon minced fresh parsley

Place potatoes in an ungreased 8-in. square baking dish. Pour butter over potatoes. Sprinkle with seasoned salt, cheese and parsley. Bake, uncovered, at 350° for 25 minutes. **Yield:** 4-6 servings.

|A "GRATE" IDEA| Firm cheeses like Parmesan are easier to grate if they're at room temperature. They can be grated ahead of time and refrigerated in a plastic bag until ready to use. If grated cheese sticks together, simply break up the pieces with your fingers.

Creamy Baked Spinach

Cream cheese turns ordinary spinach into a side dish that's pretty enough to serve company. This casserole is a snap to stir up because it relies on convenient frozen chopped spinach.
—Beverly Albrecht, Beatrice, Nebraska

2 packages (10 ounces *each*) frozen chopped spinach
2 packages (3 ounces *each*) cream cheese, softened
4 tablespoons butter, *divided*
1/4 teaspoon salt
1/2 cup seasoned bread crumbs

Cook spinach according to package directions; drain well. Stir in cream cheese, 2 tablespoons butter and salt. Transfer to a greased 1-qt. baking dish.

Melt remaining butter; toss with bread crumbs. Sprinkle over spinach mixture. Bake, uncovered, at 350° for 20 minutes or until lightly browned. **Yield:** 4-6 servings.

Glorified Hash Browns

You'll be surprised at how quick and easy it is to put together this dressed-up potato casserole! When a friend made it for a church supper, I had to have the recipe. It's great for parties, potlucks and family reunions.
—Betty Sitzman
Wray, Colorado

2 cans (10-3/4 ounces each) condensed cream of celery soup, undiluted
2 cartons (8 ounces each) spreadable chive and onion cream cheese
1 package (2 pounds) frozen cubed hash brown potatoes
1 cup (4 ounces) shredded cheddar cheese

In a large microwave-safe bowl, combine the soup and cream cheese. Cover and cook on high for 3-4 minutes or until cream cheese is melted, stirring occasionally. Add the potatoes and stir until coated.

Spoon into a greased 13-in. x 9-in. x 2-in. baking dish. Bake, uncovered, at 350° for 35-40 minutes or until the potatoes are tender. Sprinkle with cheddar cheese. Bake 3-5 minutes longer or until the cheese is melted. **Yield:** 10 servings.

Steamed Artichokes with Lemon Sauce

My husband created this smooth, tangy sauce back in the '60s. It complements the steamed artichokes, whether they're served warm or cold.
—Lois Gelzer, Oak Bluffs, Massachusetts

 Uses less fat, sugar or salt. Includes Nutritional Analysis and Diabetic Exchanges.

6 medium fresh artichokes
1-1/2 cups mayonnaise
4-1/2 teaspoons lemon juice
3/4 teaspoon seasoned salt or salt-free seasoning blend
3 drops hot pepper sauce

Place the artichokes upside down in a steamer basket; place the basket in a saucepan over 1 in. of boiling water. Cover and steam for 25-35 minutes or until tender.

In a small bowl, combine the mayonnaise, lemon juice, salt and hot pepper sauce. Cover and refrigerate until serving with the steamed artichokes. **Yield:** 6 servings.

Nutritional Analysis: One serving (prepared with fat-free mayonnaise and salt-free seasoning blend) equals 102 calories, 534 mg sodium, 0 cholesterol, 22 g carbohydrate, 4 g protein, trace fat, 7 g fiber. **Diabetic Exchanges:** 1 starch, 1 vegetable.

Pickled Pumpkin

Cubes of pickled pumpkin make a tasty addition to any meal. We like to have this side dish as part of our Thanksgiving feast. The recipe's a great way to use up any extra pumpkins you might have on hand.

—*Myra Innes, Auburn, Kansas*

2 cups water
1 cup sugar
3-1/2 cups cubed peeled pie
    pumpkin
1/2 cup cider vinegar
1 teaspoon whole cloves

In a saucepan, bring water and sugar to a boil; cook and stir for 5 minutes. Add pumpkin, vinegar and cloves. Reduce heat; simmer, uncovered, for 1 hour and 15 minutes or until pumpkin is tender. Discard cloves. Store in the refrigerator for up to 3 weeks. **Yield:** 4 cups.

|PICK OF THE PATCH| Pumpkin varieties known as pie pumpkins are smaller than the jack-o'-lantern type and make flavorful puree for use in pies and cakes. One pie pumpkin (3 pounds) yields about 2 cups cooked pureed.

Country Baked Beans

After sampling these savory beans at our local John Deere dealer's open house, I asked for the recipe. To my surprise, they had started with canned beans and easily given them a wonderful homemade taste. —*Jill Steiner, Morris, Minnesota*

4 cans (16 ounces *each*)
    baked beans, drained
1 bottle (12 ounces) chili
    sauce
1 large onion, chopped
1 pound sliced bacon,
    cooked and crumbled
1 cup packed brown sugar

In two ungreased 2-qt. baking dishes, combine all of the ingredients. Stir until blended. Bake, uncovered, at 350° for 45-60 minutes or until heated through. **Yield:** 10-12 servings.

Cheesy Cauliflower

A can of cheese soup gives me a head start on Cheesy Cauliflower. This beautiful side dish takes less than 10 minutes to fix and disappears as soon as I serve it. It's even kid-tested and approved!
—*Edna Shaffer, Beulah, Michigan*

1 medium head cauliflower
(1-1/2 pounds)
1 can (10-3/4 ounces)
condensed cheddar
cheese soup, undiluted
1/8 teaspoon salt
1/4 teaspoon paprika

Break cauliflower into florets or leave whole; place in Dutch oven or large saucepan. Add 1 in. of water. Cover and steam until tender, 7-10 minutes for florets or 15-20 minutes for the whole head.

Meanwhile, heat soup and salt; serve over cauliflower. Sprinkle with paprika. **Yield:** 4-6 servings.

|CAULIFLOWER CLUES| Cook cauliflower only until crisp-tender. Overcooking will turn the texture mushy and the flavor strong. If you do overcook cauliflower, add butter and plenty of freshly ground pepper for a still-delicious dish.

South Liberty Hall Relish

My grandparents originated this recipe that's been treasured in our family for four generations. It's named after a dance hall they ran in rural Iowa. Whenever I bite into a hot dog or hamburger dressed up with this taste bud-tingling relish, I think of them and their delicious country cooking.
—*Melinda Winchell*
Las Vegas, Nevada

1 pint dill pickles, drained
1/4 cup chopped onion
2 to 3 tablespoons sugar
1/2 cup yellow mustard

Place the pickles and onion in a food processor; cover and process until finely chopped. Transfer to a bowl; stir in sugar and mustard. Cover and store in the refrigerator for up to 1 week. **Yield:** 2 cups.

Bacon-Wrapped Corn

The incredible flavor of roasted corn combined with bacon and chili powder is sure to please your palate and bring rave reviews at your next backyard barbecue. —*Lori Bramble
Omaha, Nebraska*

8 large ears sweet corn, husks removed
8 bacon strips
2 tablespoons chili powder

Wrap each ear of corn with a bacon strip; place each corn cob on a piece of heavy-duty aluminum foil. Sprinkle with chili powder. Wrap securely, twisting ends to make handles for turning.

Grill, uncovered, over medium-hot heat for 20 minutes or until corn is tender and bacon is cooked, turning once. **Yield:** 8 servings.

|CORN COBS| Sweet corn is available with bright yellow or white kernels or a mix of both. Ears should have plump, tender, small kernels in tight rows up to the tip. Kernels should be firm enough to resist slight pressure; a fresh kernel will spurt "milk" if punctured.

Seasoned Potato Wedges

Seasoned Potato Wedges are a tasty accompaniment to hot sandwiches or most any entree. The recipe is easy because you don't peel the potatoes, and you can sprinkle different seasonings on for variety. We also like them with ranch salad dressing and sprinkled with chives. —*Linda Hartsell
Apple Creek, Ohio*

4 medium russet potatoes
2 to 3 tablespoons mayonnaise
1 to 2 teaspoons seasoned salt

Cut the potatoes in half lengthwise; cut each half lengthwise into three wedges. Place in a single layer on a greased baking sheet.

Spread mayonnaise over cut sides of potatoes; sprinkle with seasoned salt. Bake at 350° for 50-60 minutes or until tender. **Yield:** 4 servings.

Creole Rice

I've found a fast and fantastic way to turn leftover rice into a spectacular side dish. I spice it up with Creole seasoning and pepper to give it a boost of flavor, then sprinkle it with paprika for color. Rest assured that no one will figure out the zippy combination is a "second-day dish".
—*Sundra Lewis, Bogalusa, Louisiana*

1/4 cup butter
1 teaspoon Creole seasoning
1/8 teaspoon pepper
2 cups cooked long grain rice

In a saucepan, melt butter; add Creole seasoning and pepper. Cook over medium heat for 3 minutes. Stir in rice. Cover and heat through. **Yield:** 4 servings.

Editor's Note: The following spices may be substituted for the Creole seasoning—1/2 teaspoon *each* paprika and garlic powder, and a pinch *each* cayenne pepper, dried thyme and ground cumin.

Low-Fat Refried Beans

A local Mexican restaurant shared this recipe with me. It's so simple and tasty you'll never go back to canned refried beans.
—*Kitty Shelton, Ketchum, Idaho*

 Uses less fat, sugar or salt. Includes Nutritional Analysis and Diabetic Exchanges.

1 package (16 ounces) dried pinto *or* red beans
1 large onion, quartered
3 garlic cloves
1/2 teaspoon ground cumin
3 to 4 drops hot pepper sauce

Place beans in a Dutch oven; add water to cover by 2 in. Bring to a boil; boil for 2 minutes. Remove from the heat; cover and let stand for 1 hour. Drain beans; discard liquid.

Return beans to pan; add water to cover. Add onion and garlic; bring to a boil. Cover and cook over low heat for 2 hours or until beans are very tender, adding water to keep covered if needed. Discard onion and garlic. Mash beans with a potato masher, leaving some beans whole. Stir in cumin and hot pepper sauce. **Yield:** 9 servings.

Nutritional Analysis: One 1/2-cup serving equals 180 calories, 6 mg sodium, 0 cholesterol, 34 g carbohydrate, 11 g protein, 1 g fat. **Diabetic Exchanges:** 2 starch, 1 vegetable.

Crispy Mashed Potato Pancake

Here is a tasty secret for using up leftover mashed potatoes. With just a few basic ingredients, I can fry up this delightful dish in a matter of minutes. —*Mary Schuster, Scottsdale, Arizona*

2 cups cold mashed potatoes (prepared with milk and butter)
1 egg, lightly beaten
1 teaspoon Italian seasoning
1/8 teaspoon garlic powder
1 tablespoon olive oil

Combine the first four ingredients; mix well. In a small skillet, heat oil over medium-high heat. Add potato mixture; press with a spatula to flatten evenly. Cover and cook for 8 minutes or until bottom is crispy. Invert onto a serving plate. **Yield:** 3 servings.

Creamy Vegetable Casserole

Searching for a different way to prepare vegetables? Look no further. I have a fussy eater in my house who absolutely loves this medley. It can be assembled in a snap, leaving time to fix the main course, set the table or just sit back and relax. —*Tami Kratzer*
West Jordan, Utah

1 package (16 ounces) frozen broccoli, carrots and cauliflower
1 can (10-3/4 ounces) condensed cream of mushroom soup, undiluted
1 carton (8 ounces) spreadable garden vegetable cream cheese
1/2 to 1 cup seasoned croutons

Prepare vegetables according to package directions; drain and place in a large bowl. Stir in soup and cream cheese. Transfer to a greased 1-qt. baking dish. Sprinkle with croutons. Bake, uncovered, at 375° for 25 minutes or until bubbly. **Yield:** 6 servings.

|FROZEN ASSETS| Frozen vegetables such as corn and peas don't require thawing before being added to dishes like soups and casseroles. Such frozen vegetables can also be added to stir-fries, provided they'll be cooked long enough to thaw.

Roasted Tarragon Asparagus

My simple seasoning turns fresh asparagus spears into a special spring side dish that's speedy, too. Oven-roasting the asparagus gives a depth of flavor that is complemented by the tarragon.

—Joyce Speckman, Holt, California

1-1/2 pounds fresh asparagus, trimmed
2 to 3 tablespoons olive oil
1/2 teaspoon coarsely ground pepper
1/8 teaspoon salt
1-1/2 teaspoons minced fresh tarragon *or* 1/2 teaspoon dried tarragon

Place asparagus in a shallow baking dish coated with non-stick cooking spray. Drizzle with oil; sprinkle with pepper and salt. Toss to coat.

Bake, uncovered, at 450° for 13-15 minutes or until crisp-tender, turning occasionally. Sprinkle with tarragon. **Yield:** 6 servings.

Broccoli Stir-Fry

Broccoli Stir-Fry is a great way to dress up a nutritious vegetable. As a wife and mother who also works full time, I'm pleased to pass along this easy recipe to other busy cooks. Broccoli stir-fried with lemon pepper makes a mouth-watering side dish.

—Susan Davis
Vernon Hills, Illinois

3 cups fresh broccoli florets
1/4 cup butter
1-1/2 teaspoons lemon-pepper seasoning

In a skillet over medium-high heat, stir-fry broccoli in butter and lemon pepper until crisp-tender, about 2-3 minutes. **Yield:** 4 servings.

Grilled Sweet Potatoes

I love trying new recipes, so my son-in-law suggested we grill sweet potatoes. Served with steak, they're a great change of pace from traditional baked potatoes...and they're pretty, too.
—*Lillian Neer*
Long Eddy, New York

 Uses less fat, sugar or salt. Includes Nutritional Analysis and Diabetic Exchanges.

2 large sweet potatoes, halved lengthwise
2 tablespoons butter, softened
Garlic salt and pepper to taste
2 teaspoons honey

Cut two pieces of heavy-duty foil (about 18 in. x 12 in.); place a potato half on each. Spread cut side with butter. Sprinkle with garlic salt and pepper. Top each potato with another half. Fold foil over potatoes and seal tightly.

Grill, covered, over medium-hot heat for 30 minutes or until tender, turning once. To serve, fluff potatoes with a fork and drizzle with honey. **Yield:** 4 servings.

Nutritional Analysis: One serving (prepared with margarine and without garlic salt) equals 123 calories, 73 mg sodium, 0 cholesterol, 16 g carbohydrate, 1 g protein, 6 g fat. **Diabetic Exchanges:** 1 starch, 1 fat.

|HOW SWEET IT IS| Sweet potato skins that are darker tend to be sweeter and moister; they are more nutritious if cooked in their skins. Sweet potatoes have a natural affinity for maple syrup and freshly grated nutmeg.

Spicy Mustard Spread

This zippy spread makes taste buds sit up and take notice. It's super on vegetables, hot dogs and hamburgers, in potato salad and more.
—*Audrey Thibodeau, Mesa, Arizona*

1/4 cup butter, softened
2 tablespoons ground mustard
2 tablespoons vinegar
1/4 teaspoon garlic salt
4 drops hot pepper sauce

In a mixing bowl, combine all ingredients; beat until smooth. Store in the refrigerator. **Yield:** about 1/3 cup.

Carrot Parsnip Stir-Fry

Orange carrot slivers and yellow parsnips make a pretty and different side dish. If parsnips aren't available, you could substitute rutabagas or turnips. Usually, I saute the vegetables until they are crisp-tender. But they're also quite good well-cooked, almost browned.

—Lavonne Hartel
Williston, North Dakota

1-1/2 pounds parsnips, peeled and julienned
1/4 cup butter
2 pounds carrots, julienned
2 tablespoons dried minced onion

In a large skillet, saute parsnips in butter for 3-4 minutes. Add carrots and onion; cook and stir until vegetables are tender, about 10-15 minutes. **Yield:** 8 servings.

Acorn Squash Slices

Acorn squash is a favorite with my family. This recipe gets sweet maple flavor from syrup and an appealing nuttiness from pecans. It's easy, too, because you don't have to peel the squash.

—Mrs. Richard Lamb, Williamsburg, Indiana

 Uses less fat, sugar or salt. Includes Nutritional Analysis and Diabetic Exchanges.

2 medium acorn squash (about 1-1/2 pounds each)
1/2 teaspoon salt
3/4 cup maple syrup
2 tablespoons butter, melted
1/3 cup chopped pecans, optional

Wash squash. Cut in half lengthwise; discard seeds and membrane. Cut each half crosswise into 1/2-in. slices; discard the ends. Place slices in a greased 13-in. x 9-in. x 2-in. baking dish. Sprinkle with salt.

Combine syrup and butter; pour over squash. Sprinkle with pecans if desired. Cover and bake at 350° for 40-45 minutes or until tender. **Yield:** 6 servings.

Nutritional Analysis: One serving of 2 slices (prepared with sugar-free maple-flavored pancake syrup, reduced-fat margarine and pecans) equals 170 calories, 98 mg sodium, 0 cholesterol, 31 g carbohydrate, 2 g protein, 7 g fat. **Diabetic Exchanges:** 1 starch, 1 fruit, 1 fat.

Simple Saucy Potatoes

These rich and creamy potatoes are simple to prepare for potlucks. This saucy side dish always gets rave reviews wherever I take it.
—*Gloria Schroeder, Ottawa Lake, Michigan*

4 cans (15 ounces *each*) sliced white potatoes, drained
2 cans (10-3/4 ounces *each*) condensed cream of celery soup, undiluted
2 cups (16 ounces) sour cream
10 bacon strips, cooked and crumbled
6 green onions, thinly sliced

Place potatoes in a slow cooker. Combine the remaining ingredients; pour over potatoes and mix well. Cover and cook on high for 4-5 hours. **Yield:** 12 servings.

|KITCHEN HELPER| A handy attribute of a slow cooker is that if you can't get home at exactly the time the food should be done, it generally doesn't hurt to leave it cooking on low for an extra hour.

Green Beans With a Twist

Green beans get a makeover with help from fresh mushrooms, ranch salad dressing mix and crumbled bacon. For added convenience, I sometimes use canned mushrooms when fixing this side dish.
—*Nicole Orr, Columbus, Ohio*

1 package (16 ounces) frozen French-style green beans
1 cup sliced fresh mushrooms
2 tablespoons butter
1 envelope ranch salad dressing mix
4 bacon strips, cooked and crumbled

In a skillet, saute the beans and mushrooms in butter. Sprinkle with dressing mix; toss to coat. Just before serving, sprinkle with bacon. **Yield:** 4-6 servings.

Bacon Cabbage Stir-Fry

If you like cabbage, you'll enjoy this stir-fried side dish. It's not only delicious, but fast to fix when you need to get dinner on the table quickly. —*Lori Thompson, New London, Texas*

6 bacon strips, diced
1 small head cabbage,
 chopped
1 teaspoon garlic powder
3/4 teaspoon salt
1/2 teaspoon ground mustard

In a large skillet, cook bacon over medium heat until crisp. Remove to paper towels; drain, reserving 1 tablespoon drippings. Stir-fry cabbage in drippings for 5 minutes. Add garlic powder, salt, mustard and bacon; cook and stir until heated through. **Yield:** 6 servings.

Roasted Fan-Shaped Potatoes

These wonderful oven-roasted potatoes are very pretty to serve—the partially cut slices spread out in the shape of a fan. Folks at a potluck can easily take as many slices as they want. I especially like these potatoes with ham, roast pork or beef. —*Eunice Stoen, Decorah, Iowa*

12 large baking potatoes
1/2 teaspoon salt
1/2 cup butter, melted,
 divided
 6 tablespoons dry bread
 crumbs
 6 tablespoons shredded
 Parmesan cheese

With a sharp knife, slice the potatoes thinly but not all the way through, leaving slices attached at the bottom. Place the potatoes in a greased shallow baking dish. Sprinkle with salt; brush with 1/4 cup butter. Bake, uncovered, at 425° for 30 minutes.

Brush potatoes with remaining butter and sprinkle with bread crumbs. Bake 20 minutes longer. Sprinkle with Parmesan cheese. Bake 5-10 minutes more or until potatoes are tender and golden brown. **Yield:** 12 servings.

Grilled Cherry Tomatoes

Seasoned with herbs and butter, Grilled Cherry Tomatoes make a colorful and tasty side dish. Just tuck the foil packet beside any meat you happen to be grilling. —*Lucy Meyring*
Walden, Colorado

**2 pints cherry tomatoes,
   halved**
2 garlic cloves, minced
1/2 teaspoon dried oregano
3 tablespoons butter

Place tomatoes on a double thickness of heavy-duty foil (about 24 in. x 12 in.). In a skillet, saute garlic and oregano in butter for 2 minutes. Pour over tomatoes. Fold foil around tomatoes and seal tightly.

Grill, covered, over medium heat for 8-10 minutes or until the tomatoes are heated through, turning once. **Yield:** 4-6 servings.

Warm Fruit Compote

Orange marmalade is the secret to the easy sauce I spoon over canned pineapple and fresh grapes. I then sprinkle the combination with coconut and broil it to create a warm, fruity surprise.
—*Doris Heath, Franklin, North Carolina*

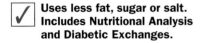 **Uses less fat, sugar or salt.
Includes Nutritional Analysis
and Diabetic Exchanges.**

**1 can (20 ounces)
   unsweetened pineapple
   chunks**
2 cups seedless grapes
**3 tablespoons orange
   marmalade**
**4 teaspoons flaked
   coconut**

Drain pineapple, reserving 2/3 cup juice. Combine the pineapple and grapes in a shallow 1-qt. broiler-proof dish.

In a saucepan, combine marmalade and reserved pineapple juice; cook over medium heat until the marmalade is melted. Pour over fruit. Sprinkle with coconut. Broil 5-6 in. from the heat for 3 minutes or until coconut is toasted. **Yield:** 4 servings.

Nutritional Analysis: One 1-cup serving (prepared with reduced-sugar marmalade) equals 168 calories, 7 mg sodium, 0 cholesterol, 43 g carbohydrate, 1 g protein, 1 g fat. **Diabetic Exchange:** 3 fruit.

Almond Currant Rice

Stirring in the almonds and currants at the last minute is a snap, and my daughter and I love the flavor of this side dish. You can substitute your favorite dried fruits and nuts if you like.
—*Felicia Johnson*
Oak Ridge, Louisiana

2 cups uncooked instant rice
2 tablespoons butter
1/4 teaspoon salt
1/4 cup chopped toasted almonds
1/4 cup dried currants

Prepare rice according to package directions, adding butter and salt. Just before serving, stir in almonds and currants. **Yield:** 4 servings.

Pasta with Basil

If you like basil, you'll enjoy the Italian flavor of this speedy side dish. This is one of my husband's favorites. It's super easy to make and tastes wonderful.   —*Jaime Hampton, Birmingham, Alabama*

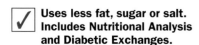 **Uses less fat, sugar or salt. Includes Nutritional Analysis and Diabetic Exchanges.**

2-1/2 cups uncooked small tube pasta
1 small onion, chopped
1 to 3 tablespoons olive oil
2 to 3 tablespoons dried basil
1 cup (4 ounces) shredded mozzarella cheese

Cook pasta according to package directions. Meanwhile, in a skillet, saute onion in oil until tender. Stir in basil; cook and stir for 1 minute.

Drain pasta; add to basil mixture. Remove from the heat; stir in cheese just until it begins to melt. Serve immediately. **Yield:** 4 servings.

Nutritional Analysis: One serving (prepared with 1 tablespoon oil and part-skim mozzarella cheese) equals 332 calories, 135 mg sodium, 16 mg cholesterol, 48 g carbohydrate, 15 g protein, 9 g fat, 2 g fiber. **Diabetic Exchanges:** 3 starch, 1 meat, 1 fat.

Vegetable Rice Skillet

A bag of frozen mixed vegetables conveniently dresses up plain rice in this recipe. It's short on ingredients and preparation time but long on satisfying flavor. —*Ruth Rigoni, Hurley, Wisconsin*

1 can (14-1/2 ounces) vegetable broth
2 tablespoons butter
1 package (16 ounces) frozen California-blend vegetables
1 package (6.2 ounces) fast-cooking long grain and wild rice mix
3/4 cup shredded cheddar cheese

In a large skillet, bring broth and butter to a boil. Stir in the vegetables and rice with seasoning packet. Return to a boil. Reduce heat; cover and simmer for 4-8 minutes or until vegetables and rice are tender. Sprinkle with cheese. **Yield:** 4-6 servings.

Caramelized Onions

These lightly golden onions have a delicate taste that complements green beans, peas and almost any type of meat. Try them over steaks, on burgers, with pork chops and more. —*Melba Lowery Rockwell, North Carolina*

4 large onions, thinly sliced
1/4 cup vegetable oil
3 tablespoons cider vinegar
2 tablespoons brown sugar

In a large skillet, saute onions in oil over medium heat until tender, about 15 minutes. Stir in vinegar and brown sugar. Cook 10 minutes longer or until onions are golden. **Yield:** 4-6 servings.

Cranberry Syrup

This flavorful syrup is so appealing over pancakes, your family will think they're in a fancy restaurant. It's very festive-looking to serve at a Christmas brunch. But we like it year-round as a change of pace from maple syrup. —*Teresa Gaetzke, North Freedom, Wisconsin*

1 cup sugar
1 cup packed brown sugar
1 cup cranberry juice
1/2 cup light corn syrup

In a saucepan, combine the sugars and cranberry juice; bring to a boil, stirring constantly. Boil for 4 minutes. Add corn syrup; boil and stir 1 minute longer. **Yield:** 2 cups.

Home-Style Mashed Potatoes

Leaving the tender skins on the spuds not only saves time, it sparks the taste and adds color to these hearty mashed potatoes. They're perfect with a pork roast and versatile enough to go well with other entrees. —*Christine Wilson Sellersville, Pennsylvania*

3 pounds red potatoes, quartered
2 teaspoons salt, *divided*
1/4 to 1/2 cup milk
5 tablespoons butter
1/4 teaspoon white pepper

Place potatoes in a large saucepan or Dutch oven; cover with water. Add 1 teaspoon salt. Cover and bring to a boil. Reduce heat; cook for 20-30 minutes or until very tender.

Drain potatoes well and place in a large mixing bowl. Add 1/4 cup milk, butter, pepper and remaining salt. Beat on low speed until potatoes are light and fluffy, adding remaining milk if needed. **Yield:** 8 servings.

Dilly Sweet Peas

A tongue-tingling side dish, Dilly Sweet Peas gets fun flavor from chopped dill pickles and pickle juice balanced with a bit of honey. My daughter and I always go back for seconds.

—*Felicia Johnson*
Oak Ridge, Louisiana

1 package (10 ounces) frozen peas
1/4 cup chopped dill pickles
2 tablespoons butter
1 tablespoon dill pickle juice
1 to 2 teaspoons honey

Prepare peas according to package directions; drain. Add remaining ingredients and toss to coat. **Yield:** 4 servings.

|COOKING PEAS| Be careful not to overcook peas; they should be crisp-tender when done. Overdone peas will lose their bright green color and much of their fresh flavor.

Gingered Squash and Pears

Butternut squash and pears are a delightful duo delicately seasoned with ginger, honey and nutmeg. This is a pretty dish, too.

—*Jane Rossi, Charlotte, North Carolina*

 Uses less fat, sugar or salt. Includes Nutritional Analysis and Diabetic Exchanges.

1 medium butternut squash, peeled, seeded and cubed (about 6-1/2 cups)
1 medium pear, peeled and cubed
1-1/2 teaspoons grated fresh gingerroot
1 tablespoon honey
1/8 teaspoon ground nutmeg

Place squash in a large skillet; cover with water. Bring to a boil. Reduce heat; cover and simmer for 10 minutes or until tender. Drain. Stir in pear and ginger. Cover and cook for 5-7 minutes or until pear is tender. Stir in honey and heat through. Sprinkle with nutmeg. **Yield:** 8 servings.

Nutritional Analysis: One serving (3/4 cup) equals 72 calories, trace fat (trace saturated fat), 0 cholesterol, 5 mg sodium, 19 g carbohydrate, 4 g fiber, 1 g protein. **Diabetic Exchange:** 1 starch.

Breads & Rolls

Cherry Cream Crescents (p. 203) and Orange Pull-Apart Bread (p. 202)

Teddy Bear Biscuits, p. 204

|ROLLS & MORE|

Banana-Nut Corn Bread, p. 207

Breads & Rolls   201

Cinnamon Nut Twists

These tender treats are good with a hot cup of coffee or a cold glass of milk. The golden twists have a pleasant cinnamon and nut filling and just a hint of sweetness.

—*Mary Van Domelen*
Appleton, Wisconsin

✓ **Uses less fat, sugar or salt. Includes Nutritional Analysis and Diabetic Exchanges.**

2 tubes (8 ounces *each*) refrigerated reduced-fat crescent rolls
2 tablespoons reduced-fat stick margarine
1/4 cup packed brown sugar
1 tablespoon ground cinnamon
1/3 cup finely chopped walnuts

Unroll both tubes of dough; press perforations and seams together to form two rectangles. Spread with margarine. Combine brown sugar and cinnamon; sprinkle over dough. Sprinkle with walnuts.

Fold each rectangle in half, starting from a short side. Cut each into eight strips. Twist each strip; tie into a knot. Place on ungreased baking sheets. Bake at 375° for 10-12 minutes or until golden brown. Serve warm. **Yield:** 16 servings.

Nutritional Analysis: One piece equals 139 calories, 7 g fat (1 g saturated fat), 0 cholesterol, 251 mg sodium, 16 g carbohydrate, trace fiber, 2 g protein. **Diabetic Exchanges:** 1 starch, 1 fat.

Orange Pull-Apart Bread

(Pictured on page 200)

The recipe for this appealing breakfast loaf came from my sister, who's an excellent cook. Brushed with a sweet orange glaze, the bread is so popular I usually double or triple the recipe.

—*Kristin Salzman, Fenton, Illinois*

1 tube (8 ounces) refrigerated crescent rolls
2 tablespoons butter, softened
2 tablespoons honey
1/2 to 1 teaspoon grated orange peel

Open tube of crescent rolls; do not unroll. Place on a greased baking sheet, forming one long roll. Cut into 12 slices to within 1/8 in. of bottom, being careful not to cut all the way through. Fold down alternating slices from left to right to form a loaf. Bake at 375° for 20-25 minutes or until golden brown. Combine butter, honey and orange peel; brush over the loaf. Serve warm. **Yield:** 6 servings.

Cherry Cream Crescents

(Pictured on page 200)

You'll need refrigerated crescent dough and just four more ingredients to assemble these fruity filled rolls. My family and friends love them. I never have any left over.
—*Elouise Bullion*
Kingsville, Texas

1 package (8 ounces)
cream cheese, softened
1 cup confectioners' sugar
1 egg, *separated*
2 tubes (8 ounces *each*)
refrigerated crescent
rolls
1 can (21 ounces) cherry
pie filling

In a mixing bowl, beat cream cheese, sugar and egg yolk. Separate dough into 16 triangles; place on lightly greased baking sheets. Spread 1 tablespoon of cream cheese mixture near the edge of the short side of each triangle. Top with 1 tablespoon pie filling.

Fold long point of triangle over filling and tuck under dough. Lightly beat egg white; brush over rolls. Bake at 350° for 15-20 minutes or until golden brown. **Yield:** 16 rolls.

Swiss-Onion Bread Ring

With the ease of prepared bread dough, this tempting cheesy bread has delicious down-home goodness. Its pleasant onion flavor goes great with any entree. You'll find it crisp and golden on the outside, rich and buttery on the inside. —*Judi Messina*
Coeur d'Alene, Idaho

2-1/2 teaspoons poppy seeds,
** *divided***
2 tubes (11 ounces *each*)
refrigerated French bread
dough
1 cup (4 ounces) shredded
Swiss cheese
3/4 cup sliced green onions
6 tablespoons butter,
melted

Sprinkle 1/2 teaspoon poppy seeds in a greased 10-in. fluted tube pan. Cut the dough into forty 1-in. pieces; place half in prepared pan. Sprinkle with half of the cheese and onions.

Top with 1 teaspoon poppy seeds; drizzle with half of the butter. Repeat layers. Bake at 375° for 30-35 minutes or until golden brown. Immediately invert onto a wire rack. Serve warm. **Yield:** 1 loaf.

Teddy Bear Biscuits

(Pictured on page 201)

Children can't resist helping to assemble these cute cinnamony bears before baking. Refrigerated biscuit dough makes them easy, convenient and fun! —*Catherine Berra Bleem, Walsh, Illinois*

1 tube (7-1/2 ounces) refrigerated buttermilk biscuits (10 biscuits)
1 egg, beaten
2 tablespoons sugar
1/4 teaspoon ground cinnamon
9 miniature semisweet chocolate chips

For each bear, shape one biscuit into an oval for the body and place on a greased baking sheet. Cut one biscuit into four pieces; shape into balls for arms and legs. Place next to body. Cut one biscuit into two small pieces and one large piece; shape into head and ears and place above body.

Brush with egg. Combine sugar and cinnamon; sprinkle over bears. Bake at 425° for 8-10 minutes (the one remaining biscuit can be baked with the bears). Place chocolate chips on head for eyes and nose while the biscuits are still warm. **Yield:** 3 bears.

Mini Cheddar Loaves

It's hard to believe you need only four ingredients to bake up a batch of these beautiful miniature loaves. Sliced warm from the oven, this golden bread is simple and delicious.
—*Melody Rowland*
Chattanooga, Tennessee

3-1/2 cups biscuit/baking mix
2-1/2 cups (10 ounces) shredded sharp cheddar cheese
2 eggs
1-1/4 cups milk

In a large bowl, combine biscuit mix and cheese. Beat eggs and milk; stir into cheese mixture just until moistened. Pour into four greased and floured 5-3/4-in. x 3-in. x 2-in. loaf pans.

Bake at 350° for 35-40 minutes or until a toothpick inserted near the center comes out clean. Cool for 10 minutes. Remove from pans; slice and serve warm. **Yield:** 4 mini loaves.

Editor's Note: Bread can also be made in one 9-in. x 5-in. x 3-in. loaf pan. Bake for 50-55 minutes.

Buttered Cornsticks

I need just three ingredients to stir together Buttered Cornsticks. Even with my family's hectic schedule, I like to prepare sit-down dinners during the week. This bread recipe is often on the menu.
—*Fran Shaffer, Coatesville, Pennsylvania*

2-2/3 cups biscuit/baking mix
1 can (8-1/2 ounces) cream-style corn
1/4 cup butter, melted

In a bowl, combine biscuit mix and corn. Stir until a soft dough forms. Knead on a lightly floured surface for 3 minutes. Roll into a 10-in. x 6-in. rectangle. Cut into 3-in. x 1-in. strips. Dip in butter.

Place in an ungreased 15-in. x 10-in. x 1-in. baking pan. Bake at 425° for 12-15 minutes or until golden brown. **Yield:** about 20 breadsticks.

Tex-Mex Biscuits

I love cooking with green chilies because they add so much flavor to ordinary dishes. Once while making a pot of chili, I had some green chilies left over and mixed them into my biscuit dough, creating this recipe. The fresh-from-the-oven treats are a wonderful accompaniment to soup or chili.
—*Angie Trolz, Jackson, Michigan*

2 cups biscuit/baking mix
2/3 cup milk
1 cup (4 ounces) finely shredded cheddar cheese
1 can (4 ounces) chopped green chilies, drained

In a bowl, combine biscuit mix and milk until a soft dough forms. Stir in cheese and chilies. Turn onto a floured surface; knead 10 times.

Roll out to 1/2-in. thickness; cut with a 2-1/2-in. biscuit cutter. Place on an ungreased baking sheet. Bake at 450° for 8-10 minutes or until golden brown. Serve warm. **Yield:** about 1 dozen.

Parmesan Breadsticks

These soft bread sticks are so easy to make and have wonderful homemade flavor. We enjoy them warm from the oven dipped in pizza sauce.
—Marlene Muckenhirn, Delano, Minnesota

3/4 cup grated Parmesan cheese
1-1/2 teaspoons dried Italian seasoning
1 loaf (1 pound) frozen white bread dough, thawed
1/4 cup butter, melted
Warm pizza sauce, optional

Combine cheese and Italian seasoning in a shallow bowl; set aside. Divide dough into 32 sections; roll each into a 5-in. rope. Twist two pieces together. Moisten ends with water and pinch to seal. Dip in butter, then in cheese mixture.

Place on a greased baking sheet. Bake at 400° for 10-14 minutes or until golden brown. Serve with pizza sauce for dipping if desired. **Yield:** 16 servings.

Savory Party Bread

It's impossible to stop nibbling on warm pieces of this cheesy, oniony bread. The sliced loaf fans out for a fun presentation at parties.
—Kay Daly
Raleigh, North Carolina

1 unsliced round loaf (1 pound) sourdough bread
1 pound Monterey Jack cheese, sliced
1/2 cup butter, melted
1/2 cup chopped green onions
2 to 3 teaspoons poppy seeds

Cut the bread lengthwise and crosswise without cutting through the bottom crust. Insert cheese between cuts. Combine butter, onions and poppy seeds; drizzle over the bread.

Wrap in foil; place on a baking sheet. Bake at 350° for 15 minutes. Uncover; bake 10 minutes longer or until the cheese is melted. **Yield:** 6-8 servings.

Cinnamon Fruit Biscuits

Because these sweet treats are so easy, I'm almost embarrassed when people ask me for the recipe. They're a snap to make with refrigerated buttermilk biscuits, sugar, cinnamon and strawberry preserves.
—Ione Burham
Washington, Iowa

1/2 cup sugar
1/2 teaspoon ground cinnamon
1 tube (12 ounces) refrigerated buttermilk biscuits, separated into 10 biscuits
1/4 cup butter, melted
10 teaspoons strawberry preserves

In a small bowl, combine the sugar and cinnamon. Dip top and sides of biscuits in butter, then in cinnamon-sugar. Place on ungreased baking sheets. With the end of a wooden spoon handle, make a deep indentation in the center of each biscuit; fill with 1 teaspoon preserves.

Bake at 375° for 15-18 minutes or until golden brown. Cool for 15 minutes before serving (preserves will be hot). **Yield:** 10 servings.

Banana-Nut Corn Bread

(Pictured on page 201)

A boxed corn bread mix gets a tasty treatment when dressed up with bananas and chopped walnuts. The moist golden loaves are a great addition to a brunch buffet or bake sale. *—Janice France*
Depauw, Indiana

2 packages (8-1/2 ounces *each*) corn bread/muffin mix
1 cup mashed ripe bananas (about 2 medium)
1 cup chopped walnuts
1 cup milk

In a bowl, combine all ingredients just until blended. Spoon into two greased 8-in. x 4-in. x 2-in. loaf pans. Bake at 350° for 35-40 minutes or until a toothpick inserted near the center comes out clean. Cool for 10 minutes before removing from pans to wire racks to cool completely. **Yield:** 2 loaves.

|GOING BANANAS| Peel and mash overripe bananas in a blender with 1 teaspoon lemon juice per banana. Spoon into an airtight container and freeze for up to 1 month. When you're ready to use the mixture, defrost overnight in the fridge.

Cordon Bleu Stromboli

My recipe has the taste of chicken cordon bleu without all the work. I roll Swiss cheese and deli meats into a swirled sandwich loaf that bakes to a golden brown. My entire gang looks forward to this stromboli.

—*Diane Schuelke, Madison, Minnesota*

1 loaf (1 pound) frozen bread dough, thawed
2 tablespoons butter, softened
8 ounces thinly sliced deli ham
1/2 cup shredded Swiss cheese
5 ounces thinly sliced deli chicken

On a lightly floured surface, roll dough into a 10-in. x 8-in. rectangle; spread with butter. Top with ham, cheese and chicken. Roll up jelly-roll style, starting with a long side; pinch seam to seal and tuck ends under.

Place seam side down on a greased baking sheet. Cover and let rise for 20 minutes. Bake at 350° for 25-30 minutes or until golden brown. Refrigerate any leftovers. **Yield:** 6 servings.

Bacon Biscuit Wreath

I showed my girl scout troop how to make this pretty golden wreath. The girls (and even some of their parents) enjoyed making and sampling the cheesy party appetizer. It's a snap to prepare with cheese spread and convenient refrigerated biscuits.

—*Kathy Kirkland*
Denham Springs, Louisiana

1 jar (5 ounces) sharp American cheese spread
3 tablespoons butter-flavored shortening
1 tube (12 ounces) flaky biscuits
4 bacon strips, cooked and crumbled
2 tablespoons minced fresh parsley

In a small saucepan, melt the cheese spread and shortening; stir until blended. Pour into a well-greased 6-cup ovenproof ring mold or 9-in. fluted tube pan. Cut each biscuit into quarters and place over cheese mixture.

Bake at 400° for 12-14 minutes or until golden brown. Immediately invert pan onto a serving platter and remove. Sprinkle with bacon and parsley. Serve warm. **Yield:** 10 servings.

Cheese Biscuits

Cheddar adds a burst of sunny flavor to these flaky biscuits. You can frequently find me in my kitchen making these tender treats. —*Donna Engel*
Portsmouth, Rhode Island

2 cups biscuit/baking mix
2/3 cup milk
1/2 cup shredded cheddar
    cheese
2 tablespoons butter,
    melted
1/2 teaspoon garlic powder

In a bowl, stir the biscuit mix, milk and cheese just until moistened. Drop by tablespoonfuls onto an ungreased baking sheet. Mix butter and garlic powder; brush over biscuits. Bake at 475° for 8-10 minutes or until golden brown. Serve warm. **Yield:** about 1-1/2 dozen.

Quick Cherry Turnovers

These fruit-filled pastries are my family's favorite at breakfast. You can substitute other fillings for cherry.
—*Elleen Oberrueter, Danbury, Iowa*

1 tube (8 ounces)
    refrigerated crescent
    rolls
1 cup cherry pie filling
1/2 cup confectioners' sugar
1 to 2 tablespoons milk

Unroll dough and separate into eight triangles; make four squares by pressing the seams of two triangles together and rolling into shape. Place on an ungreased baking sheet.

Spoon 1/4 cup pie filling in one corner of each square. Fold to make triangles; pinch to seal. Bake at 375° for 10-12 minutes or until golden. Mix sugar and milk; drizzle over turnovers. Serve warm. **Yield:** 4 servings.

Olive Pinwheel Bread

This attractive, well-seasoned loaf is perfect for parties but easy enough to prepare for every day. For extra flavor, stir in chunks of provolone cheese.
—*Barbara Manfra*
Saugus, Massachusetts

✓ **Uses less fat, sugar or salt. Includes Nutritional Analysis and Diabetic Exchanges.**

1 tube (10 ounces) refrigerated pizza crust
1 tablespoon olive oil
1 tablespoon minced fresh rosemary *or* 1 teaspoon dried rosemary, crushed
1/2 cup chopped ripe olives
1 egg yolk, lightly beaten

Unroll pizza dough and place on a lightly floured surface. Brush with oil; sprinkle with rosemary and olives. Roll up jelly-roll style, starting with a short side; pinch seam to seal and tuck ends under.

Place seam side down on a greased baking sheet. Brush with egg yolk. Bake at 350° for 20-25 minutes or until golden brown. Cool before cutting. **Yield:** 1 loaf (10 slices).

Nutritional Analysis: One slice equals 100 calories, 4 g fat (trace saturated fat), 21 mg cholesterol, 248 mg sodium, 14 g carbohydrate, 1 g fiber, 3 g protein. **Diabetic Exchanges:** 1 starch, 1/2 fat.

Tennessee Fry Bread

You'll need only four ingredients to fix this time-easing bread. We like it with scrambled eggs and fried potatoes for breakfast. Or dunk it in soup or serve it with coffee.
—*Theresa Sanchez*
Franklin, Tennessee

3 tablespoons butter
1 cup self-rising flour
1/2 cup buttermilk
All-purpose flour

Place butter in a 12-in. ovenproof skillet; place in a 450° oven for 2-3 minutes or until melted. In a bowl, combine flour and buttermilk just until moistened. Turn onto a surface dusted with all-purpose flour; knead 4-5 times.

Pat dough to 1/4-in. thickness. Cut with a 2-1/2-in. biscuit cutter. Place in a single layer in prepared pan; carefully turn to coat. Bake at 450° for 12-13 minutes or until golden brown. **Yield:** 8 servings.

Editor's Note: As a substitute for self-rising flour, place 1-1/2 teaspoons baking powder and 1/2 teaspoon salt in a measuring cup. Add all-purpose flour to measure 1 cup.

Coconut Pecan Rolls

Your family will enjoy the old-fashioned appeal of these nutty rolls. Convenient refrigerated breadsticks are dressed up with a coconut coating that's oh-so-good. —*Theresa Gingery, Blue Springs, Nebraska*

1 tablespoon sugar
1/2 teaspoon ground cinnamon
1 tube (11 ounces) refrigerated breadsticks
2/3 cup coconut pecan frosting
1/3 cup chopped pecans

In a small bowl, combine sugar and cinnamon. Remove bread-stick dough from tube (do not unroll); cut into eight slices with a serrated knife. Dip both sides of each slice in cinnamon-sugar.

Place in a greased 9-in. round baking pan. Spread with frosting; sprinkle with pecans. Bake at 350° for 25-30 minutes or until golden brown. Serve warm. **Yield:** 8 rolls.

Pull-Apart Bacon Bread

I stumbled across this recipe while looking for something different to take to a brunch. Boy, am I glad I did! Everyone asked for the recipe and could not believe it called for only five ingredients. It's the perfect item to bake for an informal get-together.
—*Traci Collins, Cheyenne, Wyoming*

12 bacon strips, diced
1 loaf (1 pound) frozen bread dough, thawed
2 tablespoons olive oil, *divided*
1 cup (4 ounces) shredded mozzarella cheese
1 envelope ranch salad dressing mix

In a skillet, cook bacon over medium heat for 5 minutes or until partially cooked; drain on paper towels. Roll out dough to 1/2-in. thickness; brush with 1 tablespoon of oil. Cut into 1-in. pieces; place in a large bowl. Add the bacon, cheese, dressing mix and remaining oil; toss to coat.

Arrange pieces in a 9-in. x 5-in. oval on a greased baking sheet, layering as needed. Cover and let rise in a warm place for 30 minutes or until doubled.

Bake at 350° for 15 minutes. Cover with foil; bake 5-10 minutes longer or until golden brown. **Yield:** 1 loaf.

Cinnamon Monkey Bread

This sweet cinnamon bread looks fancy and has an irresistible rich, buttery glaze when it comes out of the oven and is turned onto a platter. And, of course, it tastes absolutely scrumptious! We enjoy it with big glasses of cold milk.
—*Lisa Combs, Greenville, Ohio*

4 tubes (7-1/2 ounces *each*) refrigerated buttermilk biscuits
1/2 cup sugar
2 teaspoons ground cinnamon
1/2 cup butter, melted
1/2 cup packed brown sugar

Cut each biscuit into four pieces; shape into balls. In a small bowl, combine sugar and cinnamon. Roll each ball in cinnamon-sugar. Arrange evenly in a greased 10-in. fluted tube pan. Sprinkle with remaining cinnamon-sugar.

Combine butter and brown sugar; pour over the top. Bake at 350° for 35-40 minutes or until golden brown. Cool for 5 minutes before inverting bread onto a serving platter. **Yield:** 1 loaf.

Candy Bar Croissants

These croissants are a rich, buttery treat that combines convenient refrigerated crescent rolls and chocolate bars.
—*Beverly Sterling Gasport, New York*

1 tube (8 ounces) refrigerated crescent rolls
1 tablespoon butter, softened
2 plain milk chocolate candy bars (1.55 ounces *each*), broken into small pieces
1 egg, beaten
2 tablespoons sliced almonds

Unroll crescent roll dough; separate into triangles. Brush with butter. Arrange candy bar pieces evenly over triangles; roll up from the wide end.

Place point side down on a greased baking sheet; curve ends slightly. Brush with egg and sprinkle with almonds. Bake at 375° for 11-13 minutes or until golden brown. Cool on a wire rack. **Yield:** 8 servings.

Savory Biscuit Bites

These light, golden puffs are super simple to make, and their flavor is oh-so-good. Their small size makes them easy to munch, and they're wonderful warm or cold. —*Wendy Chilton, Brookeland, Texas*

1/4 cup butter, melted
2 tablespoons grated Parmesan cheese
1 tablespoon dried minced onion
1-1/2 teaspoons dried parsley flakes
1 package (12 ounces) refrigerated biscuits

In a bowl, combine butter, cheese, onion and parsley. Cut biscuits into quarters; roll in butter mixture. Place in a greased 15-in. x 10-in. x 1-in. baking pan; let stand for 25 minutes. Bake at 400° for 8 minutes or until lightly browned. **Yield:** 40 pieces.

Cheesy Corn Muffins

Meat lovers might like having little pieces of chopped ham added to these muffins. Or you could vary the shape and make a loaf of corn bread instead.
—*Joyce Hunsberger, Quakertown, Pennsylvania*

1/4 cup chopped onion
1 tablespoon butter
2 packages (8-1/2 ounces *each*) corn muffin mix
1/2 cup sour cream
1/2 cup shredded cheddar cheese

In a small skillet, saute onion in butter until tender; set aside. Prepare muffin mixes according to package directions; fold in the onion. Fill greased or paper-lined muffin cups two-thirds full. Combine sour cream and cheese; drop by rounded teaspoonfuls onto each muffin.

Bake at 400° for 15-20 minutes or until a toothpick inserted in muffin comes out clean. Cool in pan for 5 minutes before removing to a wire rack. **Yield:** 1 dozen.

Kids' Breadsticks

These cheesy breadsticks are simple to make because they start with convenient hot dog buns. I can whip up a batch in a matter of minutes...and they disappear just as quickly.
—*Mary Miller*
Fairfield, California

8 hot dog buns, split
6 tablespoons butter, melted
1 cup grated Parmesan cheese
2 to 3 tablespoons poppy *or* sesame seeds

Brush the cut sides of buns with butter. Place on ungreased baking sheets. Combine cheese and poppy or sesame seeds; sprinkle over buns. Bake at 450° for 7-9 minutes or until golden brown. **Yield:** 16 breadsticks.

Garlic Bubble Loaf

This lovely golden loaf has great garlic flavor in every bite. People go wild over this bread whenever I serve it. It's a fun change of pace from the more traditional slices of garlic bread. —*Carol Shields*
Summerville, Pennsylvania

1/4 cup butter, melted
1 tablespoon dried parsley flakes
1 teaspoon garlic powder
1/4 teaspoon garlic salt
1 loaf (1 pound) frozen white bread dough, thawed

In a bowl, combine butter, parsley, garlic powder and garlic salt. Cut dough into 1-in. pieces; dip into butter mixture. Layer in a greased 9-in. x 5-in. x 3-in. loaf pan. Cover and let rise until doubled, about 1 hour. Bake at 350° for 30 minutes or until golden brown. **Yield:** 1 loaf.

Monterey Ranch Bread

This cheesy loaf is a quick-and-easy addition to any meal. Or serve it as an appealing appetizer for a casual get-together.
—*Shirley Privratsky*
Dickinson, North Dakota

2 cups (8 ounces) shredded Monterey Jack cheese
3/4 cup ranch salad dressing with bacon
1 loaf (1 pound) unsliced French bread
2 tablespoons butter, melted
Minced fresh parsley

In a bowl, combine the cheese and salad dressing; set aside. Cut bread in half lengthwise; brush with butter. Place on baking sheets. Broil 4 in. from the heat until golden brown. Spread with cheese mixture.

Bake at 350° for 10-15 minutes or until cheese is melted. Sprinkle with parsley. Cut into 1-1/2-in. slices. **Yield:** 6-8 servings.

|FROM STALE TO SUPER| Make crostini with second-day French or Italian bread. Cut the bread into 1/4-inch-thick slices, brush one side with olive oil and broil about 30 seconds on each side or until crisp and golden brown. Crostini make great soup or salad accompaniments.

Fiesta Bread

A neighbor gave me this easy recipe more than 25 years ago, when my children were small. You can use your favorite seasoning mix, so it's very versatile.   —*Helen Carpenter, Highland Haven, Texas*

2 cups biscuit/baking mix
2/3 cup milk
4-1/2 teaspoons chili seasoning mix
2 tablespoons butter, melted

In a bowl, combine the biscuit mix, milk and seasoning mix; mix well. Pat into a greased 8-in. square baking dish; drizzle with butter. Bake at 425° for 15-17 minutes or until a toothpick inserted near the center comes out clean. **Yield:** 9 servings.

Editor's Note: Italian or ranch salad dressing mix, taco seasoning or onion soup mix may be substituted for the chili seasoning mix.

Banana Nut Bread

A yellow cake mix streamlines assembly of this moist golden bread. I searched a long while for a banana bread that was easy to make. This one takes no time at all, and makes two loaves, so one can be frozen to enjoy later.
—*Marie Davis, Pendleton, South Carolina*

1 package (18-1/4 ounces)
   yellow cake mix
1 egg
1/2 cup milk
1 cup mashed ripe bananas
   (about 2 medium)
1/2 cup chopped pecans

In a mixing bowl, combine cake mix, egg and milk. Add bananas; beat on medium speed for 2 minutes. Stir in pecans. Pour into two greased 8-in. x 4-in. x 2-in. loaf pans.

Bake at 350° for 40-45 minutes or until a toothpick inserted near the center comes out clean. Cool for 10 minutes before removing from pans to wire racks to cool completely. **Yield:** 2 loaves.

|STORING QUICK BREADS| Quick breads may be wrapped in foil or plastic wrap and stored at room temperature for up to 3 days. For longer storage, place quick breads in heavy-duty resealable plastic bags and freeze for up to 3 months.

Sausage Pinwheels

These savory spirals are very simple to fix but look special on a buffet. Our guests eagerly help themselves—sometimes the eye-catching pinwheels never make it to their plates!
—*Gail Sykora*
Menomonee Falls, Wisconsin

1 tube (8 ounces)
   refrigerated crescent
   rolls
1/2 pound uncooked bulk
   pork sausage
2 tablespoons minced
   chives

Unroll crescent roll dough on a lightly floured surface; press seams and perforations together. Roll into a 14-in. x 10-in. rectangle. Spread sausage to within 1/2 in. of edges. Sprinkle with chives.

Carefully roll up from a long side; cut into 12 slices. Place 1 in. apart in an ungreased 15-in. x 10-in. x 1-in. baking pan. Bake at 375° for 12-16 minutes or until golden brown. **Yield:** 1 dozen.

Quick Caramel Rolls

Refrigerated crescent rolls and caramel ice cream topping make these yummy, gooey treats a snap to assemble. I used to whip up a huge panful for our kids when they were growing up...now our grandchildren love them, too. They are easy to reheat in the microwave for a speedy snack.

—*Jeannette Westphal, Gettysburg, South Dakota*

1/4 cup butter
1/2 cup chopped pecans
1 cup caramel ice cream topping
2 tubes (8 ounces *each*) refrigerated crescent rolls

Place butter in a 13-in. x 9-in. x 2-in. baking pan; heat in a 375° oven until melted. Sprinkle with pecans. Add ice cream topping and mix well.

Remove dough from tubes (do not unroll); cut each section of dough into six rolls. Arrange rolls in prepared pan with cut side down. Bake at 375° for 20-25 minutes or until golden. Immediately invert onto a serving plate. Serve warm. **Yield:** 2 dozen.

Cheese Sticks

When our children were young, I'd pop these scrumptious cheesy snacks in the oven shortly before they'd get home from school. There's no need to thaw them, so they're ready to munch in under 15 minutes.

—*Ruth Peterson, Jenison, Michigan*

1 jar (5 ounces) sharp American cheese spread
1/2 cup butter, softened
1 egg white
1 loaf unsliced bread (1 pound)

In a mixing bowl, beat cheese spread, butter and egg white until fluffy. Cut crust from bread. Slice bread 1 in. thick; cut each slice into 1-in. strips. Spread the cheese mixture on all sides of each strip and place 2 in. apart on greased baking sheets.

Bake at 350° for 12-15 minutes or until lightly browned. Serve warm. Unbaked cheese sticks may be frozen for up to 4 months. Bake as directed (they do not need to be thawed first). **Yield:** 9 servings.

Swiss Onion Crescents

I put a special spin on these golden crescents by filling them with Swiss cheese, green onions and Dijon mustard. They're a snap to prepare because I use refrigerated dough.

—*Joy McMillan*
The Woodlands, Texas

1 tube (8 ounces) refrigerated crescent rolls
3 tablespoons shredded Swiss cheese, *divided*
2 tablespoons chopped green onion
1-1/2 teaspoons Dijon mustard

Unroll crescent dough and separate into eight triangles. Combine 2 tablespoons cheese, green onion and mustard; spread about 1 teaspoon over each triangle.

Roll up from the short side. Place point side down on an ungreased baking sheet and curve into a crescent shape. Sprinkle with remaining cheese. Bake at 375° for 11-13 minutes or until golden brown. **Yield:** 8 rolls.

Tasty White Bread

It's worth the rising time making this bread just to fill the house with the heavenly aroma as it bakes. But eating a thick slice is even better.
—*Angel Olvey, Kokomo, Indiana*

 Uses less fat, sugar or salt. Includes Nutritional Analysis and Diabetic Exchanges.

1 package (1/4 ounce) active dry yeast
3 teaspoons sugar, *divided*
2-1/4 cups warm water (110° to 115°), *divided*
2 teaspoons salt
6 to 6-1/2 cups all-purpose flour

In a large mixing bowl, dissolve yeast and 1 teaspoon sugar in 1/4 cup water; let stand for 10 minutes. Combine salt, remaining sugar and water; add to yeast mixture. Add 3 cups of flour; beat until smooth. Add enough remaining flour to form a soft dough. Turn onto a floured surface; knead until smooth and elastic, about 6-8 minutes. Place in a greased bowl, turning once to grease top. Cover and let rise in a warm place until doubled, about 1 hour.

Punch dough down; shape into two loaves. Place in two 8-in. x 4-in. x 2-in. loaf pans that have been coated with nonstick cooking spray. Cover and let rise until doubled, about 1 hour. Bake at 350° for 35-40 minutes. Remove from pans and cool on wire racks. **Yield:** 2 loaves (32 slices).

Nutritional Analysis: One slice equals 87 calories, 146 mg sodium, 0 cholesterol, 18 g carbohydrate, 3 g protein, trace fat. **Diabetic Exchange:** 1 starch.

Onion Rye Breadsticks

An envelope of onion soup mix provides the fast flavor you'll find in these rye snacks. They're an easy accompaniment to soup or salad when time's at a premium. The buttery mixture is terrific on multigrain bread, too.
—*Barbara Brown, Kentwood, Michigan*

1/2 cup butter, softened
1 envelope onion soup mix
14 slices rye bread

Combine butter and soup mix; spread over bread. Cut each slice into 3/4-in. strips and place on ungreased baking sheets. Bake at 350° for 5-6 minutes or until butter is melted and breadsticks are crisp. **Yield:** about 7 dozen.

Chive Garlic Bread

A purchased loaf of French bread gets a real boost with a few simple ingredients. Garlic and chives make the savory slices irresistible. Along with lasagna or another Italian meal, we munch them until the last crumbs have vanished! —*Kim Orr Louisville, Kentucky*

1/4 cup butter, softened
1/4 cup grated Parmesan cheese
2 tablespoons snipped chives
1 garlic clove, minced
1 loaf (1 pound) French bread, cut into 1-inch slices

In a bowl, combine the butter, Parmesan cheese, chives and garlic. Spread on one side of each slice of bread; wrap in a large piece of heavy-duty foil. Seal the edges. Place on a baking sheet. Bake at 350° for 25-30 minutes or until heated through. **Yield:** 12 servings.

|CUTTING CHIVES| The easiest way to cut fresh chives is to snip them with a scissors. Snip the tops of the entire bunch rather than snipping each chive individually.

Ultimate Cheese Bread

Loaded with mushrooms and cheese, this festive-looking garlic bread is a great party appetizer. Accompanied by soup or a salad, it's hearty enough to serve as a meal.

—Carolyn Hayes
Marion, Illinois

1 unsliced loaf French
   bread (1 pound)
1 package (8 ounces)
   sliced Swiss cheese
1 jar (4-1/2 ounces) sliced
   mushrooms, drained,
   optional
1/2 cup butter, melted
1/8 to 1/4 teaspoon garlic
   powder

Cut bread diagonally into 1-1/2-in. slices to within 1/2 in. of bottom. Repeat cuts in opposite direction. Cut cheese into 1-in. squares. Place one cheese square and one mushroom if desired into each slit.

Combine butter and garlic powder; spoon over the bread. Place on an ungreased baking sheet. Bake at 350° for 8-10 minutes or until cheese is melted. **Yield:** 10-12 servings.

Sausage Cheese Puffs

People are always surprised when I tell them there are only four ingredients in these tasty bite-size puffs. Cheesy and spicy, the golden morsels are a fun novelty at a breakfast or brunch...and they also make yummy party appetizers!

—Della Moore, Troy, New York

1 pound bulk Italian
   sausage
3 cups biscuit/baking mix
4 cups (16 ounces)
   shredded cheddar
   cheese
3/4 cup water

In a skillet, cook and crumble sausage until no longer pink; drain. In a bowl, combine biscuit mix and cheese; stir in sausage. Add water and toss with a fork until moistened.

Shape into 1-1/2-in. balls. Place 2 in. apart on ungreased baking sheets. Bake at 400° for 12-15 minutes or until puffed and golden brown. Cool on wire racks. **Yield:** about 4 dozen.

Editor's Note: Baked puffs may be frozen; reheat at 400° for 7-9 minutes or until heated through (they do not need to be thawed first).

English Muffins With Bacon Butter

For a change from the usual breakfast bread, I toast up a batch of English Muffins with Bacon Butter. The hint of Dijon mustard in this hearty spread really dresses up the English muffins.
—Edna Hoffman, Hebron, Indiana

1/2 cup butter, softened
1/2 to 3/4 teaspoon Dijon
   mustard
4 bacon strips, cooked and
   crumbled
4 to 6 English muffins, split

In a bowl, combine butter and mustard; stir in bacon. Toast the English muffins; spread with bacon butter. Refrigerate any leftover butter. **Yield:** 4-6 servings.

French Toast Fingers

Bite-size French Toast Fingers are great for a buffet...and kids of all ages love them. Strawberry preserves makes them pretty and taste simply scrumptious. —Mavis Diment, Marcus, Iowa

 Uses less fat, sugar or salt. Includes Nutritional Analysis and Diabetic Exchanges.

2 eggs
1/4 cup milk
1/4 teaspoon salt
1/2 cup strawberry preserves
8 slices day-old white
   bread
Confectioners' sugar, optional

In a small bowl, beat eggs, milk and salt; set aside. Spread preserves on four slices of bread; top with the remaining bread. Trim crusts; cut each sandwich into three strips. Dip both sides in egg mixture. Cook on a lightly greased hot griddle for 2 minutes on each side or until golden brown. Dust with confectioners' sugar if desired. **Yield:** 4 servings.

Nutritional Analysis: One serving of three strips (prepared with egg substitute, fat-free milk and sugar-free preserves and without confectioners' sugar) equals 235 calories, 500 mg sodium, 2 mg cholesterol, 42 g carbohydrate, 10 g protein, 4 g fat. **Diabetic Exchanges:** 2 starch, 1 meat, 1/2 fruit.

Southern Buttermilk Biscuits

The recipe for these four-ingredient biscuits has been handed down for many generations. Served warm with honey or jam, they'll melt in your mouth. —*Fran Thompson, Tarboro, North Carolina*

1/2 cup cold butter
2 cups self-rising flour
3/4 cup buttermilk
Melted butter

In a bowl, cut butter into flour until mixture resembles coarse crumbs. Stir in buttermilk just until moistened. Turn onto a lightly floured surface; knead 3-4 times.

Pat or lightly roll to 3/4-in. thickness. Cut with a floured 2-1/2-in. biscuit cutter. Place on a greased baking sheet. Bake at 425° for 11-13 minutes or until golden brown. Brush tops with butter. Serve warm. **Yield:** 9 biscuits.

Editor's Note: As a substitute for *each* cup of self-rising flour, place 1-1/2 teaspoons baking powder and 1/2 teaspoon salt in a measuring cup. Add all-purpose flour to measure 1 cup.

Pecan Pie Mini Muffins

While these are delicious year-round, you could easily turn them into an edible Christmas gift. They look festive on a decorative tray wrapped in red or green cellophane or tucked into a giveaway cookie plate. And don't forget to include the recipe so your recipient can enjoy this treat over and over again!
—*Pat Schrand, Enterprise, Alabama*

1 cup packed brown sugar
1/2 cup all-purpose flour
1 cup chopped pecans
2/3 cup butter, melted
2 eggs, beaten

In a bowl, combine brown sugar, flour and pecans; set aside. Combine butter and eggs; mix well. Stir into flour mixture. Fill greased and floured miniature muffin cups two-thirds full. Bake at 350° for 22-25 minutes. Remove immediately to cool on wire racks. **Yield:** about 2-1/2 dozen.

Editor's Note: This recipe uses only 1/2 cup flour.

Flaky Garlic Rolls

Flaky Garlic Rolls are a fun and tasty way to dress up handy refrigerator biscuits. Hot from the oven, these rolls are great alongside any meat and also are super with soup or as an evening snack.

—*Peggy Burdick*
Burlington, Michigan

1 tube (6 ounces) refrigerated flaky biscuits
1 to 2 tablespoons butter, melted
1/4 to 1/2 teaspoon garlic salt

Separate each biscuit into three pieces; place on a greased baking sheet. Brush with butter; sprinkle with garlic salt. Bake at 400° for 8-10 minutes or until golden brown. Serve warm. **Yield:** 15 rolls.

|GOT GARLIC?| A member of the lily family, garlic is sold fresh, chopped and packed in jars, or processed into garlic salt and powder. It is used in thousands of dishes in all cuisines and has been used throughout history as a medication.

Upside-Down Orange Puffs

These delicious citrusy morsels are so quick to make with refrigerated biscuits. They're our teenage son's favorite, so I make them often.
—*Rosa Griffith, Christiansburg, Virginia*

1/4 cup butter
1/4 cup sugar
2 tablespoons orange juice
1 teaspoon grated orange peel
1 can (7-1/2 ounces) refrigerated buttermilk biscuits

In a saucepan, combine butter, sugar, orange juice and peel. Cook and stir over medium heat until sugar is dissolved. Divide among 10 muffin cups. Make a hole in the center of each biscuit; place over orange mixture. Bake at 450° for 8-10 minutes or until golden brown. Immediately invert onto a wire rack to cool. **Yield:** 10 puffs.

|USE A PEELER| Always thoroughly wash citrus fruit before using their peel for anything. Pare citrus fruit rind with a vegetable peeler rather than a knife to avoid peeling the pith as well. The white pith is bitter and should be avoided.

Cinnamon Flat Rolls

I shared this recipe when 4-H leaders requested an activity for younger members. The kids had a ball rolling out the dough and enjoying the sweet chewy results. What makes these cinnamon rolls unique is you make them on the grill and not in the oven! They're quicker, too.   —Ethel Farnsworth
Yuma, Arizona

1 package (16 ounces) frozen dinner rolls, thawed
5 tablespoons olive oil
1/2 cup sugar
1 tablespoon ground cinnamon

On a floured surface, roll each dinner roll into a 5-in. circle. Brush with oil. Grill, uncovered, over medium heat for 1 minute on each side or until golden brown (burst any large bubbles with a fork). Combine sugar and cinnamon; sprinkle over rolls. **Yield:** 1 dozen.

Cheese And Sausage Muffins

These small, savory muffins are fun to serve as appetizers or at brunch. With just five ingredients, the tasty bites are easy to whip up to take to a party, the office or a friend.
—Willa Paget
Nashville, Tennessee

1 pound bulk hot pork sausage
1 can (10-3/4 ounces) condensed cheddar cheese soup, undiluted
1/2 cup milk
2 to 3 teaspoons rubbed sage
3 cups biscuit/baking mix

In a skillet over medium heat, cook sausage until no longer pink; drain. In a bowl, combine soup, milk, sage and sausage. Stir in the biscuit mix just until moistened.

Fill greased miniature or regular muffin cups two-thirds full. Bake at 400° for 15-20 minutes or until a toothpick inserted near the center comes out clean. **Yield:** 4 dozen mini-muffins or 2 dozen regular muffins.

Grandma's Popovers

Still warm from the oven, popovers are always a fun accompaniment to a homey meal. I was raised on these—my grandmother often made them for our Sunday dinners. The recipe could not be simpler.

—Debbie Terenzini, Lusby, Maryland

1 cup all-purpose flour
1/8 teaspoon salt
3 eggs
1 cup milk

In a bowl, combine flour and salt. Combine eggs and milk; whisk into dry ingredients just until blended. Using two 12-cup muffin tins, grease and flour five alternating cups of one tin and four cups of the second tin; fill two-thirds full with batter. Fill the empty cups two-thirds full with water.

Bake at 450° for 15 minutes. Reduce heat to 350° (do not open oven door). Bake 15 minutes longer or until deep golden brown (do not underbake). **Yield:** 9 popovers.

Quick Garlic Toast

Mom knew how to easily round out a meal with this crisp, cheesy garlic toast. We gobbled it up when she served it alongside of slaw or salad…and used it to soak up gravy from stew, too.

—Teresa Ingebrand, Perham, Minnesota

1/3 cup butter, softened
12 slices bread
1/2 teaspoon garlic salt
3 tablespoons grated Parmesan cheese

Spread butter on one side of each slice of bread. Cut each slice in half; place plain side down on a baking sheet. Sprinkle with garlic salt and Parmesan cheese. Broil 4 in. from the heat for 1-2 minutes or until lightly browned. **Yield:** 12 slices.

Cookies, Bars & Candies

Mint Sandwich Cookies, p. 229

Marbled Chocolate Bars, p. 228

Chewy Macaroons, p. 230

Cookies, Bars & Candies   227

Brown Sugar Shortbread

These rich buttery cookies have just three ingredients! They're a snap to make for a last-minute gift or when guests will be arriving on short notice. For best results, gradually stir the flour into the dough.

—*Shirley Gardiner*
Clearwater, Manitoba

1 cup butter, softened
1/2 cup packed brown sugar
2-1/4 cups all-purpose flour

In a mixing bowl, cream butter and sugar. Gradually stir in the flour. Turn onto a lightly floured surface and knead until smooth, about 3 minutes. Pat into a 1/3-in.-thick rectangle measuring 11 in. x 8 in. Cut into 2-in. x 1-in. strips.

Place 1 in. apart on ungreased baking sheets. Prick with a fork. Bake at 300° for 25 minutes or until bottom begins to brown. Cool for 5 minutes; remove to a wire rack to cool completely. **Yield:** 3-1/2 dozen.

Marbled Chocolate Bars

(Pictured on page 227)

These scrumptious chocolate bars with pockets of rich cream cheese are perfect for taking to a potluck. They're quick to assemble, don't need frosting and are easy to transport and serve. Best of all, folks love them!

—*Margery Bryan, Royal City, Washington*

1 package (18-1/4 ounces) German chocolate cake mix
1 package (8 ounces) cream cheese, softened
1/2 cup sugar
3/4 cup milk chocolate chips, divided

Prepare cake batter according to package directions. Pour into a greased 15-in. x 10-in. x 1-in. baking pan. In a small mixing bowl, beat cream cheese and sugar. Stir in 1/4 cup chocolate chips. Drop by tablespoonfuls over batter. Cut through batter with a knife to swirl the cream cheese mixture. Sprinkle with remaining chocolate chips.

Bake at 350° for 25-30 minutes or until a toothpick inserted near the center comes out clean. Cool on a wire rack. Cut into bars. **Yield:** 3 dozen.

Mint Sandwich Cookies

(Pictured on page 226)

Canned frosting, peppermint extract and chocolate candy coating quickly turn crackers into these wonderful little no-bake cookies. My children and I like to assemble them for parties and holidays. I hope you and your family enjoy them as much as we do. —*Melissa Thompson, Anderson, Ohio*

   1 **can (16 ounces) vanilla frosting**
1/2 **teaspoon peppermint extract**
   3 **to 5 drops green food coloring, optional**
  72 **butter-flavored crackers**
   1 **pound dark chocolate candy coating, coarsely chopped**

In a bowl, combine the frosting, extract and food coloring if desired. Spread over half of the crackers; top with remaining crackers. Place candy coating in a microwave-safe bowl. Microwave on high for 1-2 minutes or until smooth.

Dip the cookies in coating. Place on waxed paper until chocolate is completely set. Store in an airtight container at room temperature. **Yield:** 3 dozen.

Chocolate Chip Butter Cookies

At the downtown Chicago law firm where I work, we often bring in goodies for special occasions. When co-workers hear I've baked these melt-in-your-mouth cookies, they make a special trip to my floor to sample them. Best of all, these crisp, buttery treats can be made in no time. —*Janis Gruca Mokena, Illinois*

   1 **cup butter**
1/2 **teaspoon vanilla extract**
   2 **cups all-purpose flour**
   1 **cup confectioners' sugar**
   1 **cup (6 ounces) miniature semisweet chocolate chips**

Melt butter in a microwave or double boiler; stir in vanilla. Cool completely. In a large bowl, combine flour and sugar; stir in butter mixture and chocolate chips (mixture will be crumbly). Shape into 1-in. balls.

Place 2 in. apart on ungreased baking sheets; flatten slightly. Bake at 375° for 12 minutes or until edges begin to brown. Cool on wire racks. **Yield:** about 4 dozen.

Chewy Macaroons

(Pictured on page 227)

My family loves these delicious cookies on special occasions. With only three ingredients, they're a snap to make. —*Marcia Hostetter, Canton, New York*

5-1/3 cups flaked coconut
   1 can (14 ounces)
     sweetened condensed
     milk
   2 teaspoons vanilla extract

In a bowl, combine all ingredients. Drop 2 in. apart onto greased baking sheets. Bake at 350° for 10-12 minutes or until lightly browned. With a spatula dipped in water, immediately remove to wire racks to cool. **Yield:** 4-1/4 dozen.

Cookie Lollipops

A dip and a drizzle turn crunchy cream-filled sandwich cookies into a deliciously different treat! Kids love Cookie Lollipops because they taste as good as they look. You need just four ingredients and Popsicle sticks, so these fun snacks make great party favors. —*Jessie Wiggers*
Halstead, Kansas

   1 package (10 to 12
     ounces) vanilla *or* white
     chips
   2 tablespoons shortening,
     divided
   1 package (16 ounces)
     double-stuffed chocolate
     cream-filled sandwich
     cookies
  32 wooden Popsicle *or* craft
     sticks
   1 cup (6 ounces)
     semisweet chocolate
     chips

In a microwave or double boiler, melt vanilla chips and 1 tablespoon shortening; stir until smooth. Twist apart sandwich cookies. Dip the end of each Popsicle stick into melted chips; place on a cookie half and top with another half. Place cookies on a waxed paper-lined baking sheet; freeze for 15 minutes.

Reheat vanilla chip mixture again if necessary; dip frozen cookies into mixture until completely covered. Return to the baking sheet; freeze 30 minutes longer. Melt the chocolate chips and remaining shortening; stir until smooth. Drizzle over cookies. Store in an airtight container. **Yield:** 32 servings.

S'mores Bars

Glowing campfire coals are not needed to enjoy the traditional taste of s'mores with this recipe. The tasty take-along treat makes a sweet snack any time of day. —*Kristine Brown, Rio Rancho, New Mexico*

8 to 10 whole graham crackers (about 5 inches x 2-1/2 inches)
1 package fudge brownie mix (13-inch x 9-inch pan size)
2 cups miniature marshmallows
1 cup (6 ounces) semisweet chocolate chips
2/3 cup chopped peanuts

Arrange graham crackers in a single layer in a greased 13-in. x 9-in. x 2-in. baking pan. Prepare the brownie batter according to package directions. Spread over crackers. Bake at 350° for 25-30 minutes or until a toothpick inserted near the center comes out clean.

Sprinkle with marshmallows, chocolate chips and peanuts. Bake 5 minutes longer or until marshmallows are slightly puffed and golden brown. Cool on a wire rack before cutting. **Yield:** 2 dozen.

Lemon Crisp Cookies

Lemon Crisp Cookies are a snap to make using a boxed cake mix. The sunny color and lemon flavor are sure to bring smiles. —*Julia Livingston*
Frostproof, Florida

1 package (18-1/4 ounces) lemon cake mix
1 cup crisp rice cereal
1/2 cup butter, melted
1 egg, beaten
1 teaspoon grated lemon peel

In a large bowl, combine all ingredients until well mixed (dough will be crumbly). Shape into 1-in. balls. Place 2 in. apart on ungreased baking sheets. Bake at 350° for 10-12 minutes or until set. Cool for 1 minute; remove from pan to a wire rack to cool completely. **Yield:** about 4 dozen.

Easy Chocolate Drops

Friends and relatives relish these crunchy goodies. I never knew that making candy could be so simple until I tried these!
—*Heather De Cal, Terrace Bay, Ontario*

1 cup (6 ounces) semisweet chocolate chips
1 cup (6 ounces) butterscotch chips
1 cup shoestring potato sticks
1 cup salted peanuts

In a 2-qt. microwave-safe bowl, heat chips on high for 2 minutes or until melted, stirring once. Stir in potato sticks and peanuts. Drop by teaspoonfuls onto waxed paper-lined baking sheets. Chill until set, about 15 minutes. Store in airtight containers. **Yield:** 3-1/2 dozen.

Editor's Note: This recipe was tested using a 700-watt microwave.

Pretzel-Topped Sugar Cookies

It's tough to beat a three-ingredient treat...especially one that's so easy and sweet! I rely on refrigerated cookie dough to make these munchable morsels. I dress up each cookie with a white fudge-covered pretzel and melted white chocolate.
—*Michelle Brenneman, Orrville, Ohio*

2 tubes (18 ounces *each*) refrigerated sugar cookie dough
2-1/2 cups vanilla *or* white chips, *divided*
1 package (7-1/2 ounces) white fudge-covered pretzels

Crumble cookie dough into a large bowl; stir in 1-1/2 cups chips. Drop by tablespoonfuls 2 in. apart onto ungreased baking sheets. Bake at 325° for 15-18 minutes or until lightly browned. Immediately press a pretzel into the center of each cookie. Remove to wire racks to cool.

In a microwave, heat remaining chips at 70% power for 1 minute or until melted; stir until smooth. Drizzle over cookies. **Yield:** about 4-1/2 dozen.

Editor's Note: This recipe was tested with Nestle Flipz white fudge-covered pretzels.

Double Chip Bars

Our two children love these sweet, rich dessert bars. They go together so quickly that I can make them even on hectic days.
—*Victoria Lowe*
Lititz, Pennsylvania

1/2 cup butter
1-1/2 cups graham cracker crumbs
1 can (14 ounces) sweetened condensed milk
2 cups (12 ounces) semisweet chocolate chips
1 cup (6 ounces) peanut butter chips

Place butter in a 13-in. x 9-in. x 2-in. baking pan; place in a 350° oven until melted. Remove from the oven. Sprinkle the cracker crumbs evenly over butter. Pour milk evenly over crumbs. Sprinkle with chips; press down firmly.

Bake at 350° for 25-30 minutes or until golden brown. Cool on a wire rack before cutting. **Yield:** 3 dozen.

Anise Hard Candy

I like to wrap pieces of this candy in plastic wrap to share with friends. Slightly sweet, anise has a licorice-like flavor and aroma.
—*Bea Aubry, Dubuque, Iowa*

2 cups sugar
1 cup light corn syrup
1 cup water
2 teaspoons anise extract *or* 1 teaspoon anise oil
6 to 9 drops red food coloring

In a large heavy saucepan, combine sugar, corn syrup and water. Bring to a boil over medium heat, stirring occasionally. Cover and cook for 3 minutes or until sugar is dissolved. Uncover; cook on medium-high heat, without stirring, until a candy thermometer reads 300° (hard-crack stage). Remove from the heat; stir in extract and food coloring (keep face away from mixture as the aroma will be very strong).

Pour into a buttered 13-in. x 9-in. x 2-in. baking pan. When cooled slightly but not hardened, cut into 1-in. squares. Cool completely. Store in an airtight container. **Yield:** about 8-1/2 dozen.

Editor's Note: We recommend that you test your candy thermometer before each use by bringing water to a boil; the thermometer should read 212°. Adjust your recipe temperature up or down based on your test.

Snickers Cookies

Though you wouldn't know by looking, you'll find a sweet surprise inside these cookies. My mother got this recipe from a fellow teacher at her school. It's a great way to dress up refrigerated cookie dough.
—*Kari Pease, Conconully, Washington*

1 tube (18 ounces) refrigerated chocolate chip cookie dough
24 to 30 bite-size Snickers candy bars

Cut dough into 1/4-in.-thick slices. Place a candy bar on each slice and wrap dough around it. Place 2 in. apart on ungreased baking sheets. Bake at 350° for 8-10 minutes or until lightly browned. Cool on wire racks. **Yield:** 2 to 2-1/2 dozen.

Editor's Note: 2 cups of any chocolate chip cookie dough can be substituted for the refrigerated dough. Use 1 tablespoon of dough for each cookie.

Crunchy Dessert Bars

My son-in-law is diabetic and loves these five-ingredient frozen dessert bars. With their nutty crunch from Grape Nuts cereal, we think they taste like the inside of a Snickers candy bar. —*Shirley Reed*
San Angelo, Texas

 Uses less fat, sugar or salt. Includes Nutritional Analysis and Diabetic Exchanges.

1 pint sugar-free fat-free ice cream, softened
1 cup reduced-fat whipped topping
1/2 cup reduced-fat peanut butter
1 package (1 ounce) instant sugar-free butterscotch pudding mix
1 cup Grape Nuts cereal

In a mixing bowl, combine the first four ingredients; beat until smooth. Stir in cereal. Transfer to a foil-lined 8-in. square pan. Cover and freeze for 3-4 hours or until firm. Use foil to lift out of pan; discard foil. Cut into bars. **Yield:** 2 dozen.

Nutritional Analysis: One bar equals 67 calories, 122 mg sodium, 0 cholesterol, 10 g carbohydrate, 3 g protein, 2 g fat. **Diabetic Exchange:** 1 starch.

Coconut Drops

We enjoy giving friends a gift of festive candy each holiday season. With such limited time, I can rely on this recipe, which is quick and easy to make. —*Diane Rathburn, Mt. Pleasant, Michigan*

  1 package (14 ounces)
    flaked coconut
  6 drops red food coloring
  6 drops green food coloring
  1 pound white candy
    coating

Divide coconut between two bowls. Add red food coloring to one bowl and green to the other; toss to coat. In a heavy saucepan over low heat, melt candy coating. Drop by tablespoonfuls onto waxed paper.

While coating is still warm, sprinkle half of each drop with pink coconut and the other half with green; press down gently. Refrigerate until firm. **Yield:** 1-1/4 pounds.

Cookies 'n' Cream Fudge

I invented this confection for a bake sale at our children's school. Boy, was it a hit! The crunchy chunks of sandwich cookie soften a bit as the mixture mellows. It's so sweet that one panful serves a crowd. —*Laura Lane, Richmond, Virginia*

16 chocolate cream-filled
    sandwich cookies,
    broken into chunks,
    divided
  1 can (14 ounces)
    sweetened condensed
    milk
  2 tablespoons butter
2-2/3 cups vanilla *or* white
    chips
  1 teaspoon vanilla extract

Line an 8-in. square baking pan with aluminum foil; coat with nonstick cooking spray. Place half of the broken cookies in the prepared pan.

In a heavy saucepan, combine milk, butter and chips; cook and stir over low heat until chips are melted. Remove from the heat; stir in vanilla. Pour over cookies in pan. Sprinkle with remaining cookies. Cover and refrigerate for at least 1 hour. Cut into squares. **Yield:** 3 dozen.

Cookie Brittle

This recipe originally called for chocolate chips, but my family and friends like it better when I use peanut butter chips. I often make it for unexpected guests.
—*Betty Byrnes Consbruck*
Gainesville, Florida

1 cup butter, softened
1 cup sugar
2 cups all-purpose flour
1-1/4 cups peanut butter chips
1/2 cup coarsely chopped pecans

In a mixing bowl, cream the butter and sugar. Gradually add flour; mix well. Stir in peanut butter chips. Line a 15-in. x 10-in. x 1-in. baking pan with foil; coat with nonstick cooking spray. Gently press dough into the pan; sprinkle with pecans and press into dough.

Bake at 350° for 20-25 minutes or until golden brown. Cool in pan on a wire rack. Invert pan and remove foil. Break brittle into pieces; store in an airtight container. **Yield:** about 4 dozen.

Chocolate Peanut Butter Bars

To complete a meal, I often whip up a pan of Chocolate Peanut Butter Bars. These chewy cereal treats are also the perfect no-fuss contribution to a potluck or bake sale. I've discovered a few minutes in the refrigerator helps the bars' frosting set faster. Of course, the trick is getting them in there before they disappear!
—*Lorri Speer, Centralia, Washington*

1 cup sugar
1 cup light corn syrup
1 cup peanut butter
6 cups crisp rice cereal
2 cups (12 ounces) semisweet chocolate chips, melted

In a large saucepan, combine the sugar, corn syrup and peanut butter. Cook over medium-low heat until the sugar is dissolved. Remove from the heat; add cereal and stir until coated. Spread into a greased 13-in. x 9-in. x 2-in. pan; press lightly. Spread melted chocolate over bars. Chill. **Yield:** 1-1/2 to 2 dozen.

Berries 'n' Cream Brownies

If you like chocolate-covered strawberries, you'll love this sweet treat. It's an ideal ending to summer meals. A fudgy brownie, whipped topping and fresh fruit make this a fuss-free feast for the eyes as well as the taste buds. —*Anna Lapp*
New Holland, Pennsylvania

1 package fudge brownie mix (13-inch x 9-inch pan size)
1 carton (8 ounces) frozen whipped topping, thawed
4 cups quartered fresh strawberries
1/3 cup chocolate hard-shell ice cream topping

Prepare and bake brownies according to package directions, using a greased 13-in. x 9-in. x 2-in. baking pan. Cool completely on a wire rack.

Spread whipped topping over brownies. Arrange strawberries cut side down over top. Drizzle with chocolate topping. Refrigerate for at least 30 minutes before serving. **Yield:** 12-15 servings.

Cookies In a Jiffy

You'll be amazed and delighted at how quickly you can whip up a batch of these homemade cookies. Using a package of yellow cake mix hurries them along. —*Clara Hielkema, Wyoming, Michigan*

1 package (9 ounces) yellow cake mix
2/3 cup quick-cooking oats
1/2 cup butter, melted
1 egg
1/2 cup red and green Holiday M&M's *or* butterscotch chips

In a mixing bowl, beat the first four ingredients. Stir in the M&M's or chips. Drop by tablespoonfuls 2 in. apart onto ungreased baking sheets. Bake at 375° for 10-12 minutes or until lightly browned. Immediately remove to wire racks to cool. **Yield:** 2 dozen.

Tiger Butter Candy

This candy is big on peanut butter flavor and fun to make. Best of all, it's made in the microwave for added convenience.

—*Pamela Pogue, Mineola, Texas*

> 1 pound white candy coating, cut into pieces
> 1/2 cup chunky peanut butter
> 1/2 cup semisweet chocolate chips
> 4 teaspoons half-and-half cream

In a microwave-safe bowl, heat coating and peanut butter on medium for 3-4 minutes or until melted; mix well. Pour onto a foil-lined baking sheet coated with nonstick cooking spray; spread into a thin layer.

In another microwave-safe bowl, heat chips and cream on high for about 30 seconds or until chips are soft; stir until smooth. Pour and swirl over peanut butter layer. Freeze for 5 minutes or until set. Break into small pieces. **Yield:** about 1-1/2 pounds.

Editor's Note: This recipe was tested using a 700-watt microwave.

Triple Fudge Brownies

When you're in a hurry to make dessert, here's a "mix of mixes" that's so convenient and quick. The result is a big pan of very rich, fudgy brownies. Friends who ask me for the recipe are amazed that it's so easy. —*Denise Nebel, Wayland, Iowa*

> 1 package (3.9 ounces) instant chocolate pudding mix
> 1 package (18-1/4 ounces) chocolate cake mix
> 2 cups (12 ounces) semisweet chocolate chips
> Confectioners' sugar
> Vanilla ice cream, optional

Prepare pudding according to package directions. Whisk in cake mix. Stir in chocolate chips. Pour into a greased 15-in. x 10-in. x 1-in. baking pan.

Bake at 350° for 30-35 minutes or until the top springs back when lightly touched. Dust with confectioners' sugar. Serve with ice cream if desired. **Yield:** 4 dozen.

Microwave Truffles

I love to entertain and try new recipes, so I couldn't wait to make these chocolaty confections for the holidays. They're smooth, rich and so pretty topped with pecans. No one will ever guess how easy they are to make. —*Joy Neustel Jamestown, North Dakota*

1/3 cup finely chopped pecans, toasted, *divided*
8 squares (1 ounce *each*) semisweet baking chocolate
1/4 cup butter
1/4 cup heavy whipping cream
1/4 teaspoon almond extract

Place 24 small foil candy cups in miniature muffin cups or on a baking sheet. Spoon 1/2 teaspoon pecans into each; set cups and remaining pecans aside.

In a 2-qt. microwave-safe bowl, combine chocolate and butter. Microwave at 50% power for 1-1/2 to 2 minutes or until melted. Stir in cream and extract. Beat with an electric mixer until slightly thickened, scraping sides of bowl occasionally. Immediately pour into prepared cups. Top with remaining pecans. Refrigerate until set. **Yield:** 2 dozen.

Editor's Note: This recipe was tested using an 850-watt microwave.

Pecan Pie Bars

I'm always on the lookout for recipes that are quick and easy to prepare. A neighbor shared this fast favorite with me. The chewy bars taste just like pecan pie. —*Kimberly Pearce, Amory, Mississippi*

3 eggs
2-1/4 cups packed brown sugar
2 cups self-rising flour
2 cups chopped pecans
1-1/2 teaspoons vanilla extract

In a mixing bowl, beat eggs. Add brown sugar. Stir in flour until smooth. Add the pecans and vanilla (dough will be stiff). Spread in a greased 13-in. x 9-in. x 2-in. baking pan. Bake at 300° for 30-35 minutes or until a toothpick inserted near the center comes out clean. Cool before cutting. **Yield:** 2 dozen.

Editor's Note: As a substitute for *each* cup of self-rising flour, place 1-1/2 teaspoons baking powder and 1/2 teaspoon salt in a measuring cup. Add all-purpose flour to equal 1 cup.

Coated Cookie Drops

It's a good thing these no-bake drops are simple, because I like to serve them throughout the year. Their moist, cake-like center and sweet coating satisfy the chocolate lover in everyone. I'm asked for the recipe time and time again.
—*Amanda Reid, Oakville, Iowa*

1 package (14 ounces) chocolate cream-filled sandwich cookies
1 package (8 ounces) cream cheese, softened
15 ounces white candy coating
12 ounces chocolate candy coating
Red *and/or* green candy coating, optional

Place the cookies in a blender or food processor; cover and process until finely crushed. In a small mixing bowl, beat cream cheese and crushed cookies until blended. Roll into 3/4-in. balls. Cover and refrigerate for at least 1 hour.

In a small saucepan over low heat, melt white candy coating, stirring until smooth; dip half of the balls to completely coat. Melt chocolate candy coating and dip remaining balls. Place on waxed paper until hardened.

Drizzle white candies with remaining chocolate coating and chocolate candies with remaining white coating. Or melt red or green coating and drizzle over balls. Store in the refrigerator. **Yield:** about 7-1/2 dozen.

S'more Clusters

Our two sons love to help me break up the chocolate and graham crackers for these tasty treats—that way, they can tell their friends they made them! The chocolaty clusters taste just like s'mores, but without the gooey mess.
—*Kathy Schmittler, Sterling Heights, Michigan*

6 milk chocolate candy bars (1.55 ounces *each*), broken into pieces
1-1/2 teaspoons vegetable oil
2 cups miniature marshmallows
8 whole graham crackers, broken into bite-size pieces

In a large microwave-safe bowl, toss chocolate and oil. Microwave, uncovered, at 50% power for 1-1/2 to 2 minutes or until chocolate is melted, stirring once. Stir in marshmallows and graham crackers. Spoon into paper-lined muffin cups (about 1/3 cup each). Refrigerate for 1 hour or until firm. **Yield:** 1 dozen.

Editor's Note: This recipe was tested in an 850-watt microwave.

Molasses Butterballs

In a hurry to satisfy your sweet tooth? You can whip up a batch of these yummy cookies in just minutes. They're short on ingredients but long on flavor. Better hide them if you want any left—it's hard to eat just one!
—*Zelda Halloran, Dallas, Texas*

1 cup butter, softened
1/4 cup light molasses
2 cups all-purpose flour
1/2 teaspoon salt
2 cups chopped walnuts
Confectioners' sugar, optional

In a mixing bowl, cream butter and molasses. Combine flour and salt; gradually add to creamed mixture. Stir in walnuts. Roll into 1-in. balls. Place 1 in. apart on greased baking sheets.

Bake at 350° for 15 minutes or until set. Remove to wire racks to cool. Roll cooled cookies in confectioners' sugar, if desired. **Yield:** 4-1/2 dozen.

Chocolate-Covered Peanut Butter Bars

My daughter won first place in a contest with this candy, which I make at Christmas. It melts in your mouth! —*Mary Esther Holloway, Bowerston, Ohio*

3 cups sugar
1 cup light corn syrup
1/2 cup water
1 jar (18 ounces) creamy peanut butter, melted
1-1/2 pounds milk chocolate candy coating

In a large heavy saucepan, combine sugar, corn syrup and water. Cook and stir over low heat until sugar is dissolved; bring to a full rolling boil. Boil, stirring constantly, until a candy thermometer reads 290° (soft-crack stage).

Meanwhile, place melted peanut butter in a large greased heat-proof bowl. Pour hot syrup over peanut butter; stir quickly until blended. Pour onto a well-buttered baking sheet; cover with a piece of buttered waxed paper. Roll mixture into a 14-in. x 12-in. rectangle. While warm, cut into 1-1/2-in. x 1-in. bars using a buttered pizza cutter or knife. Cool completely. Melt candy coating; dip bars and place on waxed paper to harden. **Yield:** 6 dozen.

Editor's Note: We recommend that you test your candy thermometer before each use by bringing water to a boil; the thermometer should read 212°. Adjust your recipe temperature up or down based on your test.

Quick Little Devils

Enjoy the classic combination of peanut butter and chocolate in these speedy squares. A short list of ingredients, including devil's food cake mix, yields chocolaty results that are sure to satisfy any sweet tooth.
—*Denise Smith, Lusk, Wyoming*

1 package (18-1/4 ounces) devil's food cake mix
3/4 cup butter, melted
1/3 cup evaporated milk
1 jar (7 ounces) marshmallow creme
3/4 cup peanut butter

In a bowl, combine cake mix, butter and milk; mix well. Spread half the mixture into a greased 13-in. x 9-in. x 2-in. baking pan. Combine the marshmallow creme and peanut butter; carefully spread over cake mixture to within 1 in. of edge. Drop reserved cake mixture by teaspoonfuls over marshmallow mixture.

Bake at 350° for 20-22 minutes or until edges are golden brown. Cool completely. Cut into squares. **Yield:** about 2-1/2 dozen.

Surefire Sugar Cookies

You can invite kids to help make these easy treats. Sometimes I melt white coating instead of chocolate chips because it can be tinted to match the season. And for a short-cut, I purchase sugar cookies from a bakery. —*Victoria Zmarzley-Hahn Northampton, Pennsylvania*

1 tube (18 ounces) refrigerated sugar cookie dough
1-1/2 cups semisweet chocolate chips
4-1/2 teaspoons shortening
Colored sprinkles, chopped nuts *or* flaked coconut

Slice and bake the sugar cookies according to package directions. Cool on wire racks.

In a microwave-safe bowl, combine the chocolate chips and shortening. Microwave on high for 1-2 minutes or until melted; stir until smooth. Dip each cookie halfway in melted chocolate. Place on waxed paper; immediately sprinkle with colored sprinkles, nuts or coconut. Let stand until chocolate is completely set. **Yield:** 2 dozen.

Pineapple Coconut Snowballs

This is a three-ingredient candy I can whip up quickly. Canned pineapple adds refreshing taste to the frosty-looking sweet treat. —*Marlene Rhodes*
Colorado Springs, Colorado

 Uses less fat, sugar or salt. Includes Nutritional Analysis and Diabetic Exchanges.

1 package (8 ounces) cream cheese, softened
1 can (8 ounces) crushed pineapple, well drained
2-1/2 cups flaked coconut

In a small mixing bowl, beat cream cheese and pineapple until combined. Cover and refrigerate for 30 minutes. Roll into 1-in. balls; roll in coconut. Refrigerate for 6 hours or overnight. **Yield:** about 2 dozen.

Nutritional Analysis: One snowball (prepared with fat-free cream cheese) equals 67 calories, 5 g fat (5 g saturated fat), 1 mg cholesterol, 55 mg sodium, 4 g carbohydrate, 1 g fiber, 2 g protein. **Diabetic Exchanges:** 1 fat, 1/2 fruit.

Scandinavian Pecan Cookies

We enjoyed these rich, buttery cookies at a bed-and-breakfast in Galena, Illinois, and the hostess was kind enough to share her simple recipe. The pretty nut-topped treats are so special you could give a home-baked batch as a gift.
—*Laurie Knoke, DeKalb, Illinois*

1 cup butter, softened
3/4 cup packed brown sugar
1 egg, *separated*
2 cups all-purpose flour
1/2 cup finely chopped pecans

In a mixing bowl, cream butter, brown sugar and egg yolk. Gradually add flour. Shape into 1-in. balls. In a small bowl, beat egg white. Dip balls in egg white, then roll in pecans.

Place 2 in. apart on ungreased baking sheets; flatten slightly. Bake at 375° for 8-12 minutes or until edges are lightly browned. Cool on wire racks. **Yield:** 4-5 dozen.

Butterscotch Peanut Treats

I use pudding mix to stir up these sweet, crunchy no-bake bites. If you like butterscotch, you will love these delicious treats.
—*Bernice Martinoni, Petaluma, California*

1/2 cup corn syrup
1/3 cup butter, cubed
   1 package (3.5 ounces) cook-and-serve butterscotch pudding mix
   4 cups cornflakes
   1 cup coarsely chopped dry roasted peanuts

In a large heavy saucepan, cook and stir the corn syrup and butter until butter is melted. Stir in pudding mix until blended. Cook and stir until mixture comes to a boil. Cook and stir 1 minute longer.

Remove from the heat. Cool for 1 minute, stirring several times. Stir in the cornflakes and peanuts until evenly coated. Drop by rounded tablespoonfuls onto waxed paper-lined baking sheets; cool. **Yield:** about 2-1/2 dozen.

Peppermint Meringues

These melt-in-your-mouth cookies are super as a Christmas gift or to pass around when guests drop in.
—*Dixie Terry, Marion, Illinois*

 Uses less fat, sugar or salt. Includes Nutritional Analysis and Diabetic Exchanges.

   2 egg whites
1/8 teaspoon salt
1/8 teaspoon cream of tartar
1/2 cup sugar
   2 peppermint candy canes, crushed

In a mixing bowl, beat egg whites until foamy. Sprinkle with salt and cream of tartar; beat until soft peaks form. Gradually add sugar, beating until stiff peaks form, about 7 minutes. Drop by teaspoonfuls onto ungreased foil or paper-lined baking sheets; sprinkle with the crushed candy.

Bake at 225° for 1-1/2 hours. Turn off heat; leave cookies in the oven with the door ajar for at least 1 hour or until cool. Store in an airtight container. **Yield:** 3 dozen.

Nutritional Analysis: One cookie equals 21 calories, 12 mg sodium, 0 cholesterol, 5 g carbohydrate, trace protein, 0 fat. **Diabetic Exchange:** 1/2 fruit.

Graham Cracker Brownies

I enjoy making these brownies for last-minute bake sales and family gatherings alike. My grandmother first baked them nearly 50 years ago, and they're as popular today as they were then! —*Cathy Guffey Towanda, Pennsylvania*

2 cups graham cracker crumbs (about 32 squares)
1 cup (6 ounces) semisweet chocolate chips
1 teaspoon baking powder
Pinch **salt**
1 can (14 ounces) sweetened condensed milk

In a bowl, combine all the ingredients. Spread into a greased 8-in. square baking pan. Bake at 350° for 30-35 minutes or until a toothpick inserted near the center comes out clean. Cool on a wire rack. **Yield:** 1-1/2 dozen.

|BAKING BARS & BROWNIES| To easily remove bars and brownies from a pan, line the bottom of the pan with foil, then grease. Add the batter and bake as directed. It's important to evenly spread batter in the pan. If one corner is thinner than another, it will bake faster and be over-baked when the rest of the pan is done.

PB&J Bars

Big and little kids alike will love these four-ingredient bars that offer a cookie crust, a layer of jam and a crunchy peanut butter and granola topping. The delicious treats are also great for picnics or for packing into bag lunches. —*Mitzi Sentiff, Alexandria, Virginia*

1 package (18 ounces) refrigerated sugar cookie dough, *divided*
2/3 cup strawberry jam
3/4 cup granola cereal without raisins
3/4 cup peanut butter chips

Line a 9-in. square baking pan with foil and grease the foil. Press two-thirds of the cookie dough into prepared pan. Spread jam over dough to within 1/4 in. of edges. In a mixing bowl, beat the granola, peanut butter chips and remaining dough until blended. Crumble over jam.

Bake at 375° for 25-30 minutes or until golden brown. Cool on a wire rack. Using foil, lift out of pan. Cut into bars and remove from foil. **Yield:** 9-12 servings.

Christmas Bark Candy

This quick-to-fix candy is sure to please all ages when added to a homemade cookie tray. We show two versions here: vanilla chips with colorful miniature baking bits and milk chocolate chips with broken pretzels. Create your own variations by using different flavored chips and add-ins such as crushed candy canes, dried fruits or crunchy nuts.

—*Taste of Home Test Kitchen*

1 package (10 to 12 ounces) vanilla chips *or* milk chocolate chips
2 teaspoons vegetable oil
1-1/4 to 1-1/2 cups M&M miniature baking bits *or* broken pretzel pieces

In a microwave-safe bowl, heat chips and oil at 70% power for 1 minute; stir. Microwave 10-20 seconds longer or until chips are melted, stirring occasionally. Cool for 5 minutes.

Stir in baking bits or pretzels. Spread onto a waxed paper-lined baking sheet. Chill for 10 minutes. Remove from the refrigerator; break into pieces. Store in an airtight container at room temperature. **Yield:** about 1 pound.

Editor's Note: This recipe was tested in an 850-watt microwave.

Chocolate Chunk Shortbread

Chocolate is a nice addition to shortbread, as this scrumptious recipe proves. The shortbread cookies are delicious served with a cold glass of milk.
—*Brenda Mumma, Airdrie, Alberta*

3/4 cup butter, softened
1/2 cup confectioners' sugar
1 cup all-purpose flour
1/2 cup cornstarch
3 squares (1 ounce *each*) semisweet chocolate, coarsely chopped
Additional confectioners' sugar

In a mixing bowl, cream butter and sugar. Gradually add flour and cornstarch. Stir in chocolate. Shape into 1-in. balls. Place 1 in. apart on ungreased baking sheets. Flatten with a glass dipped in confectioners' sugar. Bake at 300° for 30-33 minutes or until edges are lightly brown. Remove to wire racks to cool. **Yield:** about 3-1/2 dozen.

|STORING COOKIES| Allow cookies to cool completely before storing. Store soft cookies and crisp cookies in separate air tight containers. If stored together, the moisture from the soft cookies will soften the crisp cookies, making them lose their crunch. Layer cookies in a container, separating each layer with waxed paper.

Caramel Pecan Bars

These bars are so simple to fix, yet so delicious. You'll want to cut them small because the combination of caramel, chocolate and pecans makes them rich and sweet.
—Rebecca Wyke
Morganton, North Carolina

**1-1/2 cups crushed vanilla
   wafers (about 50 wafers)
1/4 cup butter, melted
   2 cups (12 ounces)
      semisweet chocolate
      chips
   1 cup chopped pecans
   1 jar (12 ounces) caramel
      ice cream topping**

In a bowl, combine the wafer crumbs and butter. Press into a greased 13-in. x 9-in. x 2-in. baking pan. Sprinkle with chocolate chips and pecans.

In a microwave, heat caramel topping on high for 1-2 minutes or until warm. Drizzle over the top. Bake at 350° for 10 minutes or until chips are melted. Cool on a wire rack. **Yield:** 6 dozen.

Buttery Almond Crunch

This delectable candy is crisp but not as hard as peanut brittle. Some people say it reminds them of the toffee center of a well-known candy bar.
—Mildred Clothier, Oregon, Illinois

**1 tablespoon plus 1/2 cup
   butter, softened, *divided*
1/2 cup sugar
   1 tablespoon light corn
      syrup
   1 cup sliced almonds**

Line an 8-in. square pan with foil; butter the foil with 1/2 tablespoon butter. Set aside. Spread the sides of a heavy saucepan with 1/2 tablespoon butter. Add 1/2 cup of butter, sugar and corn syrup. Bring to a boil over medium-high heat, stirring constantly. Cook and stir until mixture is golden brown, about 3 minutes. Stir in almonds.

Quickly pour into prepared pan. Refrigerate until firm. Invert pan and remove foil. Break candy into pieces. **Yield:** 10 ounces.

Peanut Clusters

My husband, Greg, likes to mix up these treats with the kids. With three simple ingredients I usually have on hand, it's easy to make a batch in a matter of minutes.　　—Deb Darr, Falls City, Oregon

4 ounces milk chocolate candy coating
4 ounces white candy coating
1 can (16 ounces) salted peanuts (about 2-1/2 cups)

In a microwave, melt candy coatings, stirring often until blended. Stir in the peanuts until coated. Drop by tablespoonfuls onto a waxed paper-lined baking sheet. Refrigerate until serving. **Yield:** about 3 dozen.

|STORING CANDY| Store homemade candies in tightly covered containers unless otherwise directed. Don't store more than one kind of candy in a single container.

Swedish Butter Cookies

It's impossible to eat just one of these treats. Naturally, they're a favorite with my Swedish husband and children—but anyone with a sweet tooth will appreciate them. My recipe is "well-traveled" among our friends and neighbors.　　—Sue Soderlund
Elgin, Illinois

1 cup butter, softened
1 cup sugar
2 teaspoons maple syrup
2 cups all-purpose flour
1 teaspoon baking soda
Confectioners' sugar, optional

In a mixing bowl, cream butter and sugar. Add syrup; mix well. Combine flour and baking soda; gradually add to creamed mixture. Divide dough into eight portions. Roll each portion into a 9-in. log.

Place 3 in. apart on ungreased baking sheets. Bake at 300° for 25 minutes or until lightly browned. Cut into 1-in. slices. Remove to wire racks to cool. Dust with confectioners' sugar if desired. **Yield:** about 6 dozen.

Macaroon Bars

Guests will never recognize the refrigerated crescent roll dough that goes into these almond-flavored bars. You can assemble these chewy coconut treats in no time.   —*Carolyn Kyzer, Alexander, Arkansas*

3-1/4 cups flaked coconut, *divided*
1 can (14 ounces) sweetened condensed milk
1 teaspoon almond extract
1 tube (8 ounces) refrigerated crescent rolls

Sprinkle 1-1/2 cups coconut into a well-greased 13-in. x 9-in. x 2-in. baking pan. Combine milk and extract; drizzle half over the coconut. Unroll crescent dough; arrange in a single layer over coconut. Drizzle with remaining milk mixture; sprinkle with remaining coconut.

Bake at 350° for 30-35 minutes or until golden brown. Cool completely before cutting. Store in the refrigerator. **Yield:** 3 dozen.

Cream Cheese Candies

This four-ingredient recipe was recommended by friends and shared throughout our neighborhood. The rich, simple mints are often seen at wedding receptions and graduation parties, and they make a perfect last-minute addition to holiday candy trays.
   —*Katie Koziolek, Hartland, Minnesota*

1 package (3 ounces) cream cheese, softened
1/4 teaspoon peppermint *or* almond extract
3 cups confectioners' sugar
Green and red colored sugar, optional

In a small mixing bowl, combine cream cheese and extract. Beat in 1-1/2 cups confectioners' sugar. Knead in remaining confectioners' sugar until smooth.

Shape into 1/2-in. balls. Roll in colored sugar if desired. Place on ungreased baking sheets and flatten with a fork. Let stand for 1 hour to harden. Store in an airtight container in the refrigerator. **Yield:** 6 dozen.

Almond Bars

This is one of my favorite recipes for last-minute school bake sales. The cake-like snacks are the first items to go...that is, if they're not grabbed by a teacher first. I also include them in Christmas cookie gift baskets.
—*Sandy Kerrison, Lockport, New York*

4 eggs
2 cups sugar
1 cup butter, melted
2 cups all-purpose flour
2-1/2 teaspoons almond extract
Confectioners' sugar, optional

In a mixing bowl, beat the eggs and sugar until lemon-colored. Add the butter, flour and extract; mix well. Spread into a greased 13-in. x 9-in. x 2-in. baking pan.

Bake at 325° for 30-35 minutes or until a toothpick inserted near the center comes out clean. Cool on a wire rack. Sprinkle with confectioners' sugar if desired. **Yield:** 2 dozen.

Cranberry Crispies

At holiday rush time, you can't go wrong with these simple cookies. They're a snap to stir up with a boxed quick bread mix, and they bake up crisp and delicious.
—*LaVern Kraft, Lytton, Iowa*

1 package (15.6 ounces) cranberry quick bread mix
1/2 cup butter, melted
1/2 cup finely chopped walnuts
1 egg
1/2 cup dried cranberries

In a bowl, combine the bread mix, butter, walnuts and egg; mix well. Stir in cranberries. Roll into 1-1/4-in. balls. Place 3 in. apart on ungreased baking sheets. Flatten to 1/8-in. thickness with a glass dipped in sugar. Bake at 350° for 10-12 minutes or until light golden brown. Remove to wire racks to cool. **Yield:** 2-1/2 dozen.

Chocolate Peanut Butter Cookies

It's a snap to make a batch of tasty cookies using this recipe, which calls for a convenient boxed cake mix. My husband and son gobble them up.

—Mary Pulyer
Port St. Lucie, Florida

1 package (18-1/4 ounces) devil's food cake mix
2 eggs
1/3 cup vegetable oil
1 package (10 ounces) peanut butter chips

In a mixing bowl, beat cake mix, eggs and oil (batter will be very stiff). Stir in chips. Roll into 1-in. balls. Place on lightly greased baking sheets; flatten slightly.

Bake at 350° for 10 minutes or until a slight indentation remains when lightly touched. Cool for 2 minutes before removing to a wire rack. **Yield:** 4 dozen.

|SHAPING DOUGH INTO BALLS| Roll the dough between your palms until it forms a ball. A 1-inch ball requires about 2 teaspoons of dough. If the dough is sticky, you can refrigerate it until it is easy to handle, lightly flour your hands or spray your hands with nonstick cooking spray.

Double Chocolate Bars

A friend brought these fudgy bars a few years ago to tempt me with yet another chocolate treat. They are simple to make...and cleanup is a breeze! They're very rich, though, so be sure to cut them into bite-size pieces.

—Nancy Clark, Zeigler, Illinois

1 package (14 ounces) cream-filled chocolate sandwich cookies, crushed
3/4 cup butter, melted
1 can (14 ounces) sweetened condensed milk
2 cups (12 ounces) miniature semisweet chocolate chips, *divided*

Combine cookie crumbs and butter; pat onto the bottom of an ungreased 13-in. x 9-in. x 2-in. baking pan. Combine milk and 1 cup of chips in a microwave-safe bowl. Cover and microwave on high for 1 minute or until chips are melted; stir until smooth. Pour over crust. Sprinkle with remaining chips. Bake at 350° for 10-12 minutes or until chips are melted. Cool. **Yield:** about 4 dozen.

Editor's Note: This recipe was tested in a 700-watt microwave.

Gumdrop Cereal Bars

I was planning to make traditional marshmallow treats but didn't have enough Rice Krispies on hand, so I used Corn Pops instead. I added gumdrops for color, and the result was spectacular.—*Laura Tryssenaar Listowel, Ontario*

5 cups Corn Pops cereal
1 cup gumdrops
4 cups miniature marshmallows
1/4 cup butter
1 teaspoon vanilla extract

Place cereal and gumdrops in a large bowl; set aside. In a microwave-safe bowl, heat the marshmallows and butter on high for 2 minutes; stir until melted. Stir in vanilla. Pour over cereal mixture and toss to coat. Spread into a greased 9-in. square pan. Cool on a wire rack. Cut with a buttered knife. **Yield:** 16 bars.

Editor's Note: This recipe was tested in an 850-watt microwave.

Nutty Chocolate Marshmallow Puffs

We like to do things BIG here in Texas, so don't expect a dainty little barely-a-bite truffle from this surprising recipe. Folks are delighted to discover a big fluffy marshmallow inside the chocolate and nut coating.
—*Pat Ball, Abilene, Texas*

2 cups milk chocolate chips
1 can (14 ounces) sweetened condensed milk
1 jar (7 ounces) marshmallow creme
40 large marshmallows
4 cups coarsely chopped pecans (about 1 pound)

In a microwave or heavy saucepan, heat chocolate chips, milk and marshmallow creme just until melted; stir until smooth (mixture will be thick).

With tongs, immediately dip marshmallows, one at a time, in chocolate mixture. Shake off excess chocolate; quickly roll in pecans. Place on waxed paper-lined baking sheets. (Reheat chocolate mixture if necessary for easier coating.) Refrigerate until firm. Store in the refrigerator in an airtight container. **Yield:** 40 candies.

No-Bake Chocolate Cookies

These cookies are my oldest son's favorite. When his children tried them, the cookies became their favorites, too. I like them for two reasons—they're quick and they're chocolate!   —Connie Sackett
Glennallen, Alaska

1 can (14 ounces) sweetened condensed milk
2 cups (12 ounces) semisweet chocolate chips
3 cups crushed graham crackers (about 48 squares)
1/2 cup chopped walnuts
1 teaspoon vanilla extract
Confectioners' sugar, optional

In a microwave-safe bowl, combine milk and chocolate chips. Microwave, uncovered, on high for 1-2 minutes or until chips are melted; stir until smooth. Stir in cracker crumbs, walnuts and vanilla.

Shape into a 17-in. log; roll in confectioners' sugar if desired. Wrap in plastic wrap. Refrigerate for 1 hour or until firm. Unwrap and cut into 1/4-in. slices. **Yield:** about 5-1/2 dozen.

Editor's Note: This recipe was tested in an 850-watt microwave.

Peanut Butter Snowballs

These creamy treats are a nice change from the typical milk chocolate and peanut butter combination. This recipe is also an easy one for children to help with. I prepare them for a bake sale at my granddaughter's school and put them in gift boxes I share with neighbors at Christmas.   —Wanda Regula
Birmingham, Michigan

1 cup confectioners' sugar
1/2 cup creamy peanut butter
3 tablespoons butter, softened
1 pound white candy coating

In a mixing bowl, combine sugar, peanut butter and butter; mix well. Shape into 1-in. balls and place on a waxed paper-lined cookie sheet. Chill for 30 minutes or until firm.

Meanwhile, melt the white coating in a double boiler or microwave-safe bowl. Dip balls and place on waxed paper to harden. **Yield:** 2 dozen.

Cranberry Pecan Clusters

I have many candy recipes, and this is one of my favorites. The clusters are quick and easy to make and very festive-looking. They're so pretty on a holiday candy tray.
—Collette Tubman
St. Thomas, Ontario

6 squares (1 ounce *each*) white baking chocolate
1 cup dried cranberries
1/4 to 1/2 cup chopped pecans

Line a baking sheet with foil; set aside. In a microwave-safe bowl, heat the chocolate, uncovered, at 50% power for about 3 minutes or until melted, stirring once. Stir until smooth. Stir in cranberries and pecans. Drop by teaspoonfuls onto prepared pan. Freeze for 5 minutes, then refrigerate until firm. **Yield:** about 20 pieces.

Editor's Note: This recipe was tested in an 850-watt microwave.

Creamy Caramels

I discovered this recipe in a local newspaper several years ago and have made these soft and buttery caramels ever since. Everyone asks for the recipe once they have a taste. I make them for Christmas, picnics and charity auctions. They are so much better than store-bought caramels.
—Marcie Wolfe
Williamsburg, Virginia

1 cup sugar
1 cup dark corn syrup
1 cup butter
1 can (14 ounces) sweetened condensed milk
1 teaspoon vanilla extract

Line an 8-in. square pan with foil and butter the foil; set aside. Combine sugar, corn syrup and butter in a 3-qt. saucepan. Bring to a boil over medium heat, stirring constantly. Boil slowly for 4 minutes without stirring. Remove from the heat and stir in milk.

Reduce heat to medium-low and cook until candy thermometer reads 238° (soft-ball stage), stirring constantly. Remove from the heat and stir in vanilla. Pour into prepared pan. Cool. Remove from pan and cut into 1-in. squares. Wrap individually in waxed paper; twist ends. **Yield:** 64 pieces.

Editor's Note: We recommend that you test your candy thermometer before each use by bringing water to a boil; the thermometer should read 212°. Adjust your recipe temperature up or down based on your test.

Peanut Butter Cookie Cups

I'm a busy schoolteacher and pastor's wife who always looks for shortcuts. I wouldn't dare show my face at a church dinner or bake sale without these tempting peanut butter treats. They're quick and easy to make and always a hit.　　—Kristi Tackett
Banner, Kentucky

1 package (17-1/2 ounces) peanut butter cookie mix
36 miniature peanut butter cups, unwrapped

Prepare cookie mix according to package directions. Roll the dough into 1-in. balls. Place in greased miniature muffin cups. Press dough evenly onto bottom and up sides of each cup. Bake at 350° for 11-13 minutes or until set.

Immediately place a peanut butter cup in each cup; press down gently. Cool for 10 minutes; carefully remove from pans. **Yield:** 3 dozen.

Editor's Note: 2-1/4 cups peanut butter cookie dough of your choice can be substituted for the mix.

Praline Grahams

Someone brought these crunchy, nutty treats to a meeting I attended, and I wouldn't leave without the recipe. They're super easy to fix, inexpensive and delicious. The recipe makes a lot, so it's a great snack for a crowd.　　—Marian Platt
Sequim, Washington

12 graham crackers (4-3/4 inches x 2-1/2 inches)
1/2 cup butter
1/2 cup packed brown sugar
1/2 cup finely chopped walnuts

Line a 15-in. x 10-in. x 1-in. baking pan with heavy-duty foil. Break the graham crackers at indentations; place in a single layer in pan. In a small saucepan, combine butter and brown sugar. Bring to a rolling boil over medium heat; boil for 2 minutes. Remove from the heat; add nuts. Pour over crackers.

Bake at 350° for 10 minutes or until lightly browned. Let stand for 2-3 minutes. Remove to a wire rack to cool. **Yield:** 4 dozen.

Cakes, Pies & Desserts

Light Berry
Mousse, p. 263

Peppermint Stick Pie, p. 259

Peach Pudding, p. 264 and
Red, White & Blue Refresher, p. 258

Root Beer Float
Cake, p. 260

Cranberry Shiver

Cool and refreshing, this pretty dessert is delightfully sweet-tart and makes the perfect ending for a bountiful holiday meal. You can make it ahead and keep it in the freezer, so there will be one less thing to do before serving. —Audrey Thibodeau
Mesa, Arizona

✓ Uses less fat, sugar or salt. Includes Nutritional Analysis and Diabetic Exchanges.

- 1 **package (12 ounces) fresh *or* frozen cranberries**
- 3 **cups water, *divided***
- 1-3/4 **cups sugar**
- 1/4 **cup lemon juice**
- 1 **teaspoon grated orange peel**
- **Fresh mint, optional**

In a saucepan, bring cranberries and 2 cups of water to a boil. Reduce heat; simmer for 5 minutes. Press through a strainer to remove skins; discard skins. To the juice, add sugar, lemon juice, orange peel and remaining water; mix well.

Pour into an 8-in. square pan. Cover and freeze until ice begins to form around the edges of the pan, about 1-1/2 hours; stir. Freeze until mushy, about 30 minutes. Spoon into a freezer container; cover and freeze. Remove from the freezer 20 minutes before serving. Scoop into small dishes; garnish with mint if desired. **Yield:** 10 servings.

Nutritional Analysis: One 1/2-cup serving equals 154 calories, 1 mg sodium, 0 cholesterol, 40 g carbohydrate, trace protein, trace fat. **Diabetic Exchange:** 2-1/2 fruit.

Red, White & Blue Refresher

(Pictured on page 257)

A colorful combination of pineapple sherbet, berries and grape juice makes a refreshing dessert on a hot summer day.
—Carol Gillespie, Chambersburg, Pennsylvania

- 1 **quart pineapple *or* lemon sherbet**
- 1 **cup sliced strawberries**
- 1/2 **cup blueberries**
- 1/2 **cup white grape juice**

Divide the sherbet between four dessert cups or bowls. Top with the berries and grape juice. **Yield:** 4 servings.

Peppermint Stick Pie

(Pictured on page 256)

What's a cook to do when days are filled with holiday preparations and you need to fix a dessert in time for dinner? Try this delicious pie! It's very festive looking, and folks fall for the minty flavor.

—*Mildred Peachey, Wooster, Ohio*

4-1/2 cups crisp rice cereal
1 cup (6 ounces) semisweet chocolate chips, melted
2 quarts peppermint stick ice cream, softened
Chocolate syrup *or* chocolate fudge topping
Crushed peppermint candies

Combine cereal and chocolate; mix well. Press into the bottom and up the sides of an ungreased 10-in. pie plate. Freeze for 5 minutes. Spoon ice cream into the crust. Freeze until serving. Garnish with chocolate syrup and peppermint candies. **Yield:** 6-8 servings.

Editor's Note: Pie may be made ahead and frozen. Remove from freezer 15 minutes before serving.

Rhubarb Custard Cake

Rhubarb thrives in my northern garden and is one of the few crops the pesky moose don't bother! Of all the rhubarb desserts I've tried, this pudding cake is my No. 1 choice. It has old-fashioned appeal but is simple to prepare.   —*Evelyn Gebhardt Kasilof, Alaska*

1 package (18-1/4 ounces) yellow cake mix
4 cups chopped fresh *or* frozen rhubarb
1 cup sugar
1 cup heavy whipping cream
Whipped cream and fresh mint, optional

Prepare cake batter according to package directions. Pour into a greased 13-in. x 9-in. x 2-in. baking dish. Sprinkle with rhubarb and sugar. Slowly pour cream over top.

Bake at 350° for 40-45 minutes or until golden brown. Cool for 15 minutes before serving. Garnish with whipped cream and mint if desired. Refrigerate leftovers. **Yield:** 12-15 servings.

Root Beer Float Cake

(Pictured on page 257)

I add root beer to both the cake batter and fluffy frosting of this summery dessert to get that great root beer float taste. Serve this moist cake to a bunch of hungry kids and watch it disappear.

—Kat Thompson, Prineville, Oregon

1 package (18-1/4 ounces) white cake mix
1-3/4 cups cold root beer, *divided*
1/4 cup vegetable oil
2 eggs
1 envelope whipped topping mix

In a mixing bowl, combine dry cake mix, 1-1/4 cups root beer, oil and eggs. Beat on low speed for 2 minutes or stir by hand for 3 minutes. Pour into a greased 13-in. x 9-in. x 2-in. baking pan. Bake at 350° for 30-35 minutes or until a toothpick inserted near the center comes out clean. Cool completely on a wire rack.

In a mixing bowl, combine the whipped topping mix and remaining root beer. Beat until soft peaks form. Frost cake. Store in the refrigerator. **Yield:** 12-16 servings.

Quick Coconut Cream Pie

I've found a way to make coconut cream pie without a lot of fuss and still get terrific flavor. Using a convenient purchased crust, instant pudding and frozen whipped topping, I can enjoy an old-time dessert even when time is short.

—Betty Claycomb
Alverton, Pennsylvania

1 package (5.1 ounces) instant vanilla pudding mix
1-1/2 cups cold milk
1 carton (8 ounces) frozen whipped topping, thawed, *divided*
3/4 to 1 cup flaked coconut, toasted, *divided*
1 pastry shell, baked *or* graham cracker crust (8 *or* 9 inches)

In a mixing bowl, beat pudding and milk on low speed for 2 minutes. Fold in half of the whipped topping and 1/2 to 3/4 cup of coconut. Pour into crust. Spread with remaining whipped topping; sprinkle with remaining coconut. Refrigerate until serving. **Yield:** 6-8 servings.

White Chocolate Tarts

White Chocolate Tarts are scrumptious but really no fuss, because they call for prepared tart shells, instant pudding and whipped topping.
—*Traci Maloney, Toms River, New Jersey*

1 can (14 ounces) sweetened condensed milk
1 cup cold water
1 package (3.4 ounces) instant white chocolate pudding mix
2 cups whipped topping
2 packages (6 count *each*) individual graham cracker tart shells

In a mixing bowl, combine milk, water and pudding mix. Beat on low speed for 2 minutes. Cover and refrigerate for 10 minutes. Fold in whipped topping. Spoon about 1/3 cup into each tart shell. Refrigerate until serving. **Yield:** 12 servings.

Nutty Peach Crisp

A co-worker brought this easy, delicious dessert to work, and I couldn't resist asking for the recipe. A moist bottom layer made with canned peaches and boxed cake mix is covered with a lovely golden topping of coconut and pecans. It tastes wonderful served warm with ice cream.
—*Nancy Carpenter Sidney, Montana*

1 can (29 ounces) sliced peaches, undrained
1 package (18-1/4 ounces) yellow *or* butter pecan cake mix
1/2 cup butter, melted
1 cup flaked coconut
1 cup chopped pecans

Arrange peaches in an ungreased 13-in. x 9-in. x 2-in. baking dish. Sprinkle dry cake mix over top. Drizzle with butter; sprinkle with coconut and pecans. Bake at 325° for 55-60 minutes or until golden brown. Let stand for 15 minutes. Serve warm or cold. **Yield:** 12-15 servings.

Creamy Lemonade Pie

This luscious lemon pie looks quite elegant for a special dinner, yet it requires little effort. Guests will never suspect they're eating a quick-and-easy dessert. —*Carolyn Griffin, Macon, Georgia*

1 can (5 ounces) evaporated milk
1 package (3.4 ounces) instant lemon pudding mix
2 packages (8 ounces *each*) cream cheese, softened
3/4 cup lemonade concentrate
1 graham cracker crust (9 inches)

In a mixing bowl, combine milk and pudding mix; beat on low speed for 2 minutes (mixture will be thick). In another mixing bowl, beat cream cheese until light and fluffy, about 3 minutes. Gradually beat in lemonade concentrate. Gradually beat in pudding mixture. Pour into crust. Cover and refrigerate for at least 4 hours. **Yield:** 6-8 servings.

Fruit-Topped Almond Cream

Fruit-Topped Almond Cream is a light and refreshing dessert. It's delicious with fresh berries, but it can be made all year using whatever fruit is available. —*Donna Friedrich, Fishkill, New York*

1 package (3.4 ounces) instant French vanilla pudding mix
2-1/2 cups cold milk
1 cup heavy whipping cream
1/2 to 3/4 teaspoon almond extract
3 cups assorted fruit (strawberries, grapes, raspberries, blueberries, mandarin oranges)

In a large mixing bowl, combine pudding mix and milk. Beat on low speed for 2 minutes; set aside. In a small mixing bowl, beat cream and extract until stiff peaks form. Fold into pudding. Spoon into a shallow 2-qt. serving dish. Chill. Top with fruit just before serving. **Yield:** 8 servings.

Coconut Cake Supreme

I make most of my cakes from scratch, but during the holiday rush, this recipe that starts with a mix buys me some time. Most eager eaters don't suspect the shortcut when you dress up the cake with fluffy coconut filling and frosting.

—*Betty Claycomb*
Alverton, Pennsylvania

1 package (18-1/4 ounces) yellow cake mix
2 cups (16 ounces) sour cream
2 cups sugar
1-1/2 cups flaked coconut
1 carton (8 ounces) frozen whipped topping, thawed
Fresh mint and red gumdrops, optional

Prepare and bake cake according to package directions in two 9-in. round baking pans. Cool in pans for 10 minutes before removing to a wire rack to cool completely.

For filling, combine sour cream and sugar; mix well. Stir in coconut (filling will be soft). Set aside 1 cup of filling for frosting.

To assemble, split each cake into two horizontal layers. Place one layer on a serving platter; cover with a third of the filling. Repeat layers. Fold reserved filling into whipped topping; frost cake. Refrigerate for at least 4 hours. Garnish with mint and gumdrops if desired. **Yield:** 10-12 servings.

Light Berry Mousse

(Pictured on page 256)

Members of my family are diabetic, so I'm always looking for sugar-free recipes. This light, fluffy dessert flavored with fresh strawberries is a refreshing ending to a summer meal. —*Peggy Key*
Grant, Alabama

 Uses less fat, sugar or salt. Includes Nutritional Analysis and Diabetic Exchanges.

3/4 cup boiling water
1 package (.3 ounce) sugar-free strawberry gelatin
1 cup ice cubes
1-1/2 cups sliced fresh strawberries
3/4 cup light whipped topping

In a blender, combine water and gelatin. Cover and process until gelatin is dissolved. Blend in ice cubes until partially melted. Add strawberries; process well. Pour into a bowl; fold in whipped topping. Chill for 2 hours. **Yield:** 4 servings.

Nutritional Analysis: One serving equals 57 calories, 55 mg sodium, 0 cholesterol, 8 g carbohydrate, 2 g protein, 2 g fat. **Diabetic Exchanges:** 1/2 fruit, 1/2 fat.

Peach Pudding

(Pictured on page 257)

This light peach dessert is so fresh it tastes just like summertime. It's a quick way to dress up instant vanilla pudding.
—*Shelby Nicodemus, New Carlisle, Ohio*

1/4 cup peach gelatin powder
1/2 cup hot milk
1-1/2 cups cold milk
1 package (3.4 ounces) instant vanilla pudding mix
Sliced fresh peaches and whipped topping, optional

In a bowl, dissolve gelatin in hot milk; set aside. Meanwhile, in a mixing bowl, beat cold milk and pudding mix on low speed for 2 minutes. Add the gelatin mixture and mix well. Let stand for 5 minutes. Spoon into individual dishes. Garnish with peach slices and whipped topping if desired. **Yield:** 4 servings.

Apple Cream Pie

My four daughters have always shared my love of baking. By their teens, the girls were turning out breads, pies and cakes. This pretty pie is still a family favorite.
—*Eilene Bogar, Minier, Illinois*

4 cups sliced peeled baking apples
1 unbaked pie shell (9 inches)
1 cup sugar
1 cup heavy whipping cream
3 tablespoons all-purpose flour

Place apples in pie shell. Combine sugar, cream and flour; pour over the apples. Bake at 400° for 10 minutes. Reduce heat to 375°; bake for 35-40 minutes or until pie is set in center. Cover crust edges with foil during the last 15 minutes if needed. Cool on a wire rack. Serve, or cover and refrigerate. **Yield:** 6-8 servings.

Easy Cherry Tarts

Refrigerated crescent rolls simplify preparation of these delightful cherry bites. I cut the dough into circles with a small juice glass. —*Frances Poste*
Wall, South Dakota

1 tube (8 ounces) refrigerated crescent rolls
1 package (3 ounces) cream cheese, softened
1/4 cup confectioners' sugar
1 cup canned cherry pie filling
1/4 teaspoon almond extract

Place crescent dough on a lightly floured surface; seal seams and perforations. Cut into 2-in. circles. Place in greased miniature muffin cups. In a small mixing bowl, beat cream cheese and confectioners' sugar until smooth. Place about 1/2 teaspoon in each cup. Combine pie filling and extract; place about 2 teaspoons in each cup.

Bake at 375° for 12-14 minutes or until edges are lightly browned. Remove to wire racks to cool. Refrigerate until serving. **Yield:** 2 dozen.

Raspberry Pudding Parfaits

These parfaits are a fresh, flavorful dessert that have been in my family for ages. They're so easy to prepare, and you can substitute strawberries or blueberries with equally tempting results.—*Fran Shaffer*
Coatesville, Pennsylvania

1-1/2 cups cold milk
1 package (5.1 ounces) instant vanilla pudding mix
1 package (12 ounces) unsweetened frozen raspberries, thawed
Whipped topping, optional

In a mixing bowl, combine milk and pudding mix; beat for 2 minutes or until thickened. Spoon half into four parfait glasses. Top with half of the raspberries. Repeat layers. Garnish with whipped topping if desired. **Yield:** 4 servings.

Cherry Mousse

If you're looking for something to tickle your sweet tooth, consider this cheery mousse. This three-item treat is a cinch to whip up no matter how busy you are. The fluffy dessert is a wonderful way to end a meal. I just know your family will find it as tasty as mine does.
—Becky Lohmiller
Monticello, Indiana

1 tablespoon cherry gelatin powder
1 can (14-1/2 ounces) tart cherries, drained
1 carton (8 ounces) frozen whipped topping, thawed

In a bowl, combine gelatin powder and cherries; fold in the whipped topping. Serve immediately. **Yield:** 4 servings.

Black Forest Trifle

When I want a dessert that's fit for a feast, I turn to this trifle. The recipe calls for a convenient brownie mix, so it's simple to make.
—Peggy Linton
Cobourg, Ontario

1 package brownie mix (13-inch x 9-inch pan size)
2 packages (2.8 ounces each) chocolate mousse mix
1 can (21 ounces) cherry pie filling
1 carton (16 ounces) frozen whipped topping, thawed
4 Skor candy bars, crushed

Prepare and bake brownies according to package directions; cool completely on a wire rack. Prepare mousse according to package directions.

Crumble brownies; sprinkle half into a 4-qt. trifle dish or glass bowl. Top with half of the pie filling, mousse, whipped topping and candy bars. Repeat layers. Cover and refrigerate for 8 hours or overnight. **Yield:** 16 servings.

Raspberry Mallow Pie

Raspberry Mallow Pie is a delightful way to end a meal. It's quick to fix and tastes wonderful either refrigerated or frozen.
—*Judie Anglen*
Riverton, Wyoming

- 35 **large marshmallows**
- 1/2 **cup milk**
- 1 **package (10 ounces) frozen sweetened raspberries**
- 1 **carton (8 ounces) frozen whipped topping, thawed**
- 1 **graham cracker crust (9 inches)**

In a large microwave-safe bowl, combine marshmallows and milk. Cook on high for 1-2 minutes; stir until smooth. Stir in raspberries. Fold in the whipped topping. Pour into crust. Refrigerate or freeze. **Yield:** 6-8 servings.

Editor's Note: This recipe was tested using a 700-watt microwave.

|TAKE THE CHILL OFF| Allow frozen and ice cream desserts to sit at room temperature for 10 minutes before serving. This will make cutting them into slices easier.

Cantaloupe Sherbet

I make this sherbet very early in the day, then we sit outside under the evening Texas sky and enjoy it! It's simply delicious.
—*Rolanda Crawford, Abilene, Texas*

 Uses less fat, sugar or salt. Includes Nutritional Analysis and Diabetic Exchanges.

- 1 **medium ripe cantaloupe**
- 1 **can (14 ounces) fat-free sweetened condensed skim milk**
- 2 **tablespoons honey**

Cut cantaloupe in half; discard seeds. Peel and slice cantaloupe; cut into large pieces. Place in a blender container. Add milk and honey; cover and blend until smooth. Pour into a freezer-proof container. Freeze overnight or until firm. **Yield:** 9 servings.

Nutritional Analysis: One 1/2-cup serving equals 158 calories, 52 mg sodium, 3 mg cholesterol, 35 g carbohydrate, 4 g protein, trace fat. **Diabetic Exchanges:** 1-1/2 starch, 1 fruit.

Frozen Mud Pie

Here's one of those "looks like you fussed" desserts that is so easy it's become a standard for me. I love the mocha version, but pure chocolate lovers may prefer using chocolate chip ice cream. The cookie crust is a snap to make.
—*Debbie Terenzini, Lusby, Maryland*

1-1/2 cups crushed cream-filled chocolate sandwich cookies (about 15)
1-1/2 teaspoons sugar, optional
1/4 cup butter, melted
2 pints chocolate chip *or* coffee ice cream, softened
1/4 cup chocolate syrup, *divided*
Additional cream-filled chocolate sandwich cookies, optional

In a bowl, combine cookie crumbs and sugar if desired. Stir in butter. Press onto the bottom and up the sides of an ungreased 9-in. pie plate. Refrigerate for 30 minutes.

Spoon 1 pint of ice cream into crust. Drizzle with half of the chocolate syrup; swirl with a knife. Carefully top with remaining ice cream. Drizzle with remaining syrup; swirl with a knife. Cover and freeze until firm.

Remove from the freezer 10-15 minutes before serving. Garnish with whole cookies if desired. **Yield:** 8 servings.

Quick Banana Splits

Quick Banana Splits are a simple but special way to serve ice cream. Made with just five ingredients, there's no need to make a trip to the ice cream stand.   —*Doreen Stein, Ignace, Ontario*

2 medium bananas
1 pint vanilla ice cream
Chocolate syrup *or* ice cream topping
Chopped nuts
Maraschino cherries

Slice bananas into four dessert dishes. Top each with 1/2 cup of ice cream. Drizzle with chocolate syrup. Sprinkle with nuts; top with cherries. **Yield:** 4 servings.

Gingered Pear Sorbet

During the hot summer here in Florida, we enjoy this refreshing sorbet. Sometimes I dress up servings with berries, mint leaves or crystallized ginger. —*Donna Cline, Pensacola, Florida*

1 can (29 ounces) pear halves
1/4 cup sugar
2 tablespoons lemon juice
1/8 teaspoon ground ginger
Yellow food coloring, optional

Drain pears, reserving 1 cup syrup (discard remaining syrup or save for another use); set pears aside. In a saucepan, bring the sugar and reserved syrup to a boil. Remove from the heat; cool.

In a blender, process the pears, lemon juice and ginger until smooth. Add cooled syrup and food coloring if desired; cover and process until pureed. Pour into an 11-in. x 7-in. x 2-in. dish. Cover and freeze for 1-1/2 to 2 hours or until partially frozen.

Return mixture to blender; cover and process until smooth. Place in a freezer container; cover and freeze for at least 3 hours. Remove from the freezer 20 minutes before serving. **Yield:** 3 cups.

Blueberry Angel Dessert

Make the most of angel food cake, pie filling and whipped topping by creating this light impressive dessert that doesn't keep you in the kitchen for hours. It's the perfect way to end a summer meal. I frequently get requests for the recipe.
—*Carol Johnson, Tyler, Texas*

1 package (8 ounces) cream cheese, softened
1 cup confectioners' sugar
1 carton (8 ounces) frozen whipped topping, thawed
1 prepared angel food cake (14 ounces), cut into 1-inch cubes
2 cans (21 ounces *each*) blueberry pie filling

In a large mixing bowl, beat the cream cheese and sugar; fold in whipped topping and cake cubes. Spread evenly into an ungreased 13-in. x 9-in. x 2-in. dish; top with pie filling. Cover and refrigerate for at least 2 hours before cutting into squares. **Yield:** 12-15 servings.

Biscuit Apple Cobbler

I like to top off many meals with this comforting cobbler. The sweet treat requires only three ingredients but tastes like you fussed.
—*Claudine Moffatt, Manchester, Missouri*

1 can (21 ounces) apple
  pie filling
1/2 teaspoon ground
  cinnamon
1 tube (6 ounces)
  refrigerated flaky
  buttermilk biscuits
Whipped topping and mint,
  optional

Place pie filling in an ungreased 9-in. pie plate. Sprinkle with cinnamon. Separate each biscuit into three layers and arrange over apples.

Bake at 400° for 12-14 minutes or until the biscuits are browned. Garnish with whipped topping and mint if desired. **Yield:** 4-6 servings.

Chocolate Mousse Pie

Sky-high and scrumptious, this fluffy chocolate delight is super to serve to company. You can put the pie together in a wink—and it'll disappear just as fast! For a nice option, mound the filling in a purchased chocolate crumb crust.
—*Lois Mulkey, Sublimity, Oregon*

1 milk chocolate candy bar
  with almonds (6 ounces)
16 large marshmallows
  or 1-1/2 cups miniature
  marshmallows
1/2 cup milk
2 cups heavy whipping
  cream, whipped
1 pastry shell, baked *or*
  graham cracker *or*
  chocolate crumb crust
  (8 *or* 9 inches)

Place the candy bar, marshmallows and milk in a heavy saucepan; cook over low heat, stirring constantly until chocolate is melted and mixture is smooth. Cool. Fold in whipped cream; pour into crust. Refrigerate for at least 3 hours. **Yield:** 6-8 servings.

Banana Split Shortcake

My shortcut shortcake uses purchased pound or sponge cake instead of from-scratch biscuits. By varying the fruits, it's a treat for any season. Kids enjoy adding their choice of sundae toppings.
—*Christi Gillentine, Tulsa, Oklahoma*

8 slices pound cake (1/2 inch thick) *or* **4 individual round sponge cakes**
2 medium firm bananas, cut into 1/4-inch slices
4 scoops vanilla ice cream
1/4 cup chocolate sauce

Place cake slices on four dessert plates. Top each with bananas and ice cream. Drizzle with chocolate sauce. **Yield:** 4 servings.

Peanut Butter Sundaes

Peanut Butter Sundaes are a peanutty change of pace from the traditional ice cream sundae with chocolate sauce. This delicious recipe proves that even a quick meal doesn't have to go without dessert. —*Susan Mowery, Newville, Pennsylvania*

1 cup sugar
1/2 cup water
1/2 cup creamy peanut butter
Vanilla ice cream
Salted peanuts, optional

In a saucepan, combine sugar and water. Bring to a boil; boil 1 minute or until sugar is dissolved. Remove from the heat; stir in peanut butter. Place in a blender; blend on high until smooth. Cool slightly; pour over ice cream. Sprinkle with peanuts if desired. Refrigerate any leftovers. **Yield:** 1-1/2 cups sauce.

Fudge Berry Pie

I've made this pie several times and it always gets great reviews. With its refreshing berry flavor and chocolate crust, the no-bake delight is sure to receive thumbs-up approval from your gang, too.   —Sharlene Cullen, Robbinsdale, Minnesota

2 packages (10 ounces *each*) frozen sweetened raspberries *or* sliced strawberries, thawed and drained
1/4 cup corn syrup
1 carton (12 ounces) frozen whipped topping, thawed, *divided*
1 chocolate crumb crust (9 inches)
1 cup (6 ounces) semisweet chocolate chips

In a blender, process the berries until pureed. Pour into a large bowl. Add the corn syrup; mix well. Fold in 2 cups of whipped topping. Spoon into the crust. Freeze for 2 hours or until firm.

In a saucepan, combine 1 cup of whipped topping and chocolate chips; cook and stir over low heat until smooth. Spread over filling. Cover and freeze for 4 hours or until firm.

Remove from the freezer 30 minutes before serving. Garnish with remaining whipped topping. **Yield:** 6-8 servings.

Apricot Sorbet

I end a summer meal with this refreshing treat. With only three ingredients, it's simple to blend and freeze.   —Ruth Kahan, Brookline, Massachusetts

1 can (15 ounces) apricot halves, undrained
1 to 2 tablespoons sugar
1 tablespoon lemon juice

Freeze the apricots in a freezer-proof container. Place frozen apricots in a blender or food processor; add sugar and lemon juice. Cover and process until combined. Serve immediately or freeze. **Yield:** 4 servings.

Double Chocolate Torte

If you love chocolate, you won't be able to resist this rich, fudgy torte. I often make it for company because it's easy to prepare yet looks so impressive. For special occasions, I place it on a fancy cake plate and I use a can of whipped topping to decorate it. It looks and tastes awesome! —*Naomi Treadwell Swans Island, Maine*

1 package fudge brownie mix (13-inch x 9-inch pan size)
1 cup (6 ounces) semisweet chocolate chips, melted
1/2 cup butter, softened
2 cups whipped topping
1 teaspoon chocolate sprinkles

Prepare brownie mix according to package directions for fudge-like brownies. Spread batter in a greased and floured 9-in. round baking pan. Bake at 350° for 38-42 minutes or until center springs back when lightly touched. Cool for 10 minutes. Invert onto a serving plate; cool completely.

In a bowl, stir the chocolate and butter until smooth. Spread over brownie layer; refrigerate for 30 minutes. Just before serving, top with whipped topping. Decorate with sprinkles. **Yield:** 9-12 servings.

Burnt Custard

The recipe for this smooth-as-silk custard came from a local restaurant years ago. With its broiled topping, it looks pretty in individual cups. —*Heidi Main, Anchorage, Alaska*

2 cups heavy whipping cream
4 egg yolks
1/2 cup plus 6 teaspoons sugar, *divided*
3 teaspoons vanilla extract

In a saucepan, heat cream over medium-low until almost simmering; remove from the heat. In a mixing bowl, beat egg yolks and 1/2 cup sugar until thick and lemon-colored. Gradually beat in cream; add vanilla. Pour into six ungreased 6-oz. custard cups. Place cups in a 13-in. x 9-in. x 2-in. baking pan. Fill pan with boiling water to a depth of 1 in.

Bake at 350° for 45 minutes or until custard center is almost set. Remove cups from pan to a wire rack; cool for 15 minutes. Refrigerate for at least 2 hours or until chilled. Sprinkle with remaining sugar. Broil 4-6 in. from the heat for 2 minutes or until golden brown. Serve immediately. **Yield:** 6 servings.

Cream Cheese Cupcakes

It's hard to believe these cupcakes can taste so delicious, yet be so easy. Frost them if you wish, but my family likes them plain, which is great when I'm having an especially busy day.

—*Nancy Reichert, Thomasville, Georgia*

1 package (3 ounces) cream cheese, softened
1 package (18-1/4 ounces) yellow cake mix
1-1/4 cups water
1/2 cup butter, melted
3 eggs

In a mixing bowl, beat cream cheese until smooth. Add cake mix, water, butter and eggs; mix well. Spoon batter by 1/4 cupfuls into paper-lined muffin cups. Bake at 350° for 25 minutes or until golden brown. Remove to a wire rack to cool completely. **Yield:** 2 dozen.

Tart Cherry Pie

My aunt and I are diabetic. We both enjoy this yummy, fruity pie...and our friends even request this dessert when they come to visit.

—*Bonnie Johnson, DeKalb, Illinois*

✓ Uses less fat, sugar or salt. Includes Nutritional Analysis and Diabetic Exchanges.

2 cans (16 ounces *each*) pitted tart cherries
1 package (.8 ounce) cook-and-serve sugar-free vanilla pudding mix
1 package (.3 ounce) sugar-free cherry gelatin
Artificial sweetener equivalent to 4 teaspoons sugar
1 pastry shell (9 inches), baked

Drain cherries, reserving juice; set cherries aside. In a saucepan, combine cherry juice and dry pudding mix. Cook and stir until mixture comes to a boil and is thickened and bubbly. Remove from the heat; stir in gelatin powder and sweetener until dissolved. Stir in the cherries; transfer to pastry shell. Cool completely. Store in the refrigerator. **Yield:** 8 servings.

Nutritional Analysis: One serving equals 176 calories, 293 mg sodium, 0 cholesterol, 24 g carbohydrate, 3 g protein, 8 g fat. **Diabetic Exchanges:** 1 starch, 1/2 fruit, 1/2 fat.

Banana Butterfinger Pudding

As for my dessert, you can substitute other kinds of candy bars to suit your preference. The pudding flavor can be changed as well—perhaps to vanilla or butterscotch.
—*LaVerna Mjones*
Moorhead, Minnesota

1 cup cold milk
1 package (3.4 ounces) instant banana pudding mix
3 Butterfinger candy bars (2.1 ounces *each*), crushed
1 carton (8 ounces) frozen whipped topping, thawed
3 medium firm bananas, sliced

In a mixing bowl, combine milk and pudding mix until thickened and smooth. Set aside 1/3 cup crushed candy bars for topping. Fold whipped topping, bananas and remaining candy bars into pudding. Spoon into serving dishes; refrigerate until serving. Sprinkle with the reserved candy bars. **Yield:** 4-6 servings.

Gingered Melon

For get-togethers, let guests spoon their melon from a large serving bowl and put on their own topping. Combine the fruit with ice cream or frozen yogurt and ginger ale to make a melon float.
—*Patricia Richardson, Verona, Ontario*

1/2 medium honeydew, cut into 1-inch cubes
1/4 cup orange juice
1-1/2 teaspoons ground ginger
1/2 to 1 cup whipped cream
1/4 cup fresh *or* frozen unsweetened raspberries

In a bowl, combine the melon, orange juice and ginger; refrigerate for 5-10 minutes. Spoon into tall dessert glasses or bowls. Top with whipped cream and raspberries. **Yield:** 4 servings.

Lemon Graham Freeze

For a cool and economical treat, try Lemon Graham Freeze. This light, pleasantly tart dessert is convenient since you make it ahead.

—Barbara Husband, Dorchester, Wisconsin

1 can (5 ounces) evaporated milk
1/2 cup sugar
2 tablespoons lemon juice
4 drops yellow food coloring, optional
6 whole graham crackers

Place milk in a mixing bowl; add beaters to bowl. Freeze for 25-30 minutes or until soft crystals form around edges of bowl. Beat milk until stiff peaks form. Gradually add sugar, lemon juice and food coloring if desired; mix well.

Place five graham crackers in an ungreased 11-in. x 7-in. x 2-in. dish; pour milk mixture over crackers. Crush remaining graham cracker and sprinkle over top. Cover and freeze until firm. **Yield:** 6 servings.

Frozen Berry Fluff

My family loves this cool, refreshing dessert no matter what flavor pie filling I use, but I must admit raspberry is their favorite.

—Donetta Brunner
Savanna, Illinois

2 cans (21 ounces *each*) raspberry *or* strawberry pie filling
1 can (14 ounces) sweetened condensed milk
1 can (8 ounces) crushed pineapple, undrained, optional
1 carton (12 ounces) frozen whipped topping, thawed
Fresh berries, optional

In a bowl, combine pie filling, milk and pineapple if desired. Fold in whipped topping. Spread into an ungreased 13-in. x 9-in. x 2-in. pan. Cover and freeze for 8 hours or overnight.

Remove from the freezer 10-15 minutes before serving. Cut into squares. Garnish each with berries if desired. **Yield:** 12-15 servings.

Swiss Meringue Shells

Folks will know you fussed when you bring out these sweet, cloud-like cups topped with fresh berries (or a tart fruit filling if you like). These meringues from the American Egg Board make an elegant ending to a company dinner.

3 egg whites
1/4 teaspoon cream of tartar
3/4 cup sugar
1/2 teaspoon vanilla extract
Berries of your choice

In a mixing bowl, beat egg whites and cream of tartar until foamy, about 1 minute. Gradually beat in sugar, 1 tablespoon at a time, on high until stiff glossy peaks form and sugar is dissolved. Beat in vanilla.

Cover a baking sheet with parchment paper or greased foil. Spoon meringue into eight mounds on paper. Using the back of the spoon, shape into 3-in. cups. Bake at 225° for 1 to 1-1/2 hours or until set and dry. Turn oven off; leave meringues in oven 1 hour. Cool on wire racks. Store in an airtight container. Fill shells with berries. **Yield:** 8 servings.

Danish Rhubarb Pudding

My grandmother came to the U.S. from Denmark at the age of 16, and she was an excellent cook. A delightful rhubarb pudding that she made often is one of my favorite traditional desserts. It has a sweet, delicious, distinctive flavor and clear, deep color. Since the pudding is soft-set, it could also be used as a sauce over ice cream or pound cake. —*Kay Sundheim, Nashua, Montana*

6 cups chopped fresh *or*
**   frozen rhubarb, thawed**
6 cups water
2 cups sugar
1/4 cup cornstarch
3 tablespoons cold water

In a saucepan, bring rhubarb and water to a boil. Reduce heat; simmer, uncovered, for 10-15 minutes or until rhubarb is tender. Drain, reserving liquid; discard pulp. Measure 4 cups liquid; return to the pan.

Add sugar; bring to a boil. Combine cornstarch and cold water until smooth; stir into rhubarb liquid. Cook and stir for 1-2 minutes or until slightly thickened. Pour into individual dishes. Refrigerate for at least 4 hours before serving. **Yield:** 8 servings.

Cherry Cheesecake

When I worked full time and needed a quick dessert to take to a potluck or a friend's home, this pie was always the answer. You can substitute a graham cracker crust or use another type of fruit pie filling for a change of pace. Even the chilling time is flexible if you're in a big hurry.
—*Mary Smith*
Bradenton, Florida

2 packages (one 8 ounces, one 3 ounces) cream cheese, softened
1 cup confectioners' sugar
1 carton (8 ounces) frozen whipped topping, thawed
1 shortbread *or* graham cracker crust (8 *or* 9 inches)
1 can (21 ounces) cherry pie filling

In a mixing bowl, beat the cream cheese and sugar until smooth. Fold in whipped topping; spoon into crust. Top with pie filling. Refrigerate until serving. **Yield:** 6-8 servings.

|CUTTING CHEESECAKE| Cheesecake can be covered and refrigerated for up to 3 days. Use a straight-edge knife to cut cheesecake. Warm the blade in hot water, dry and slice. Clean and rewarm the knife after each cut.

Hot Apple Sundaes

After dinner, everyone usually dashes off, but this ice cream treat makes them linger around the table. It's that good!
—*Delia Gurnow, New Madrid, Missouri*

1 can (21 ounces) apple pie filling
1/4 cup apple juice
1 tablespoon sugar
1/2 teaspoon ground cinnamon
Vanilla ice cream

In a saucepan, combine the first four ingredients. Cook and stir over medium heat until heated through. Serve over ice cream. **Yield:** 2 cups.

Chocolate Cookie Mousse

I have family members who beg me to bring this rich yummy dessert whenever I visit. It calls for just four ingredients, and it's handy to keep in the freezer for a special occasion. —*Carol Mullaney*
Pittsburgh, Pennsylvania

1 package (14 ounces) cream-filled chocolate sandwich cookies, *divided*
2 tablespoons milk
2 cups heavy whipping cream, *divided*
2 cups (12 ounces) semisweet chocolate chips

Crush 16 cookies; sprinkle into an 8-in. square dish. Drizzle with milk. In a microwave-safe bowl, combine 2/3 cup cream and chocolate chips. Microwave, uncovered, on high for 1 minute. Stir; microwave 30-60 seconds or until chips are melted. Stir until smooth; cool to room temperature.

Meanwhile, in a mixing bowl, beat remaining cream until soft peaks form. Fold into chocolate mixture. Spread a third of the chocolate mixture over crushed cookies. Separate eight cookies; place over chocolate mixture. Repeat. Top with remaining chocolate mixture. Garnish with remaining whole cookies.

Cover; freeze for up to 2 months. Thaw in refrigerator for at least 3 hours before serving. **Yield:** 16 servings.

Editor's Note: This recipe was tested in an 850-watt microwave.

Lemon Ice

Pucker up for this sweet-tart treat. The delicious lemon dessert is a perfectly refreshing way to end a summer meal or any meal, for that matter.
—*Concetta Maranto Skenfield, Bakersfield, California*

2 cups sugar
1 cup water
2 cups lemon juice
1 tablespoon grated lemon peel

In a saucepan over low heat, cook and stir sugar and water until sugar is dissolved. Remove from the heat; stir in lemon juice. Pour into a freezer container. Freeze for 4 hours, stirring every 30 minutes, or until mixture becomes slushy. Sprinkle servings with lemon peel. **Yield:** 6 servings.

Kool-Aid Pie

A fun crust of vanilla wafers is easy for kids to make and holds an eye-catching, fluffy filling that's refreshing in summer. Use different flavors of Kool-Aid to vary the pie's taste.

—Ledia Black
Pineland, Texas

1 can (12 ounces)
  evaporated milk
36 vanilla wafers
1 cup sugar
1 envelope (.14 ounce)
  unsweetened lemon-lime
  Kool-Aid
Whipped topping, optional

Pour milk into a small metal or glass mixing bowl. Add beaters to the bowl. Cover and chill for at least 2 hours.

Coat a 9-in. pie plate with nonstick cooking spray. Line bottom and sides of plate with wafers. Beat milk until soft peaks form. Add sugar and drink mix; beat until thoroughly mixed. Spoon over wafers; freeze for at least 4 hours. Garnish with whipped topping if desired. **Yield:** 6-8 servings.

Berry Good Ice Cream Sauce

I started cooking in earnest as a bride over 40 years ago. I'm thankful to say I improved in time—though I made something once even the dog refused to eat! Now, my three children are grown and I'm the grandmother of four.

—Joy Beck
Cincinnati, Ohio

1-3/4 cups sliced fresh *or*
  frozen rhubarb
2/3 cup pureed fresh *or*
  frozen strawberries
1/4 cup sugar
1/4 cup orange juice
2 cups sliced fresh *or*
  frozen strawberries

In a saucepan, combine the first four ingredients. Cook over medium heat until rhubarb is tender, about 5 minutes. Stir in the sliced strawberries. Store in the refrigerator. **Yield:** 3-1/2 cups.

Watermelon Ice

If you're one of many folks who just can't wait for the county fair, you'll love these snow cones that exhibit plenty of good taste. This sweet, frosty snack is so refreshing on hot summer days. Store it in the freezer, so it's a snap to scoop and serve in snow cone cups. —*Darlene Markel, Mt. Hood, Oregon*

1/2 cup sugar
1/4 cup watermelon *or* mixed fruit gelatin powder
3/4 cup boiling water
5 cups seeded cubed watermelon

In a bowl, dissolve sugar and gelatin in boiling water; set aside. Place watermelon in a blender; cover and puree. Stir into gelatin mixture. Pour into an ungreased pan. Cover and freeze overnight. Remove from the freezer 1 hour before serving. Spoon into paper cones or serving dishes. **Yield:** 4-6 servings.

Layered Pudding Dessert

High on our list of long-time favorites, this fluffy, fruity refrigerated treat continues to hold its own against new dessert recipes I try. —*Pat Habiger Spearville, Kansas*

1 cup crushed vanilla wafers, *divided*
1 package (3 ounces) cook-and-serve vanilla pudding mix
2 medium ripe bananas, *divided*
1 package (3 ounces) strawberry gelatin
1 cup whipped topping

Spread half of the crushed wafers in the bottom of a greased 8-in. square pan. Prepare pudding mix according to package directions; spoon hot pudding over crumbs. Slice one banana; place over pudding. Top with remaining crumbs. Chill for 1 hour.

Meanwhile, prepare gelatin according to package directions; chill for 30 minutes or until partially set. Pour over crumbs. Slice the remaining banana and place over gelatin. Spread whipped topping over all. Chill for 2 hours. **Yield:** 9 servings.

Frozen Banana Pineapple Cups

You can stir together this sweet tangy fruit mixture with just five ingredients, then pop it in the freezer overnight. The frosty results are a refreshing addition to a summer dinner. —*Alice Miller*
Middlebury, Indiana

3 cups water
2-2/3 cups mashed ripe
      bananas (5 to 6 medium)
1-1/2 cups sugar
  1 can (20 ounces) crushed
      pineapple, undrained
  1 can (6 ounces) frozen
      orange juice
      concentrate, thawed

In a 2-qt. freezer container, combine all of the ingredients and mix well. Cover and freeze for 5 hours or overnight. Remove from the freezer 15 minutes before serving. **Yield:** 9-12 servings.

Caramel Apple Cupcakes

Bring these extra-special cupcakes to your next bake sale and watch how quickly they disappear—if your family doesn't gobble them up first! Kids will go for the fun appearance and tasty toppings while adults will appreciate the moist spiced cake underneath.
—*Diane Halferty, Corpus Christi, Texas*

  1 package (18-1/4
      ounces) spice *or* carrot
      cake mix
  2 cups chopped peeled tart
      apples
 20 caramels
  3 tablespoons milk
  1 cup finely chopped
      pecans, toasted

Prepare cake batter according to package directions; fold in apples. Fill 12 greased or paper-lined jumbo muffin cups three-fourths full. Bake at 350° for 20 minutes or until a toothpick comes out clean. Cool for 10 minutes before removing from pans to wire racks to cool completely.

In a saucepan, cook the caramels and milk over low heat until smooth. Spread over cupcakes. Sprinkle with pecans. Insert a wooden stick into the center of each cupcake. **Yield:** 1 dozen.

Sherbet Dessert

This refreshing dessert was served at a baby shower I attended. It was so delicious I asked the hostess to share her secret. I couldn't believe it was made with only three ingredients, and it was low-fat as a bonus.
—Shirley Colvin
Tremonton, Utah

✓ **Uses less fat, sugar or salt. Includes Nutritional Analysis and Diabetic Exchanges.**

1/2 gallon orange sherbet *or* flavor of your choice, softened
1 package (10 ounces) frozen sweetened raspberries, thawed
2 medium ripe bananas, mashed

Place the sherbet in a large bowl; stir in raspberries and bananas. Freeze until firm. **Yield:** 18 servings.

Nutritional Analysis: One 1/2-cup serving equals 150 calories, 40 mg sodium, 4 mg cholesterol, 34 g carbohydrate, 1 g protein, 2 g fat. **Diabetic Exchanges:** 1 starch, 1 fruit, 1/2 fat.

Editor's Note: Rainbow sherbet is not recommended for this recipe.

Cranberry Crumble

My family likes this crumble so much I make it year-round. But I especially like to serve it warm on cool winter evenings.
—Karen Riordan, Louisville, Kentucky

1-1/2 cups quick-cooking oats
1 cup packed brown sugar
1/2 cup all-purpose flour
1/3 cup cold butter
1 can (16 ounces) whole-berry cranberry sauce
Whipped cream *or* ice cream, optional

In a bowl, combine oats, brown sugar and flour. Cut in butter until crumbly. Press half into a greased 8-in. square baking dish. Spread the cranberry sauce evenly over crust. Sprinkle with remaining oat mixture.

Bake at 350° for 35-40 minutes or until golden brown and filling is hot. Serve warm with whipped cream or ice cream if desired. **Yield:** 9 servings.

Lime Sherbet

You don't need an ice cream maker to churn out this light, green refresher. The mild lime flavor and frosty consistency make it a perfect treat.

—*Carolyn Hannay, Antioch, Tennessee*

✓ **Uses less fat, sugar or salt. Includes Nutritional Analysis and Diabetic Exchanges.**

    1 package (3 ounces) lime gelatin
    1 cup boiling water
    3 cups 1% milk
    1/2 cup sugar
    1/4 cup lemon juice

In a bowl, dissolve gelatin in boiling water. Add the milk, sugar and lemon juice; stir until sugar is dissolved. Pour into a freezer container; freeze for 4 hours or until frozen.

Remove from the freezer and let stand for 10 minutes or until slightly softened. Beat with a mixer until light and fluffy. Refreeze for at least 1 hour. **Yield:** about 1 quart.

Nutritional Analysis: One serving (1 cup) equals 260 calories, 2 g fat (1 g saturated fat), 11 mg cholesterol, 156 mg sodium, 54 g carbohydrate, trace fiber, 9 g protein. **Diabetic Exchanges:** 2 starch, 1-1/2 fruit.

Cake with Lemon Sauce

This is a family favorite on hot summer nights. Cream cheese, milk and pudding mix are all that's needed for the sunny sauce drizzled over prepared pound cake and topped with a few berries. You could also use sponge cake dessert shells instead.

—*Claire Dion*
Canterbury, Connecticut

    1 package (3 ounces) cream cheese, softened
1-3/4 cups cold milk
    1 package (3.4 ounces) instant lemon pudding mix
    4 slices pound cake *or* angel food cake
Fresh raspberries, optional

In a small mixing bowl, beat the cream cheese until smooth. Add milk and pudding mix; beat for 2 minutes or until smooth and thickened. Serve with cake. Garnish with raspberries if desired. **Yield:** 4 servings.

Cookie Ice Cream Sandwiches

Endulge in your love for ice cream by assembling these sandwiches. The tempting treats take advantage of store-bought oatmeal raisin cookies, ice cream and peanut butter. You can roll them in crushed candy bars or nuts for an even fancier look. *—Melissa Stevens, Elk River, Minnesota*

Peanut butter
12 oatmeal raisin cookies
1 pint vanilla ice cream *or* flavor of your choice
Miniature chocolate chips

Spread peanut butter over the bottom of six cookies. Top with a scoop of ice cream. Top with another cookie; press down gently. Roll sides of ice cream sandwich in chocolate chips. Wrap in plastic wrap and freeze until serving. **Yield:** 6 servings.

Pineapple Upside-Down Cake

I need just a few easy ingredients to dress up a boxed mix and create this classic cake. It bakes up so moist and pretty, no one will believe it wasn't made from scratch. *—Gloria Poyer Hackettstown, New Jersey*

6 canned pineapple slices
6 maraschino cherries
1 cup chopped walnuts, *divided*
1 package (18-1/4 ounces) white cake mix

Place pineapple slices in a greased and floured 10-in. tube pan. Place a cherry in the center of each slice. Sprinkle half of the walnuts around the pineapple. Prepare cake mix according to package directions; spoon batter over pineapple layer. Sprinkle with remaining nuts.

Bake at 350° for 40-45 minutes or until a toothpick inserted near the center comes out clean. Cool for 10 minutes before inverting onto a wire rack to cool completely. **Yield:** 10 servings.

Pineapple Ice Cream

I rely on my ice cream maker when whipping up this five-ingredient frozen treat. The creamy concoction has just the right amount of pineapple to keep guests asking for more. —*Phyllis Schmalz* *Kansas City, Kansas*

3 eggs, beaten
2 cups milk
1 cup sugar
1-3/4 cups heavy whipping cream
1 can (8 ounces) crushed pineapple, undrained

In a saucepan, cook the eggs and milk over medium heat for 8 minutes or until a thermometer reads 160° and mixture coats a metal spoon. Stir in sugar until dissolved. Cool. Stir in the cream and pineapple.

Fill cylinder of ice cream freezer two-thirds full; freeze according to manufacturer's directions. Refrigerate remaining mixture until ready to freeze. Allow ice cream to ripen in refrigerator freezer for 2-4 hours before serving. May be frozen for up to 2 months. **Yield:** 6 servings.

Pistachio Pudding Tarts

For St. Patrick's Day, Christmas or anytime you want a treat that's green, refreshing and delightful, try these tempting tarts. —*Bettye Linster* *Atlanta, Georgia*

1 cup butter, softened
1 package (8 ounces) cream cheese, softened
2 cups all-purpose flour
1 package (3.4 ounces) instant pistachio pudding mix
1-3/4 cups cold milk

In a mixing bowl, combine butter, cream cheese and flour; mix well. Shape into 48 balls (1 in. each); press onto the bottom and up the sides of ungreased miniature muffin cups. Bake at 400° for 12-15 minutes or until lightly browned. Cool for 5 minutes; carefully remove from pans to a wire rack to cool completely.

For filling, combine pudding and milk in a mixing bowl; beat on low speed for 2 minutes. Cover and refrigerate for 5 minutes. Spoon into tart shells; serve immediately. **Yield:** 4 dozen.

Flowerpot Cupcakes

A strip of fruit roll is used to wrap a chocolate cupcake and form a mini flowerpot. Giving color to each pot are easy gumdrop blossoms growing from pretzel stick stems. They're great for a spring or summer birthday party.

—*Judi Oudekerk*
Buffalo, Minnesota

1 package (18-1/4 ounces) devil's food cake mix
16 pieces Fruit by the Foot
24 large green gumdrops
48 large assorted gumdrops
48 pretzel sticks

Prepare cake batter according to package directions. Fill greased muffin cups two-thirds full. Bake at 350° for 18-20 minutes or until a toothpick comes out clean. Cool for 5 minutes; remove from pans to wire racks to cool completely.

Cut three 9-in. pieces from each fruit roll piece (save small pieces for another use). With a small pastry brush, lightly brush water on one end of a fruit strip. Wrap around bottom of cupcake; press ends together. Repeat with remaining cupcakes. Lightly brush water on one side of remaining fruit strips; fold in half lengthwise. Brush one end with water; wrap around cupcake top, slightly overlapping bottom fruit strip.

Press each gumdrop into a 1-1/4-in. circle. With scissors, cut each green gumdrop into four leaf shapes; set aside. Cut one end of each remaining gumdrop into a tulip shape. Gently press a pretzel into each tulip-shaped gumdrop. Gently press gumdrop leaves onto pretzels. Press two flowers into the top of each cupcake. **Yield:** 2 dozen.

Five-Minute Blueberry Pie

If you like the taste of fresh blueberries, you'll love this pie. Since it's a breeze to whip up, I make it often, especially in summer.
—*Milda Anderson, Osceola, Wisconsin*

1/2 cup sugar
2 tablespoons cornstarch
3/4 cup water
4 cups fresh or frozen blueberries, thawed
1 graham cracker crust (9 inches)

In a saucepan, combine sugar and cornstarch. Stir in water until smooth. Bring to a boil over medium heat; cook and stir for 2 minutes. Add blueberries. Cook for 3 minutes, stirring occasionally. Pour into crust. Refrigerate until serving. **Yield:** 6-8 servings.

Chocolate Mint Ice Cream

When the weather gets hot, my family enjoys this cool combination of chocolate and mint. It doesn't require an ice cream maker—all that you need is an ordinary freezer. My ice cream's versatile, too. We've used crushed Heath bars, Oreo cookies and miniature chocolate chips in place of the Andes candies.
—*Fran Skaff, Egg Harbor, Wisconsin*

   1 can (14 ounces) sweetened condensed milk
1/2 cup chocolate syrup
   2 cups heavy whipping cream
   1 package (4.67 ounces) mint Andes candies (28 pieces), chopped

In a small bowl, combine the milk and chocolate syrup; set aside. In a mixing bowl, beat cream until stiff peaks form. Fold in chocolate mixture and candies. Transfer to a freezer-proof container; cover and freeze for 5 hours or until firm. Remove from the freezer 10 minutes before serving. **Yield:** 1-1/2 quarts.

Caramel Chocolate Sauce

Chocolate lovers, rejoice! This quick fix takes ice cream toppings to new heights. Melted caramels give the rich fudge-like sauce extra appeal, making it hard to resist a second helping. —*June Smith Byron Center, Michigan*

30 caramels
   1 cup (6 ounces) semisweet chocolate chips
   1 can (5 ounces) evaporated milk
1/2 cup butter
Ice cream

In a 1-qt. microwave-safe bowl, combine the caramels, chocolate chips, milk and butter. Microwave, uncovered, on high for 2 minutes; stir.

Heat 1-2 minutes longer or until the caramels are almost melted; stir until smooth. Serve warm if desired over ice cream (sauce will thicken upon standing). Refrigerate leftovers. **Yield:** 2 cups.

Editor's Note: This recipe was tested in an 850-watt microwave.

S'more Tarts

I bring a fireside favorite indoors with the taste-tempting treats I fix for movie and game nights. Kids of all ages will quickly gobble up the individual graham cracker tarts filled with a fudgy brownie and golden marshmallows before asking, "Can I have s'more?"

—Trish Quinn
Cheyenne, Wyoming

>   1 package fudge brownie mix (13-inch x 9-inch pan size)
> 12 individual graham cracker shells
> 1-1/2 cups miniature marshmallows
>   1 cup milk chocolate chips

Prepare brownie batter according to package directions. Place graham cracker shells on a baking sheet and fill with brownie batter. Bake at 350° for 20-25 minutes or until a toothpick inserted in the center comes out with moist crumbs.

Immediately sprinkle with marshmallows and chocolate chips. Bake 3-5 minutes longer or until marshmallows are puffed and golden brown. **Yield:** 1 dozen.

Layered Toffee Cake

This is a quick and yummy way to dress up a purchased angel food cake. To keep the plate clean while assembling this pretty layered dessert, cut two half circles of waxed paper to place under the bottom layer and remove them after frosting the cake and sprinkling on the toffee.

—Pat Squire
Alexandria, Virginia

>   2 cups heavy whipping cream
> 1/2 cup caramel *or* butterscotch ice cream topping
> 1/2 teaspoon vanilla extract
>   1 prepared angel food cake (16 ounces)
>   9 Heath candy bars (1.4 ounces *each*), chopped

In a mixing bowl, beat cream just until it begins to thicken. Gradually add ice cream topping and vanilla, beating until soft peaks form.

Cut cake horizontally into three layers. Place the bottom layer on a serving plate; spread with 1 cup cream mixture and sprinkle with 1/2 cup candy bar. Repeat. Place top layer on cake; frost top and sides with remaining cream mixture and sprinkle with the remaining candy bar. Store in the refrigerator. **Yield:** 12-14 servings.

Praline Parfaits

The recipe for this sweet, nutty ice cream sauce comes from a famous New Orleans restaurant. When we entertain, I top each pretty parfait with whipped cream and a pecan half. —*Cindy Stephenson*
Houston, Texas

1 bottle (16 ounces) dark corn syrup
1/3 cup sugar
1/3 cup water
1 cup chopped pecans
3 to 4 cups vanilla ice cream

In a saucepan, combine the corn syrup, sugar and water; bring to a boil, stirring constantly. Remove from the heat; stir in pecans. Cool completely.

Spoon half of the ice cream into four parfait glasses or dishes. Top each with 2 tablespoons sauce. Repeat layers. Refrigerate leftover sauce. **Yield:** 4 servings (about 2-1/2 cups sauce).

Dipped Strawberries

(Also pictured on front cover)

I dip plump red berries in chocolate and vanilla chips, and they're always a hit. They'll be the delicious red, white and "ooh" center of attention at your place, too.
—*Marlene Wiczek*
Little Falls, Minnesota

1 quart medium fresh strawberries (with stems)
1-2/3 cups vanilla *or* white baking chips
2 tablespoons shortening, *divided*
1 cup (6 ounces) semisweet chocolate chips

Wash strawberries and gently pat until completely dry. In a microwave or double boiler, melt vanilla chips and 1 tablespoon shortening. Dip each strawberry until two-thirds of the berry is coated, allowing the excess to drip off. Place on a waxed paper-lined tray or baking sheet; refrigerate for 30 minutes or until set.

Melt chocolate chips and remaining shortening. Dip each strawberry until one-third is coated. Return to tray; refrigerate for 30 minutes or until set. **Yield:** 2-1/2 to 3 dozen.

Raspberry Cupcake Dessert

A light and fun finish, my cream cake dessert is a hit with kids of all ages. When I'm in a hurry, store-bought cupcakes work fine. And while I prefer homemade whipped cream, purchased whipped topping is an easy option. —*Edith Ruth Muldoon*
Baldwin, New York

2 creamed-filled chocolate cupcakes, cut in half
1 to 2 cups heavy whipping cream
3 tablespoons confectioners' sugar
1/2 teaspoon vanilla extract
1 to 1-1/2 cups fresh *or* frozen raspberries, thawed and drained
Additional raspberries, optional

Place one cupcake half each in four dessert dishes. In a mixing bowl, beat cream until soft peaks form. Beat in sugar and vanilla until stiff peaks form. Fold in raspberries. Spoon over cupcakes. Garnish with additional berries if desired. Refrigerate until serving. **Yield:** 4 servings.

Editor's Note: This recipe was prepared with Hostess brand cupcakes.

Caramel Apple Burritos

These are such fun to experiment with. I've made them with different varieties of apples and have substituted applesauce or pie filling. Topped with ice cream, caramel or chocolate sauce, they make a memorable dessert. —*Cindy Reams*
Philipsburg, Pennsylvania

3 large tart apples, peeled and sliced
10 caramels
5 flour tortillas (8 inches), warmed

Place apple slices in a saucepan; cover and cook over medium heat for 3-4 minutes or until tender. Reduce heat. Add caramels; cook and stir until caramels are melted. Spoon apple mixture off center on each tortilla; fold sides and ends over filling and roll up. **Yield:** 5 servings.

Pumpkin Ice Cream

This ice cream is as simple as opening a can, stirring and freezing. Plus, if you're like me and looking for a good way of using up your homegrown pumpkins, feel free to substitute fresh-picked for canned.
—*Linda Young*
Longmont, Colorado

1 cup canned pumpkin
1/4 teaspoon pumpkin pie spice
1 quart vanilla ice cream, softened
Gingersnaps, optional

In a medium bowl, mix the pumpkin and pie spice until well blended. Stir in ice cream. Freeze until serving. Garnish with gingersnaps if desired. **Yield:** 4-6 servings.

Raspberry Pear Delight

Raspberry Pear Delight is a fast-to-fix yet fairly fancy dessert that's a perfect ending to a meal anytime.
—*Marion Tipton, Phoenix, Arizona*

1 package (10 ounces) frozen sweetened raspberries, thawed
1 can (15 ounces) pear halves, drained
1 pint raspberry sorbet *or* sherbet
Hot fudge ice cream topping
Fresh raspberries, optional

In a blender or food processor, puree raspberries; strain seeds. Pour onto four dessert plates. Top with pears and a scoop of sorbet. Drizzle with hot fudge topping. Garnish with fresh berries if desired. **Yield:** 4 servings.

Candy Bar Pie

I've made this no-bake dessert for many occasions because the recipe is so simple and easy to remember. I freeze the candy bars and use a rolling pin to make crushing them easy.

—*Sharlie Hanson*
Tulsa, Oklahoma

1 package (8 ounces) cream cheese, softened
1 carton (8 ounces) frozen whipped topping, thawed
4 Butterfinger candy bars (2.1 ounces *each*)
1 prepared graham cracker crust (9 inches)

In a small mixing bowl, beat the cream cheese until smooth. Fold in whipped topping. Crush the candy bars; fold 1 cup into cream cheese mixture. Spoon into crust. Sprinkle with remaining candy bar crumbs. Refrigerate for 2-4 hours before slicing. **Yield:** 6-8 servings.

Frosty Cranberry Pie

It's nice to have this light, not-too-sweet pie in the freezer when unexpected guests stop over for coffee. It's so easy to put together, and everyone always asks for the recipe.
—*Mildred Skrha*
Oak Brook, Illinois

1 package (8 ounces) cream cheese, softened
1 cup confectioners' sugar
1 can (16 ounces) whole-berry cranberry sauce
1 carton (8 ounces) frozen whipped topping, thawed
2 pastry shells (9 inches), baked
Additional whipped topping, optional

In a mixing bowl, beat cream cheese and sugar. Stir in cranberry sauce. Fold in whipped topping. Spoon into crusts. Cover and freeze for up to 3 months. Remove from the freezer 10-15 minutes before serving. Garnish with whipped topping if desired. **Yield:** 2 pies (6-8 servings each).

Editor's Note: Shortbread or graham cracker crusts may be substituted for the pastry shells.

Granola Sundaes

My kids like to mix the no-bake granola topping themselves and sprinkle it over ice cream. The versatile granola mix can top off yogurt, fresh fruit and pie filling...or be rolled into a ball for a sweet snack.
—*Kim Dunbar, Willow Springs, Illinois*

1 cup quick-cooking oats
1/2 cup packed brown sugar
1/4 cup peanut butter
1/4 cup butter, softened
Ice cream

In a bowl, combine oats and brown sugar. Stir in peanut butter and butter until mixture forms coarse crumbs. Sprinkle over ice cream. **Yield:** 2 cups topping.

|ABOUT OATS| Old-fashioned oats and quick-cooking oats can usually be interchanged in recipes. Store oats in an airtight container in a cool, dry place for up to 6 months.

Honey Baked Apples

These tender apples smell so good while they're in the oven—and taste even better. We enjoy the golden raisins inside and the soothing taste of honey. They're a yummy change from the cinnamon and sugar seasoning traditionally used with apples.
—*Chere Bell*
Colorado Springs, Colorado

2-1/4 cups water
3/4 cup packed brown sugar
3 tablespoons honey
6 large tart apples
1 cup golden raisins

In a saucepan, bring water, brown sugar and honey to a boil. Remove from the heat. Core apples and peel the top third of each. Place in an ungreased 9-in. baking dish.

Fill apples with raisins; sprinkle any remaining raisins into pan. Pour sugar syrup over apples. Bake, uncovered, at 350° for 1 hour or until tender, basting occasionally. **Yield:** 6 servings.

Easy Black Forest Torte

Easy Black Forest Torte couldn't be simpler—all you need is a boxed cake mix, pie filling, miniature marshmallows and whipped topping. I sampled this fancy-looking dessert during a visit with my grandmother. The marshmallows and cherries trade places during baking, and the flavor is excellent.

—Deb Morrison, Skiatook, Oklahoma

4 to 5 cups miniature marshmallows
1 package (18-1/4 ounces) chocolate cake mix
1 can (21 ounces) cherry pie filling
1 carton (8 ounces) frozen whipped topping, thawed

Sprinkle marshmallows in a greased 13-in. x 9-in. x 2-in. baking pan. Prepare cake batter according to package directions; pour over the marshmallows. Spoon pie filling over batter. Bake at 350° for 1 hour or until a toothpick inserted near the center comes out clean. Cool. Frost with whipped topping. Store in the refrigerator. **Yield:** 12-16 servings.

Quick Strawberry Cobbler

Blueberry or cherry pie filling also work great with this easy cobbler. A good friend shared the recipe with me.
—Sue Poe, Hayden, Alabama

2 cans (21 ounces *each*) strawberry pie filling *or* fruit filling of your choice
1/2 cup butter, softened
1 package (3 ounces) cream cheese, softened
2 teaspoons vanilla extract
2 packages (9 ounces *each*) yellow cake mix

Pour pie filling into a greased 13-in. x 9-in. x 2-in. baking dish. Bake at 350° for 5-7 minutes or until heated through.

Meanwhile, in a mixing bowl, cream butter, cream cheese and vanilla. Place cake mixes in another bowl; cut in cream cheese mixture until crumbly. Sprinkle over hot filling. Bake 25-30 minutes longer or until topping is golden brown. **Yield:** 12 servings.

No–Bake Cheesecake Pie

I came up with this creamy white chocolate cheesecake after remembering one evening that I needed to bring a treat to the office the next day. It was a tremendous hit. It's quick to fix yet tastes like you fussed.   —*Geneva Mayer, Olney, Illinois*

1 cup vanilla *or* white chips
2 packages (8 ounces *each*) cream cheese, cubed
1 carton (8 ounces) frozen whipped topping, thawed
1 graham cracker crust (9 inches)
1/3 cup English toffee bits *or* almond brickle chips

In a heavy saucepan, melt chips over medium-low heat; stir until smooth. Remove from the heat; stir in cream cheese until smooth. Fold in whipped topping. Pour into the crust.

Cover and refrigerate overnight or until set. Just before serving, sprinkle with toffee bits. **Yield:** 6-8 servings.

Cinnamon Graham Sundaes

For a swift sweet dessert, try four-ingredient Cinnamon Graham Sundaes. Many Mexican restaurants serve ice cream in deep-fried shells. I use cinnamon graham crackers and honey to get a similar taste. You can replace the honey with caramel or chocolate syrup with good results.   —*Jennifer Villarreal Texas City, Texas*

20 cinnamon graham cracker squares
1/2 gallon vanilla ice cream
3 tablespoons honey
2 teaspoons ground cinnamon

For each serving, place two graham cracker squares on a plate. Top with ice cream and drizzle with honey. Sprinkle with cinnamon. **Yield:** 10 servings.

Peach-Glazed Cake

After tasting this cake, guests always ask for a second slice and the recipe. Everyone is surprised when they learn this dessert is so easy to make. I often garnish servings with pear slices instead of peaches.
—*Samantha Jones*
Morgantown, West Virginia

1 can (15 ounces) pear halves, drained
1 package (18-1/4 ounces) white cake mix
3 eggs
1 jar (12 ounces) peach preserves, *divided*
Fresh *or* frozen sliced peaches, thawed

In a blender or food processor, cover and process pears until pureed. Transfer to a mixing bowl; add the cake mix and eggs. Beat on medium speed for 2 minutes. Pour into a greased and floured 10-in. fluted tube pan. Bake at 350° for 30-35 minutes or until a toothpick inserted near the center comes out clean. Cool for 10 minutes before removing from pan to a wire rack.

In a microwave-safe bowl, heat 1/2 cup of peach preserves, uncovered, on high for 60-90 seconds or until melted. Slowly brush over warm cake. Cool completely. Slice cake; top with peaches. Melt remaining preserves; drizzle over top. **Yield:** 10-12 servings.

Dessert Waffles

Everyone raves about the contrast between the crunchy waffles and creamy ice cream in this easy dessert.
—*Sheila Watson, Stettler, Alberta*

1/2 cup flaked coconut
1/2 cup packed brown sugar
1/4 cup butter, softened
6 frozen waffles, lightly toasted
6 scoops butter pecan ice cream *or* flavor of your choice

In a small bowl, combine the first three ingredients; mix well. Spread over waffles. Broil for 3-4 minutes or until bubbly. Top with ice cream. **Yield:** 6 servings.

Peach Melba Dessert

My dessert's a no-fuss one. In fact, when we have company, I'll put it together while the after-dinner coffee is perking.
—*Kathryn Awe, International Falls, Minnesota*

4 individual round sponge cakes *or* shortcakes
4 canned peach halves in syrup
4 scoops vanilla *or* peach ice cream
2 tablespoons raspberry jam
1 tablespoon chopped nuts

Place cakes on dessert plates. Drain the peaches, reserving 2 tablespoons syrup; spoon 1-1/2 teaspoons syrup over each cake. Place peach halves, hollow side up, on cakes. Put a scoop of ice cream in each peach. Heat jam; drizzle over ice cream. Sprinkle with nuts and serve immediately. **Yield:** 4 servings.

Brownie Caramel Parfaits

I easily transform brownies, ice cream and caramel topping into a tempting treat. Layers of toasted coconut and nuts add nice crunch and make this dessert seem fancy. But it really couldn't be simpler to put together.
—*Chris Schnittka Charlottesville, Virginia*

1/2 cup chopped pecans
1/2 cup flaked coconut
1 package brownie mix (8-inch x 8-inch pan size)
1 pint vanilla ice cream
1 jar (12-1/4 ounces) caramel ice cream topping

Place pecans and coconut in an ungreased baking pan. Bake at 350° for 10-12 minutes or until toasted, stirring frequently. Meanwhile, prepare brownies according to package directions. Cool; cut into small squares.

When ready to serve, layer the brownies, ice cream, caramel topping and pecan mixture in parfait or dessert glasses; repeat layers one or two times. **Yield:** 6 servings.

Editor's Note: Any type of nuts, ice cream or topping may be used in these parfaits.

Raspberry Cream Croissants

This heavenly dessert takes only seconds to assemble because it begins with bakery croissants, whipped topping and store-bought jam. A friend and I came up with the recipe. —*Sherry Horton*
Sioux Falls, South Dakota

4 to 6 croissants
1/2 cup seedless raspberry jam
Whipped cream in a can *or* whipped topping
1-1/4 cups fresh *or* frozen unsweetened raspberries, thawed
Confectioners' sugar, optional

Cut the croissants in half horizontally; spread cut halves with jam. Spread whipped cream over bottom halves; top with raspberries. Replace tops. Dust with confectioners' sugar if desired. Serve immediately. **Yield:** 4-6 servings.

Coconut Gingerbread Cake

This unusual dessert came from a little book I bought at a flea market many years ago. The broiled orange-coconut topping really dresses up a boxed gingerbread mix. When I bring it to potlucks and family get-togethers, it never lasts long!
—*Paula Hartlett, Mineola, New York*

1 package (14-1/2 ounces) gingerbread mix
1 large navel orange
1-1/3 cups flaked coconut
1/2 cup packed brown sugar
2 tablespoons orange juice

Prepare and bake cake according to package directions, using a greased 8-in. square baking pan. Meanwhile, grate 1 tablespoon of peel from the orange; set aside. Peel and section the orange, removing white pith; dice the orange. When cake tests done, remove from the oven and cool slightly.

Combine coconut, brown sugar, orange juice, diced orange and reserved peel; spread over warm cake. Broil 4 in. from the heat for 2-3 minutes or until the top is lightly browned. Cool on a wire rack. **Yield:** 9 servings.

Fancy Fuss-Free Torte

This pretty layered torte relies on convenient frozen pound cake and canned pie filling. It's a snap to assemble. I put toothpicks through the ends to hold the layers in place, then remove them before serving.
—Joan Causey
Greenwood, Arkansas

1 loaf (10-3/4 ounces)
  frozen pound cake,
  thawed
1 can (21 ounces) cherry
  pie filling *or* flavor of your
  choice
1 carton (8 ounces) frozen
  whipped topping, thawed
1/2 cup chopped pecans

Split cake into three horizontal layers. Place bottom layer on a serving plate; top with half of the pie filling. Repeat layers. Top with third cake layer. Frost top and sides with whipped topping. Sprinkle with pecans. Store in the refrigerator. **Yield:** 8-10 servings.

Yogurt Berry Pies

Yogurt Berry Pies have just two ingredients in the filling, so they're a snap to assemble, yet they look and taste like you fussed. Topped with fresh berries, they're irresistible.
—Dawn Fagerstrom
Warren, Minnesota

1 carton (8 ounces) mixed
  berry yogurt *or* flavor of
  your choice
2 cups whipped topping
1 package (6 count)
  individual graham
  cracker tart shells
Blueberries and raspberries

In a bowl, stir the yogurt and whipped topping until combined. Spoon into tart shells. Cover and freeze for 20 minutes. Top with berries. **Yield:** 6 servings.

Cinnamon Apple Pizza

My son asked me to make something the night before a bake sale. He was pleased with this pizza that I created using on-hand ingredients.

—*Cherron Walker*
Columbus, Ohio

1 tube (12.4 ounces) refrigerated cinnamon roll dough
1 can (21 ounces) apple pie filling
1/4 cup packed brown sugar
1 tablespoon butter, melted

Set cinnamon roll icing aside. Separate dough into individual rolls; roll out each into a 4-in. circle. Arrange on a greased 12-in. pizza pan, overlapping edges. Bake at 400° for 8 minutes.

Spoon the apple pie filling over rolls to within 1/2 in. of edge. Combine the brown sugar and butter; sprinkle over pie filling. Bake 6-8 minutes longer or until the crust is golden brown. Cool. Drizzle with the reserved icing. **Yield:** 10-12 servings.

Spiced Peaches

Canned peaches get special attention from cinnamon and brown sugar. Served warm, these peaches offer down-home comfort. Chilled, they make a refreshing treat with frozen yogurt.

—*Debbie Schrock, Jackson, Mississippi*

 Uses less fat, sugar or salt. Includes Nutritional Analysis and Diabetic Exchanges.

1 can (15 ounces) reduced-sugar peach halves
2 tablespoons brown sugar
1 teaspoon lemon juice
1 teaspoon orange juice
2 cinnamon sticks (3-1/2 inches)

Drain peaches, reserving juice; set the peaches aside. Pour juice into a saucepan; add brown sugar and lemon and orange juices. Bring to a boil over medium heat; add cinnamon sticks. Reduce heat; simmer, uncovered, for 5 minutes. Add peach halves; heat through. Discard cinnamon sticks. Serve warm or cold. **Yield:** 4 servings.

Nutritional Analysis: One serving equals 74 calories, trace fat (0 saturated fat), 0 cholesterol, 7 mg sodium, 19 g carbohydrate, 1 g fiber, 1 g protein. **Diabetic Exchange:** 1 fruit.

Grilled Pineapple

Fresh pineapple adds an elegant touch to a barbecue when grilled, topped with butter and maple syrup and sprinkled with nuts. I cut each pineapple quarter into bite-size pieces before serving.

—*Polly Heer, Cabot, Arkansas*

1/4 cup maple syrup
3 tablespoons butter, melted
1 fresh pineapple
2 tablespoons chopped macadamia nuts *or* hazelnuts, toasted

Combine syrup and butter; set aside. Quarter the pineapple lengthwise, leaving top attached. Grill, uncovered, over medium heat for 5 minutes. Turn; brush with maple butter. Grill 5-7 minutes longer or until heated through; brush with maple butter and sprinkle with nuts. Serve with remaining maple butter. **Yield:** 4 servings.

Fluffy Mint Dessert

The cool, minty flavor of this fluffy dessert is perfect for Christmas or the hot summer months. Since it has to be made ahead of time, it's a great time-saver on potluck day. I received the recipe from a neighbor a couple years ago. —*Carol Mixter Lincoln Park, Michigan*

1 package (14 ounces) cream-filled chocolate sandwich cookies, crushed
1/2 cup butter, melted
2 cartons (12 ounces *each*) frozen whipped topping, thawed
2 cups pastel miniature marshmallows
1-1/3 cups small pastel mints (5-1/2 ounces)

Reserve 1/4 cup of crushed cookies for garnish. Combine the remaining cookies with butter; press into an ungreased 13-in. x 9-in. x 2-in. baking dish.

Fold together whipped topping, marshmallows and mints; pour over crust. Garnish with reserved cookies. Cover and refrigerate for 1-2 days before serving. **Yield:** 18-20 servings.

Butterscotch Chocolate Cake

Butterscotch Chocolate Cake is an easy ending to dinner because it can be made ahead and kept in the fridge. A moist chocolate cake is covered with rich butterscotch ice cream topping, spread with whipped topping, then sprinkled with crushed Butterfinger candy bars.
—*Shelley McKinney*
New Castle, Indiana

1 package (18-1/4 ounces) chocolate cake mix
1 jar (17 ounces) butterscotch ice cream topping
1 carton (8 ounces) frozen whipped topping, thawed
3 Butterfinger candy bars (2.1 ounces *each*), coarsely crushed

Prepare and bake cake according to package directions, using a greased 13-in. x 9-in. x 2-in. baking pan. Cool on a wire rack for 30 minutes.

Using the end of a wooden spoon handle, poke 12 holes in warm cake. Pour butterscotch topping over cake; cool completely. Spread with whipped topping; sprinkle with candy bars. Refrigerate for at least 2 hours before serving. **Yield:** 12-16 servings.

Caramel Banana Dessert

This dessert leaves plenty of room for imagination. Chocolate sauce can replace the caramel...you can substitute your favorite nut topping...or you can create a mini sundae by serving the bananas along with scoops of ice cream.
—*Carolene Esayenko*
Calgary, Alberta

4 medium firm bananas, sliced
4 to 6 tablespoons caramel ice cream topping
4 to 6 tablespoons chopped pecans
Whipped topping, optional

Place the bananas in individual serving dishes. Top with caramel topping and pecans. Garnish with whipped topping if desired. **Yield:** 4-6 servings.

Pear Bundt Cake

Five simple ingredients are all I need to fix this lovely light dessert. Tiny bits of pear provide sweetness to the moist slices. —*Veronica Ross Columbia Heights, Minnesota*

✓ **Uses less fat, sugar or salt. Includes Nutritional Analysis and Diabetic Exchanges.**

1 can (15-1/4 ounces) pears in light syrup
1 package (18-1/4 ounces) white cake mix
2 egg whites
1 egg
2 teaspoons confectioners' sugar

Drain pears, reserving the syrup; chop pears. Place pears and syrup in a mixing bowl; add dry cake mix, egg whites and egg. Beat on low speed for 30 seconds. Beat on high for 4 minutes.

Coat a 10-in. fluted tube pan with nonstick cooking spray and dust with flour. Add batter. Bake at 350° for 50-55 minutes or until a toothpick inserted near the center comes out clean. Cool for 10 minutes before removing from pan to a wire rack to cool completely. Dust with confectioners' sugar. **Yield:** 16 servings.

Nutritional Analysis: One slice equals 163 calories, 4 g fat (1 g saturated fat), 13 mg cholesterol, 230 mg sodium, 30 g carbohydrate, 1 g fiber, 2 g protein. **Diabetic Exchanges:** 1 starch, 1 fruit, 1 fat.

Raspberry Sorbet

With an abundant crop of fresh raspberries from the backyard, it's no wonder I rely on this sorbet in the summer months for a no-fuss frozen dessert. This treat is popular whenever I serve it.

—*Karin Bailey, Golden, Colorado*

1/4 cup plus 1-1/2 teaspoons lemon juice
3-3/4 cups unsweetened raspberries
2-1/4 cups confectioners' sugar

In a blender or food processor, combine all ingredients; cover and process until smooth. Pour into six dessert dishes. Cover and freeze for 1 hour or until set. Remove from the freezer 15 minutes before serving. **Yield:** 6 servings.

Eggnog Pudding

For a festive dessert in a hurry, I jazz up instant pudding mix to create Eggnog Pudding. Anyone who likes eggnog loves this creamy concoction—it tastes like the real thing. This recipe is easy to double and serve in a no-fuss graham cracker crust. —*Kim Jorgensen, Coulee City, Washington*

✓ Uses less fat, sugar or salt. Includes Nutritional Analysis and Diabetic Exchanges.

2 cups cold milk
1 package (3.4 ounces) instant vanilla pudding mix
1/2 teaspoon ground nutmeg
1/4 teaspoon rum extract
Additional ground nutmeg, optional

In a bowl, combine the first four ingredients. Beat for 2 minutes. Spoon into individual dishes. Sprinkle with nutmeg if desired. **Yield:** 4 servings.

Nutritional Analysis: One 1/2-cup serving (prepared with sugar-free pudding and fat-free milk) equals 117 calories, 328 mg sodium, trace cholesterol, 23 g carbohydrate, 7 g protein, trace fat. **Diabetic Exchanges:** 1 starch, 1/2 skim milk.

Chocolate Caramel Cupcakes

A few baking staples are all you need to throw together these chewy delights. Boxed cake mix and a can of frosting make them fast, but caramel, walnuts and chocolate chips tucked inside make them memorable. We like them with ice cream. —*Bev Spain, Bellville, Ohio*

1 package (18-1/4 ounces) chocolate cake mix
24 caramels
3/4 cup semisweet chocolate chips
1 cup chopped walnuts
Chocolate frosting
Additional walnuts, optional

Prepare cake batter according to package directions. Fill 24 greased or paper-lined muffin cups one-third full; set remaining batter aside. Bake at 350° for 7-8 minutes or until top of cupcake appears set.

Gently press a caramel into each cupcake; sprinkle with chocolate chips and walnuts. Top with remaining batter. Bake 15-20 minutes longer or until a toothpick inserted near the center of cake comes out clean. Cool for 5 minutes; remove from pans to wire racks to cool completely. Frost with chocolate frosting. Sprinkle with additional nuts if desired. **Yield:** 2 dozen.

Editor's Note: This recipe was tested with Betty Crocker cake mix.

General Recipe Index

This handy index lists every recipe by food category, major ingredient and/or cooking method, so you can easily locate recipes to suit your needs.

✓Recipe includes Nutritional Analysis and Diabetic Exchanges

Alphabetical Index

This handy index lists every recipe in alphabetical order so you can easily find your favorite recipes.

✓ Recipe includes Nutritional Analysis and Diabetic Exchanges